D0225053

THE POSTMODERN ARTS
An introductory reader

Modernism and postmodernism are now the two most comprehensive and influential terms applied to twentieth-century culture. *The Postmodern Arts: An introductory reader* begins by establishing definitions of both words, while also demonstrating the inconsistencies and contradictions which are inherent within them.

As with all books in the *Critical Readers in Theory and Practice* series, the volume is divided into two halves: the first, a comprehensive and thorough introduction by the editor, offering a schematic survey of the major themes and positions taken in the debates around modernism and postmodernism. The second half is a collection of pertinent essays grouped into four sections to demonstrate how the debates have been applied to specific cultural activities:

• Popular Culture
• Architecture and Visual Arts
• Literature
• Documentary Film

The Postmodern Arts provides essential material and invaluable guidance for students of modern literature and culture.

Nigel Wheale teaches in the Faculty of Humanities at Anglia Polytechnic University. He is the co-editor, with Lesley Aers, of *Shakespeare in the Changing Curriculum* (Routledge 1991).

Critical Readers in Theory and Practice

GENERAL EDITOR: Rick Rylance, *Anglia Polytechnic University*

The gap between theory and practice can often seem far too wide for the student of literary theory. *Critical Readers in Theory and Practice* is a new series which bridges that gap: it not only offers an introduction to a range of literary and theoretical topics, but also *applies* the theories to relevant texts.

Each volume is split into two parts: the first consists of an in-depth and clear introduction, setting out the theoretical bases, historical developments and contemporary critical situation of the topic. The theory is then applied to practice in the second part in an anthology of classic texts and essays.

Designed specifically with the student in mind, *Critical Readers in Theory and Practice* provides an essential introduction to contemporary theories and how they relate to textual material.

IN THIS SERIES:

THE POSTMODERN ARTS

An introductory reader

EDITED BY

NIGEL WHEALE

LONDON AND NEW YORK

First published 1995
by Routledge
11 New Fetter Lane, London EC4P 4EE

Simultaneously published in the USA and Canada
by Routledge
29 West 35th Street, New York, NY 10001

© 1995 Nigel Wheale and contributors

Typeset in Janson by
Ponting–Green Publishing Services, Chesham, Bucks

Printed and bound in Great Britain by
Biddles Ltd, Guildford and King's Lynn

All rights reserved. No part of this book may be reprinted or
reproduced or utilized in any form or by any electronic,
mechanical, or other means, now know or hereafter
invented, including photocopying and recording, or in any
information storage or retrieval system, without permission
in writing from the publishers.

British Library Cataloguing in Publication Data
A catalogue record for this book is available from
the British Library

Library of Congress Cataloguing in Publication Data
A catalogue record for this book has been requested

ISBN 0–415–07776–1
0–415–12611–8 (pbk)

For Joe and for Josh

Contents

Part II Essays on Postmodernism

One: Popular Culture

Two: Architecture and Visual Arts

[ix]

Plates

Contributors

ANDREW GOODWIN is a critic, musician and teacher. He is the author of *Dancing in the Distraction Factory: Music, Television and Popular Culture* (1993) and co-editor (with Simon Frith) of *On Record: Rock, Pop and Written Word* (1990). He is Associate Professor of Communication at the University of San Francisco, from where he also broadcasts about pop music and culture, on KUSF.

HILARY GRESTY was Curator at Kettle's Yard Gallery, Cambridge, from 1983 to 1989, and now works as a freelance writer and visual arts consultant. She is also Director of the Visual Arts and Galleries Association.

YVE LOMAX studied at St Martin's School of Art and the Royal College of Art. Her photographic work has been exhibited widely and regularly, including *Three Perspectives on Photography* (Hayward Gallery 1979), *Beyond the Purloined Image* (Riverside Studios 1983), *Difference* (The New Museum of Contemporary Arts, New York, 1984), and *Questioning Europe* (Rotterdam 1988). Her essay 'Telling Times. Tales of Photography and Other Stories' is included in *Public Bodies / Private States. New Views on Photography, Representation and Gender*, edited by Jane Brettel and Sally Rice (Manchester University Press 1994).

JULIAN ROBERTS teaches philosophy at the University of Bayreuth. He is the author of *Walter Benjamin* (1982), *German Philosophy. An Introduction* (1988) and *The Logic of Reflection* (1992).

GAYATRI CHAKRAVORTY SPIVAK is Professor of English and Comparative Literature and Adjunct Professor of Philosophy at Columbia University. She is the translator of Jacques Derrida's *Of Grammatology* (1976) and author of *In Other Worlds* (1987), *The Post-Colonial Critic* (1990), *Identity Talk* (1991) and *Outside in the Teaching Machine* (1993). She has published widely in the areas of feminist–marxist literary and cultural theory.

TRINH T. MINH-HA is a writer, film-maker and composer. Her works include the films *Reassemblage* (1982), *Naked Spaces* (1985), *Surname Viet Given Name Nam* (1989) and *Shoot for the Contents* (1991), and her most recent books are *Woman, Native, Other: Writing Postcoloniality and Feminism* (1989), *When the Moon Waxes Red. Representation, Gender and Cultural Politics* (1991) and *Framer Framed* (1992). She teaches as Chancellor's Distinguished Professor of Women's Studies at the University of California, Berkeley, and as Associate Professor of Cinema at San Francisco State University.

NIGEL WHEALE teaches English with Text and Image Studies at Anglia Polytechnic University, Cambridge campus. He co-edited *Shakespeare in the Changing Curriculum* (1991) with Lesley Aers, and contributed to *Cultural Icons* edited by James Park (1991), *Poets on Writing. Britain 1970–1991*, edited by Denise Riley (1992), and *The Oxford Companion to Twentieth-Century Poetry in English* edited by Ian Hamilton (1994). His latest collection of poetry is *Phrasing the Light* (1994).

General editor's preface

The interpretation of culture never stands still. Modern approaches to familiar problems adjust our sense of their importance, and new ideas focus on fresh details or remake accepted concepts. This has been especially true over recent years when developments across the humanities have altered so many ideas.

For many this revolution in understanding has been exciting but difficult, involving the need to integrate advanced theoretical work with attention to specific texts and issues. This series attempts to approach this difficulty in a new way by putting together a new balance of basic texts and detailed, introductory exposition.

Each volume in the series will be organized in two parts. Part I provides a thorough account of the topic under discussion. It details important concepts, historical developments and the contemporary context of interpretation and debate. Part II provides an anthology of classic texts or – in the case of very recent work – essays by leading writers which offer focused discussions of particular issues. Commentary and editorial material provided by the author connect the explanations in Part I to the materials in Part II, and in this way the reader moves comfortably between original work and enabling introduction.

The series will include volumes on topics which have been of particular importance recently. Some books will introduce specific theoretical ideas; others will re-examine bodies of literary or other material in the light of current thinking. But as a whole the series aims to reflect, in a clear-minded and approachable way, the changing ways in which we understand the expanding field of modern literary and cultural studies.

Rick Rylance

Acknowledgements

Andrew Goodwin's 'Popular music and postmodern theory' first appeared in *Cultural Studies* 5/2 May 1991. A shorter form of Nigel Wheale's 'Recognizing a "human-Thing"': cyborgs, robots and replicants in Philip K. Dick's *Do Androids Dream of Electric Sheep?* and Ridley Scott's *Blade Runner'* appeared in *Critical Survey* 3/3 1991, the issue dedicated to 'Text into Performance', edited by Peter Reynolds. Thanks to Philippa Hurd for picture research towards Chapter 3 and for her photograph of Ricardo Bofill's 'Les Espaces d'Abraxas'. Hilary Gresty's contribution incorporates quotations from Yve Lomax's 'The World Is Indeed a Fabulous Tale', first published in *Other than Itself: Writing Photography*, edited by John X. Berger and Olivier Richon (1989). Thanks to Yve Lomax for permission to reproduce five plates from *Sometime(s)* (1994). Thanks to Tom Phillips for permission to reproduce stills from *A TV Dante* (1990), page 159 from *A Humument* (1985), and 'The Greyhound' from his *Dante's Inferno* (1985). Thanks to John Ashbery for permission to quote extensively from *Three Poems* (1972). Gayatri Spivak's 'Reading *The Satanic Verses*' appeared in *Public Culture* 2.i (Fall 1989), in a developed form in *Third Text: Beyond the Rushdie Affair* (1990) Summer, no. 11, and in *Outside in the Teaching Machine* (1993). The present reprint omits pp. 53–8 of the second version. A shortened version of Trinh T. Minh-ha's 'The totalizing quest of meaning' appeared as 'Documentary is/not a name' in *October* 52 (Summer 1990), and the present version also appears in *When the Moon Waxes Red. Representation, Gender and Cultural Politics* (1991). Thanks to Trinh T. Minh-ha for permission to reproduce three stills from *Naked Spaces – Living Is Round* (1985), and two stills from *Surname Viet Given Name Nam* (1989). Thanks to the Photography Department, Cambridge University Library, for reproductions of Dürer's *Melancholia* and Schinkel's *Museum* elevation, and to the Library for permission to reprint them; to the Academy Group Ltd for permission to reproduce Michael Graves' 'Fifth Avenue elevation' of his Portland Public Services Building, which is taken from *Architectural Design* 5/6, 1980, *Post-Modern Classicism*, guest-edited by

Charles Jencks; to Thames and Hudson and Corvina Verlag, Hungary, for permission to reproduce Tatlin's sketch of a *Project for a Monument to the Third International*; and to Media Production Division, Anglia Polytechnic University, for photographic work. Thanks to the editors of all the journals and books concerned, and to my contributors for their patience.

Thanks to the Department of Arts and Letters at Anglia Polytechnic University, Cambridge campus, for remission from some teaching over several years in order to work on this book, and to my colleagues for their support; also to my students whose interest and scepticism focuses my teaching. Thanks to the staff at Routledge for their efficiency, in particular Talia Rodgers, Tricia Dever, Jemma Kennedy, Patricia Stankiewicz and Alison Kelly; Christine Shuttleworth for indexing, and to the three anonymous readers of the typescript who pointed out some errors. And thanks to the following friends for diverse help: Will Meister enabled me to change horses at a crucial moment; David Mosley taught his teacher a lot about current science fiction and graphic novels; Cathy Pompe for sharing with me her work with primary schoolchildren on the BFI 'Science and SF' project; Stephanie Newell, whose undergraduate dissertation *The Other God: Salman Rushdie's 'New Aesthetic'* (Anglia Polytechnic 1991) was immediately accepted for publication by *Literature & History*; Andrea Bassil, Will Hill, John James, Penelope Kenrick, Elaine Ward and Arvon Wellen for discussion about various aspects of visual arts in theory and practice; Peggy and Robert Ellsberg for facilitating visits to Barnard College, Columbia University, New York, where some of the materials on Salman Rushdie and Tom Phillips were presented, and to Cary and Marie-Thérèse Plotkin for their hospitality; Rod Macdonald of the Media Production Division, Anglia, for an eight-year night school in television and video, and to all our evening-class students who theorized and practised so well; Charlie Ritchie also for media education; Jan Ayton, Roger Langley, Tom Lowenstein Denise Riley, Peter Riley and John Welch for discussion of poetry and painting; David Oppedisano for the truth about Jean Gabin; Gilly Maude for helping to cut (some of) the flannel; Rajiv Krishnan of Kerala State for discussion and enlightenment about Islam in India, and for specific materials on allegory and imagism from his doctoral dissertation on Ezra Pound; to all those friends who refuse to take postmodernism seriously, and so helped to shape the argument, particularly Ewan Smith and Ed Esche. Many thanks to Rick

Rylance for asking me to do this in the first place, and for his insistence – probably in vain – that it should be sensible and clear. Very special thanks to Kate and Dan for being the main interest. All the remaining obscurity, errors and non sequiturs are of course down to me.

PART I

Postmodernism: a new representation?

Paradigms of the Postmodern

During the late 1960s a distracting advert was to be seen on the walls of bars and restaurants in Italy: it was an aerial photograph of St Mark's Square in Venice, where bird seed had been arranged in the shape of huge letters on the flagstones of the piazza so as to spell out COCA-COLA. But the food was invisible under thousands of pigeons fighting to eat it, and the mass of their bodies figured the commodity while they consumed its name. As a keen student of quattrocento art and architecture, avidly reading my John Ruskin and Adrian Stokes, I was annoyed to find that the Coke ad distracted me, and in a disconcerting way it began to mean as much and more than Ruskin's eccentric account of the development of the ogee arch, which I was trying to follow, with difficulty, among the crush of mere tourists.

Was this my first brush with postmodernity? Elite traditions overlaid by mass consumption; the co-option of the aesthetic to commodity; the devouring nature of the advertising sign, which could shape anything to its own consuming logic; the subordination of the natural to artifice. Ten years later the photograph of the massed pigeons would also come to signify an ecology out of balance, a threat to architecture and health. How well Roland Barthes might have written about the image, and of how the pigeons in fact during those seasons were more often scattered by the formation squads of riot police as they tackled demonstrators from the industrial mainland who were protesting against Venice's tourist hegemony....

Using this book

For better or worse, modernism and postmodernism are now the two most comprehensive and influential terms applied to twentieth-century culture. *The Postmodern Arts* begins by establishing definitions of both words, while also demonstrating the inconsistencies and contradictions which are inherent in them. Five of the eight contributions in Part II have been written specifically for the book, and the essays are grouped into four sections to demonstrate how the debates over postmodernism have been applied to specific cultural activities. These are [1] Popular Culture, [2] Architecture and Visual Arts, [3] Literature, and finally [4] Documentary Film. The contributions represent a variety of different positions as to the truth and usefulness of postmodernism as a critical concept, and this reflects the wide range of often conflicting arguments about the general category of the postmodern which are surveyed in Part I of the book. Both Part I and the commentaries introducing each of the four sections in Part II are intended to be as clear as possible, surveying arguments and themes so that readers can arrive at their own conclusions. I do however take a position about the idea of postmodernity and culture, which is argued in the final section of Part I.

Cultural production – film and video, writing, architecture, visual arts, photography and design, and popular culture in all its forms – is exceptionally vigorous and diverse at the moment. The entire literature on postmodernism amounts at one level to an attempt to understand what is particular about this activity, in what ways it is absolutely new, in what ways it expresses our modernity. This vast critical literature offers postmodernity as a universal category, and the adjective 'postmodern' has by now been applied to almost everything, from trainer shoes to the nature of our subjectivity – from 'sole to soul' as the rappers might say. And there has been a good deal of 'Post-What-Not fashionableness', as was said long ago in 1913 during the aesthetic squabbles provoked by the first modernism (Symons 1987: 42). But I have focused this book specifically on discussion of popular culture and the arts because these are the forms through which most of us experience 'the postmodern'. Themes and debates within philosophy, anthropology, sociology, and other more strictly academic disciplines will only be represented here when they inform a view of specific films, novels and poems, buildings or art works.

The use of quotation marks around 'the postmodern' is also significant, because postmodern art is fundamentally ironic, often quoting another work in order to imply a meaning indirectly: *Twin Peaks* is an ironic version of popular narrative television entertainment; *The Satanic Verses* is an ironized version of the founding of Islam. Quotation marks around terms are therefore often used to demonstrate that a particular meaning is being 'put into question' by postmodernist irony: what is the status of 'the truth' in this text, or picture (or even, 'text' or 'picture')? The political journalist Ian Aitken once proposed a new typeface, to be called 'ironic',

[4]

which would indicate to the reader that any statement printed in it was not to be taken literally; this 'ironica' typeface would be heavily used by postmodern typesetters. But in writing a plain description of post-modernism such as this book, there would be no end to the ironizing of terms, and so from now on quotation marks will not be used in this way. Finally, as a category, postmodernism is so unstable that the word is even written in different ways. Throughout this account it will not be capitalized or hyphenated, but kept penny-plain as 'postmodernism'.

Part I offers a schematic survey of the major themes and positions taken in these debates. The sequence of categories is organized chrono-logically; it begins with socio-economic diagnoses of postmodernity, and then describes the cultural responses which flow from these in the form of postmodernism. An extended discussion of modernism is included in order to examine what kinds of continuity and disruption can be found between the first period of modern cultural innovation, generally located in the period 1880–1930, and the onset of postmodernity during the 1960s (a more disputed date). The shortcomings of these headings and general groupings will quickly become obvious, but they do allow us to establish initial terms of reference.

This review of definitions begins then with a brief survey of the socio-economic analyses of postmodernity. These are in many ways the most interesting kinds of paradigm because they are the most ambitious, and they seem to give answers to our perception of dramatic changes which we can all recognize at work around us. For arts-based readers they are often also the most difficult definitions to understand, because they rely on complex historical and sociological descriptions which are also linked to philosophical and political analyses. This section will therefore be more than usually schematic, but will indicate where the arguments can be followed in more detail.

Modern, modernity, modernize

All discussions of postmodernism have to begin with definitions of modernity and modernism, the period and cultural phase which have supposedly been superseded by the *post*-modern's prefix. Various ana-lyses locate the onset of modernity specifically in Western Europe from the mid-seventeenth century onwards, or else emphasize the develop-ment of America as an economic and cultural catalyst during the twentieth century. Descriptions of the earliest development of a modern mentality concentrate on the rise of rationalist philosophies from the early seventeenth century which were dedicated to establishing systematic, pragmatic knowledge of the natural world which could then be extended into the material exploitation of nature (Whimster and Lash: 1987). These accounts also emphasize the revolutionary forms of philosophical enquiry pursued by thinkers such as René Descartes which placed knowledge of the self and subjectivity on a new foundation (Rorty 1984: 170). This rapport between sophisticated philosophical analysis of identity and the surrounding, material development of modernity is paralleled in the literature on postmodernism, which also hopes to establish causal relations between mentality and social change.

The tensions between philosophical tradition and the social developments characteristic of European societies from the eighteenth century onward provide the next chronological phase of arguments about modernity. This period is said to have developed what was in effect a programme dedicated to a conception of social progress which relied on a notion of human perfectibility. This is often called 'the Enlightenment project', taking its name from the eighteenth-century philosophical movement which included thinkers such as Diderot, Voltaire and Rousseau, through to Kant and Hegel. This European-wide revaluation of intellectual method had consequences not only for culture but also for political science, and in due course for the actual conduct of politics: the republican revolutions in France and America were both deeply influenced by enlightenment thinking. A clear example of the continuing vitality of this tradition is the influence of enlightenment debates over human rights on the drafting of the United Nations Universal Declaration of Human Rights (Freeman 1990: 166).

In part it was the universalism of the Enlightenment's ambitions which was so compelling, because it proposed a universal form of reason together with an aspiration to universal rights. But in other forms this supreme confidence could also appear as a triumphalism or absolutism. Therefore another characteristic of the period was the self-conscious definition of Europe as the most advanced region of the world, with a related tendency to disparage other cultures as under-developed and therefore implicitly ripe for exploitation. But it should not be forgotten that many enlightenment texts also parodied this over-bearing self-confidence, for example using the genre of travel literature as a means to criticize European arrogance and expansionism: Lemuel Gulliver, the anti-hero of Jonathan Swift's *Travels into Several Remote Nations of the World*

(1726) and most unlovely of explorers, is a good instance of this self-critical tradition.

Taking a very long view, it is possible to see a number of the central debates concerning the nature of postmodernity as continuing (or being condemned to repeat) central arguments from the enlightenment period. These debates are represented throughout this collection, as the following list indicates; the number of the chapter most relevant to the discussion is bracketed. The Enlightenment displayed:

> Anxiety about the relation of cultural elites to common experience, and the kinds of contribution made by intellectual minorities to the civil values and political forms of the majority (1, 3).

> Doubts about the universal applicability of particular conceptions of reason and right, alongside the practical application of just such values (4, 7 and 8).

> Debate over the relative values ascribed to European and non-European cultures (7 and 8).

> Continuing argument between secularists and people maintaining religious faith (2, 6, 7).

> Unresolved disputes over the relations between immediate, visual meanings, and verbal – spoken or written – language (2, 4, 5, 8).

The nineteenth-century contribution to the development of modernity is inevitably associated with the rise of mass urban existence. From the mid-nineteenth century more than half of the population of England lived in cities, establishing a pattern of development for the rest of the world as it too modernized. The more strictly conceptual revolutions of the two previous centuries now became individualized in each person's experience of city life. The poet Charles Baudelaire is often credited with formulating the modernity of mid-nineteenth-century Paris in terms of a new, fragmented and distracted sense of time as it was experienced in the city (Benjamin 1973A). The influential German sociologist Georg Simmel developed a compelling analysis of the various effects of modernity-as-metropolis, concentrating on the fracturing of the sense of both time and space as experienced by the modern city dweller (Frisby 1986, 1992). In broad terms, the optimism with which the progress of modernity had been viewed up to this point began increasingly to be qualified by a range of competing objections to its implications and consequences. Individual subjectivity seemed to be cast adrift from the kinds of institution and belief which had previously conferred feelings of solidarity and purposiveness. Modernity at this point comes to be in part described as a pathology, experienced in isolation and characteristically through intense anxiety. In this view, the operations of both the state and commerce can seem to occur inhumanly, no longer in service of individuals, but separated from them, if not actively hostile to them. This experience is bound up with a recoil from the worst depredations of industrialism and the romantic reaction to them, as found in the poetry of Blake or Wordsworth and, later, in the novels of Dickens.

In the course of the twentieth century, modernity has been increasingly described as an irresistible process of the 'Americanization' of the entire world, as the United States displaced Europe as the most powerful region. This process is defined as the remorseless triumph of production and consumption values developed in the United States, together with the adaptation of American mass or popular culture which displaces the cultures of localities. This equating of the painful process of becoming-modern with the acquisition of Western, specifically American, culture and values, may be welcomed as a liberating experience, bringing new freedoms and possibilities. Or it can be resented and resisted as another example of the creation of misleading and oppressive categories, in this case of Western as opposed to non-Western values.

Japan, for example, is often cited as the only non-Western nation to have achieved the condition of postmodernity owing to its singular culture and a post-war history of purposive material reconstruction. The central business district of Tokyo is worth more in real estate terms than the whole of Canada; every stride an executive makes there covers a quarter-million dollars. The Japanese conception of the self is said to be defined more in terms of group allegiances than as an autonomous individual agency; Japanese culture is said to be able to 'erase the consequences of history' through the ritual practices of shinto religion; parody, pastiche, and an overwhelmingly visual dimension to culture are all well-established, apparently postmodern traits; Japanese politics as a forum for public debate and dissension is overwhelmed by the dedication of state and corporate structures to production and consumption: Japanese citizens are de-politicized consumers – but: 'This is a caricature, of course' (Miyoshi 1989: 148). For Masao Miyoshi, the attempt to describe 'Japaneseness' as the postmodern condition is itself another example of 'orientalism', that is, of the systematic misrecognition of other cultures by the West. As the latest seductive universalizing analysis, post-

[8]

modernism and postmodernity themselves may be performing the sort of abolition of local particularity which they claim to be diagnosing.

Is there a science of postmodernism? Jean-François Lyotard's *The Postmodern Condition: A Report on Knowledge* ([1979] 1984) was one of the most influential descriptions of postmodernity viewed as a radical development stemming from the European Enlightenment. He proposed that the idea of progress itself had become increasingly untenable since the eighteenth century in the face of the violence and destruction which seemed to be intrinsic to modern experience. A combination of technological mastery, scientific rationalism, and totalitarian politics (of the left or right) had destroyed confidence in the enlightenment project of a rationally administered progress. Here as elsewhere the 'rationally administered' mass extermination of the European Jewish populations by the German National Socialists became the prime instance of the failure of 'universal emancipation', spreading 'a kind of sorrow in the Zeitgeist' (Lyotard 1986: 6). This realization brought about 'the failure of the grand narratives', that is, the loss of confidence in the systematic bodies of knowledge which were the product of the Enlightenment, and which had been the European humanists' best hope for constructively acting on the world. These grand narratives are often characterized as Marxism, Freudianism, and the applied sciences.

There are broadly three kinds of response to this catastrophic analysis. The first can be called weak postmodernism, which welcomes the failure of analytical rationality and moral argument, and accepts this groundlessness as a reason to act out of a pure relativism and nihilism. The second is strong postmodernism (Lyotard's position) which calls for ever greater analysis and reflection on the nature of modernity's failure through self-critical practices, whether in philosophy, the arts, or politics. Third, there is the option of rejecting the analysis as quite mistaken and arguing against the 'cognitive relativism' implied by postmodern thinking (Gellner 1992). This third position argues for the need to persevere with the Enlightenment project, rather than despair of it, and maintains that the kinds of logic deployed in arguments about postmodernism can only have application in the purely speculative disciplines of the 'human sciences', rather than in the empirically verifiable practices of the physical and natural sciences such as physics, biology and chemistry. This argument maintains that issues concerning interpretation, meaning, discourse and textuality are central to the debates about postmodernism, and brute empirical facts are beyond its scope.

[9]

Postmodernism remains a subject of opinion and theory, and never of verifiable demonstration. Applied quantum mechanics enables me to type on this word processor, but postmodern theory, it is claimed, will never deliver anything so useful.

Economic transformation, commodity and consumption

Modernity is also defined as the social condition brought about by the development of the Western world's characteristic economic formation, that of capitalism, and its incorporation to itself of other societies' modes of production. The economic processes of capitalism are driven by a perpetual demand for new resources required to produce innovative commodities which can then be sold to new markets (Callinicos 1989: 132–44). This remorseless economic engine also necessarily brings with it social transformation, creating novel 'historical geographies' and new modes of experience (Harvey 1989: 343). Theorists of the postmodern argue that the irresistible expansion of the capitalist economies, which can be said to originate in the seventeenth century in close association with the modern mentalities described above, has now gathered such a momentum and scale that it creates new kinds of perception and cultural formation. The collapse of central command economies in the USSR and Eastern Europe, and comparable crises in China and state-socialist African economies, arguably have left capitalist processes as the dominant global economic form. As a consequence, postmodernity is poised to become the most extensive and highly integrated socio-economic mode, if these accounts are to be credited. The postmodern is the experience of modernity raised to a new level of intensity which saturates culture and subjectivity alike.

For these analysts, to live under late capitalism in the postmodern condition is primarily to be defined as one who consumes: our subjectivity is therefore most clearly exhibited through the patterns of consumption which we choose (Bourdieu [1979] 1984; Featherstone 1991). For many postmodern theorists commodity consumption characterizes our social being and inter-relations, and drawing up a profile of an individual's 'lifestyle niche' within the shopping malls is the most effective indicator of personality. Postmodernity is defined as a strenuous new form of capitalist social organization, where leisure and culture, formerly marginal activities for the majority of people, have been co-opted to the production process itself. Mass-spectating of sport, often on a global

[10]

scale, can be taken as a characteristic postmodern leisure event. Commodities therefore pleasure us – or they may fill us with nauseated boredom. But even if this is the case, resistance to the hegemony of consumption can only be expressed through deviant patterns of consumption (Hebdige 1988: 17–36).

Jean Baudrillard is the writer who has done most to promote this aspect of postmodern theory. Extending some aspects of the work of Roland Barthes, Baudrillard argued that commodities as objects have less importance now than their symbolic value within the all-pervasive regime of mediatized images through which they are promoted (Baudrillard 1989, 1990). The stable, intrinsic values which attached to goods during the earlier phases of capitalist development, when production dictated to consumption, have been overwhelmed by endlessly shifting patterns of hysterical desire. Contemporary consumption is perpetually whipped up through image campaigns, one demand displacing another without reference to the actual merits of the commodities concerned. For Baudrillard, postmodern existence is literally 'hectic', a diagnostic word used since the middle ages to categorize the feverish, all-consuming condition produced by tuberculosis. Roy Porter, however, who studies the social history of medicine, points out that from the time of the seventeenth century tuberculosis was called 'consumption', and by the late eighteenth century the disease was being linked to the giddy, enervating nature of contemporary urban life. Social commentators, doctors, even poets, exclaimed against the debilitating effects of the new kind of consumer society that was growing by 1800, one moralist labelling it 'the English Malady': 'Since our Wealth has increas'd, and our Navigation has been extended, we have ransack'd all the Parts of the *Globe* to bring together its whole Stock of Materials for *Riot, Luxury,* and to provoke *Excess*' (Porter 1993: 11). In other words, Porter argues, the diagnosis which Baudrillard makes specifically for late twentieth-century hyperconsumption in fact was being made in not dissimilar terms from the earliest development of modern economic society during the seventeenth and eighteenth centuries (Porter 1992). Here, as with many other aspects of the definition of postmodernity, it is possible to push back the boundary at which a decisive mutation is supposed to have occurred.

At the centre of economic activity is the commodity which is produced and exchanged, and as the scale and nature of consumption has increased, people's perception of the commodity as an object has altered. Therefore the ways in which things-as-such have been represented in writing and painting since the eighteenth century is a rewarding area of research in sociology and philosophy (Frisby 1992: 165–8; Asendorf [1984] 1993). The excess of things does seem to have produced quite particular responses from the beginning of the twentieth century, during the period which comes to be defined as modernist. The nausea which objects may induce, or else an attitude of mute reproach bestowed on the animal creation, figure in countless twentieth-century texts, paintings and films. The use of collage and assemblage by artists during the modernist period can be seen as a way of responding to this increasing 'strangeness of things' which is characteristic of modernity. By the early twentieth century, objects were already perceived as separated, and as existing over-against human experience. Therefore they were endlessly described or repro-duced enigmatically, as if the act of addressing them so persistently would make them speak. Things of course continued to take absolutely no notice whatsoever, and animals only a little less so; but by this obsessive address to the isolated Thing writing and painting did articu-late many new ways of representing the nature of perception. What was actually being portrayed was the projection of fantasy, anxiety, and hopes of various kinds:

> ... Sind wir vielleicht hier, um zu sagen: Haus,
> Brücke, Brunnen, Tor, Krug, Obstbaum, Fenster, –
> höchstens: Säule, Turm ... aber zu sagen, verstehs,
> oh zu sagen so, wie selber die Dinge niemals
> innig meinten zu sein.

> [... Are we, perhaps, *here* just for saying: House,
> Bridge, Fountain, Gate, Jug, Fruit tree, Window, –
> possibly: Pillar, Tower? ... but for *saying*, remember,
> oh, for such saying as never the things themselves
> hoped so intensely to be.]

> (Rilke [1922] 1963: 85)

This interest in things-as-perceived also developed in a complicated tension with the endless, nauseating proliferation of objects produced for circulation and exchange within the social economy, that is, in the material circumstances of commodity production. An artist who illus-trates these developments is Kurt Schwitters (1887–1948) who developed the practice of collage and assemblage begun by Picasso and Braque in 1912. From 1918 until his death 30 years later, Schwitters produced several thousand laminations made from found-paper, card and paint. He described his collage-practice and associated working methods, including his poetry, by a new word, MERZ:

> That is the second syllable of Kommerz [commerce]. It originated from the Merzbild [Merzpicture], a picture in which the word MERZ, cut-out and glued-on from an advertisement for the KOMMERZ UND PRIVATBANK [Commercial and Private Bank], could be read in between abstract forms ... Now I call myself MERZ.
>
> (Elderfield 1985: 12–13)

Commerce provoked the plague of objects which proliferated in the world of the international market; object-nausea provoked a significant element of the modernist formal innovation. Schwitters very acutely transformed the name of the process itself, and applied it to the analytical fragmentation by which he explored the new world of unrelated objects (Steel 1990). A comparable case of object phobia is 'A Chair', Chapter XXVI of D. H. Lawrence's *Women in Love* (1920). Here Birkin and Ursula visit a flea-market to look for bits and pieces as they tentatively begin their life together. But since Birkin is so critical of conventional marriage and the accepted kinds of relation between a man and a woman, the expedition is fraught with tension. Birkin lights on a rickety Georgian chair in the flea-market which his cultivated taste finds it hard to ignore as he launches into a nostalgic lament for the authenticity and virtues of pre-industrial production:

> 'So beautiful, so pure!' Birkin said. 'It almost breaks my heart.' They walked along between the heaps of rubbish. 'My beloved country – it had something to express even when it made that chair... it had living thoughts to unfold even then, and pure happiness in unfolding them. And now, we can only fish among the rubbish heaps for the remnants of their old expression. There is no production in us now, only sordid and foul mechanicalness.'
>
> (Lawrence [1920] 1988: 327)

Birkin fantasizes a vitalistic happiness through the inert object, and celebrates the truth of a craftsmanship that supposedly is instinct with the virtues of its time precisely because it is pre-modern, innocent of the corruption of machines. In the words of an influential theorist of postmodernity, Birkin is celebrating the 'particular status of the bygone object', which is its 'definitive being' (Baudrillard 1990: 36). But at the other end of the flea-market we can just catch a sight of Kurt Schwitters gleefully picking over heaps of last week's newspapers, some bus-tickets and a few catalogues, not for 'remnants of their old expression', but for use in the forensic collage of MERZ – which does derive from *Kommerz*, but also from *ausmerzen* (to eliminate), *Schmerz* (pain, grief) and tellingly, from *Herz* – the heart (Paz 1970: [37]). Therefore, in discussing some of the qualities that are attributed to postmodern representation below (p. 42) we can contrast the place of commodities in late twentieth-century taste with these modernist objects.

We have broadly established the description of postmodernity as a socio-economic mode that has intensified and surpassed modernity itself. We can now move on to the more specifically cultural descriptions of postmodernism which are said to be produced in response to this new form of hyper-modernity. But in order to discuss the culture of the postmodern, we must first establish what is meant by the modernism from which it is said to derive.

Modernism and Its Consequences: Continuity or Break?

The best way of understanding the relation between postmodernism and modernism is to be clear about the inadequacies and contradictions which are inherent in both terms (Iversen 1989). As we have seen from the initial description, postmodernism is a very elusive concept, and a major reason for the lack of agreement over its meaning stems from the difficulty of defining the meaning of its precursor: what was the modernism which gave rise to postmodernity? The following aspects are major elements which can be found in most definitions of the cultural phase called modernism.

The forms of art

No-one could deny that there was a revaluation and transformation of practices in all the arts throughout Europe, usually thought to have taken place between 1880 and 1930. Assigning the time-scale like this creates problems, because the relationship between this 'first wave' of artistic activity and later developments is obscured by the cut-off date at 1930, and the long-range continuities extending from late eighteenth-century romanticism to the development of modernism are also effaced by the boundary at 1880. But accepting this conventional time-span for the moment, it is the case that all cultural production participated in these developments, even if in negative reaction. Innovations occurred in every literary genre – novel, poetry and drama; in painting and sculpture, music and dance; in the graphic, decorative and applied arts such as fashion and interior design; in architecture and, crucially, in the emerging, lens-based arts of photography and cinema. All of this artistic activity was accompanied by vigorous, often violent argument, which changed conventional assumptions about aesthetic value and the place of the arts in society. Therefore as with all profound cultural change, new practices were accompanied by related changes in perception and thinking.

Many of these developments were initiated by relatively small coteries or groupings in the new European metropolises, with Paris and Berlin acting as the major engines of artistic change, followed by complex networks of reaction and liaison in other centres such as Vienna, Rome, London and Moscow. The modernizing artist-activists were often emigres or exiles from their own countries, or migrant from the provinces to the great cities – though we should be aware of the existence of regional centres of cultural activity which were also often significant. The final words of James Joyce's *Ulysses* ([1922] 1986) are usually remembered as being the enveloping, breathless embrace of Molly Bloom's night-speech: '... and his heart was going like mad and yes I said yes I will Yes.' But there is beyond this a coda which gives the period and places of the novel's construction: 'Trieste–Zurich–Paris 1914–1921' (ibid.: 644). This strict deixis, a pointing outside of the fiction to real contexts, works contrastively against the fiction which has just absorbed us, and which was located in one, now distant day and a peripheral city. The fictional specificity of the novel based in Ireland is contradicted by the record of its construction – three European cities, the period of the First World War and its aftermath – and these indicate the scope of the audience for whom the novel was intended.

This modernist revolution in the arts inevitably and quickly spread to the continents which shared strong cultural traditions with Europe, everywhere producing characteristic local variations, in particular throughout Latin America. It would however be difficult to say what African or Asian modernism might have been in that period, though for example in India there were responses which drew on indigenous traditions and which were shaped by powerful anti-imperialist feeling. A complex exchange and interaction quickly developed between European cultural emigres and the vangardist writers, artists and photographers of New York, where there was also a vigorous cultural renaissance within the black community of Harlem (Baker 1987; Hull 1987). By the mid-century, in the era of high or late modernism, New York had become estabished as the metropolis which exerted predominant influence, and the modernist initiative, originally west European, had passed to North America as a part of the post-Second World War settlement.

What does modernism look like? In the visual arts an early tendency of the modernizing painters was to use unmodulated colours to present a fresh, direct version of perception, which appeared to be realistic in very obvious ways, as in the work of Impressionists such as Camille Pissarro (1831–1903) and Claude Monet (1840–1926), and then with the

Fauves (the 'Wild Beasts') such as Henri Matisse (1869–1954) and André
Derain (1880–1954). Because these paintings conveyed an impression of
the visible world on the eye in such apparently naive terms, they
provoked scandal, contravening the elaborate visual conventions associated with Art to such an extent that for many people they were
unrecognizable as painting. This rejection of the accumulated visual
traditions and iconography of European painting represents one of the
decisive fractures established by the new cultural forms. In refusing the
visual manners of traditional art, which had often been closely allied to
Christian symbolism and wealthy patronage, the modernist painters
turned to new and, once more, shocking sources of visual reference.
Forms of art previously regarded as naive or uncivilized now provided
the inspiration for the new painting and sculpture: in particular, pre-
modern cultures were valued for the direct expressiveness of their art, as
in African and Polynesian traditions of sculpture, or the remnants of
European peasant art. Serge Diaghileff's ballet, *The Fire Bird* (1910) was
profoundly influential in this way through its use of Russian neo-
primitivist designs. This paradox whereby modernizing artists exploited
pre-modern values and traditions is a contradiction which has large
consequences, as we shall see.

[handwritten margin note: Impressionist flirtation with Japanese art]

These tendencies within modernist visual art at least retained some
visual relation to the known world. But there also developed, partly as a
consequence of the first revolution in seeing, another broad movement
in painting and drawing which altogether abandoned the world of
appearances. Modernism in the visual arts was not simply the triumphant
exploitation of optical knowledge, the painterly dwelling on what is seen
as primordially true. The more challenging interface between perception
and cognition was also explored by the new art which led towards an
abstracting of the art image, and a conceptual presentation of psychological processes. A series of anti-visual artists attempted to think beyond
the apparencies of the visual field, in order to articulate the underlying
foundations of physiology and psychology. This project began with
Cubism, initiated by Pablo Picasso (1881–1973) and Georges Braque
(1882–1963), and was quickly followed by Russian Suprematism, invented
by Kasimir Malevich (1878–1935). The extraordinary career of Marcel
Duchamp (1887–1968) anticipated many of the strategies associated with
postmodernism, in particular the notion of a Conceptual Art. Paintings,
sculptures and assemblages of this kind explored the complex relations
between perception, memory and identity, and in the process produced

works which ironized and reflected upon the assumptions of traditional painting and conventional perception. In order to make these quite new connections, the abstracting artists often combined visual images with written texts, or produced collages of disparate materials which had never previously been considered to be appropriate to Art. Written and graphic forms also began to draw intimately on the new modes of mechanical reproduction – photography, cinema, radio – developing technicized styles in emulation. These working practices of collage and bricolage – the eclectic combination of diverse, apparently incongruous materials, as in Duchamp's *The Bride Stripped Bare by her Bachelors, Even (The Large Glass)* (1915–23) – established a kind of writerly art practice in opposition to the cult of painterly conventions, and this has become very influential for late twentieth-century artists working in what is known as the postmodern period (Krauss 1986A; Harrison 1991).

What is modernist writing? Modernist novels, drama and poetry articulate a new frankness through new kinds of narrative or formal organization. During the last decades of the nineteenth century fiction and drama increasingly focused on emergent social divisions and conflict. The great nineteenth-century achievements in the novel had also addressed class division and tensions between the individual and her or his place in relation to marriage and desire, but modernist and near-modernist authors wrote with increasing explicitness, as their narratives gave voice to the textures of subjective life and the agonized development of relationships with startling effect. Through narrative techniques such as stream of consciousness, free-indirect narration, graphic description and the juxtaposition of scenes through montage, the novel at the turn of the century was articulating sharpened forms of awareness for its authors and readership.

This vivid, frank writing intensified the representation of people's subjective experience of class and gender. A poignant contrast which demonstrates this new development can be made between two novels, *The Ragged Trousered Philanthropists* by 'Robert Tressell' (pseudonym of Robert Noonan), published in 1914, and D. H. Lawrence's *Sons and Lovers*, published in 1913. Both novels describe attempts to escape from the poverty and restriction of English working-class life at the same period, drawing respectively on Noonan's experience of Hastings, and Lawrence's of Eastwood, near Nottingham. Noonan's hero, Frank Owen, is crushed by the drudgery and exploitation of work in the building trade within the oppressive snobberies of 'Mugsborough'. The vindictive pettiness of Edwardian class relations is closely portrayed through characters who are marked by allegorical names such as Crass the Foreman, Grinder the Greengrocer, and the Reverend Belcher of the Shining Light Chapel – while the hero's own surname, Owen, recalls Robert Owen, the early nineteenth-century philanthropist and industrial reformer. *The Ragged Trousered Philanthropists* is one of the great portrayals of early twentieth-century working-class life, and its subsequent publication history is an eloquent record of suppressions and enthused reception (Ball 1973). But when compared with Lawrence's *Sons and Lovers*, Noonan's novel reads like a work from the nineteenth century, relying on caricature and moralistic tableaux to convey its message of Socialist redemption.

Although Lawrence only developed a decisively innovative style in the period following the composition of *Sons and Lovers*, when contrasted with *The Ragged Trousered Philanthropists*, his novel clearly marks a new kind of writing. The subjectivities of his characters are shaped at their most profound levels by familial experience which is also class-based experience, and this is true of their most intimate feelings. Both novels for example describe a particular rite of passage in working-class families where the hair of the young male child is cut for the first time. This shearing marks a crucial stage in the mother's relinquishing of the child, where the cropping is a confirmation of its male gender. In 'Tressell's' novel, the child Frankie prattles precociously, urging his mother to cut his hair so that he won't be teased any more (Tressell [1914] 1965: 164–5). The pathos of the situation is real enough, but it recalls some of the sentimentality of Dickens' presentation of childhood. In *Sons and Lovers* the parallel incident is focused at the level of psychological latency. Without consulting his wife, Walter Morel cuts the hair of his first, one-year-old son William. Gertrude Morel is deeply wounded by this action, which becomes a trauma expressing the failure of their relationship, and it marks a permanent transformation in the marriage:

> She was one of those women who cannot cry: whom it hurts as it hurts a man. It was like ripping something out of her, her sobbing ... She remembered the scene all her life, as one in which she had suffered the most intensely.
> This act of masculine clumsiness was the spear through the side of her love for Morel.

> (Lawrence [1913] 1992: 24)

The scale of the consequences, and the way in which the couple's separation is articulated through a small, naturalistic incident, demonstrates the psychological acuity of an early-modernist fiction, as against the more external pathos of Noonan's 'Dickensian' narrative. These formal differences between the two novels are real enough, but *The Ragged Trousered Philanthropists* employs a range of conventions in some ways no less impressive than the new tone of *Sons and Lovers*. What is also at stake for the two authors is a different conception of readership, and it must be partly this which encouraged Lawrence's innovative style.

The genders of modernism

Were modernist cultural developments of equal value to men and women? How was the representation of gendered relations and sexuality affected by modernism's revolution? When studying the early-modern period in Europe (that is, the sixteenth and seventeenth centuries) feminist historiography has asked 'Did women enjoy a Renaissance?' and the same question can be put for twentieth-century modernism. The argument which says that women did not benefit from the innovations of modernism is less often made, but has persuasive elements. Here the presence of the idea-of-woman in many male texts, paintings, and films is presented not as a liberation from repressive conventional attitudes, but often as a violent intensification of traditional misrepresentations. Modernist frankness and its exploitation of sexuality often only confirmed the figure of woman as an etherial ideal or as erotic object to be plundered (Segal 1988; Showalter 1987: 121–64; Taylor 1987: 54–5).

As for all earlier periods, the recognition – and often even the basic awareness – of many women's careers as writers and artists have only begun to be established within academic criticism and literary history since the 1970s. The difficulties for women in earning a living by writing during the early twentieth century, and of making a serious reputation, clearly affected their lives and the kinds of writing which they produced (Benstock 1987). In addition, a significant number of female authors also committed their energies to the social issues of the time such as the campaigns for female suffrage, equality of educational opportunity, law reform in respect of divorce and property rights, combating the gendered division of labour, and campaigning for greater awareness of the need for sexual hygiene and contraception (Hollis 1979; Kings 1987). Therefore the modernist definition fits even more imperfectly for many women's careers than for those male authors in respect of whose writing the paradigm was painstakingly constructed (Scott 1990; Joannou 1995). A similar case is made for women painters – and no doubt could be made for female composers, architects, film-makers – where art history and theory are now being redefined in terms of hitherto overlooked careers, and through analysis of the historical construction of gender difference. The established paradigms for modernism and postmodernism are both very effectively called into question from the perspectives of contemporary research into the history of women's cultural contributions (Pollock 1988: 50–90).

Female authors often produced work which has been overlooked by the grand narrative of literary-critical theory because it is generically inappropriate: some examples of this from among many cases would be the massively influential translations from Russian by Constance Garnett (1861–1946), who declined to interpret for Lenin in 1907; the wry children's fiction of Edith Nesbit (1858–1924); the popular fiction of May Sinclair (1863–1946) which was among the first to incorporate Freudian and Jungian psychology in attacking conventional hypocrisies and repressions. Or else women's writing only gained attention through notoriety when its frankness was read as 'impropriety', as in the cases of 'George Egerton' (Mary Chavelita Dunne, 1859–1945), and 'Ralph Iron' (Olive Schreiner, 1855–1920). These indirections and intransigencies marked the lives and production of writers such as Katherine Mansfield (1888–1923) and Jean Rhys (1890–1979). Other women such as Harriet Shaw Weaver, Sylvia Beach and Adrienne Monnier acted tirelessly as patrons and propagandists for modernist writing (Benstock 1987: 194–229; Symons 1987: 72–106). These careers and many others like them can be researched in detail in the collections edited by Virginia Blain, Patricia Clements and Isobel Grundy (1990), Bonnie Kime Scott (1990), and Janet Todd (1989).

The female authors whose work is most often described in terms of modernist innovation are Gertrude Stein (1874–1946), H.D. (Hilda Doolittle, 1886–1961), and Virginia Woolf (1882–1941). They are cited as demonstrating the ways in which modernist texts became fundamentally 'writerly', producing the materiality of language as an inextricable element of subjectivity, writing and reading. Avant-garde female authors therefore used these techniques of fragmentation and textuality to represent the pressures of patriarchal culture in a new way. Pictorial art of the period had focused on the surface of the painting itself as the locus of attention, as the flatbed or plain where abstraction articulated the exchanges of perception and memory; this was done in reaction against

[21]

the pre-modernist view of painting as a perspective on a version of the visual world. Similarly, the modernist page became 'writerly' by interposing the mechanisms of language as constitutive of meaning, rather than allowing language to be a transparent vehicle for its narrative or humane content. This reflexivity is in fact present in different ways in all texts, but modernist writing foregrounded the process as an inseparable aspect of literary consumption.

This emphasis on writerly process was common to all of the innovative work of the period, and structuralist and post-structuralist, deconstructive criticism since the 1970s has demonstrated how reflexive processes are the condition of reading modernist epics such as James Joyce's *Ulysses* (1922), *Finnegans Wake* (1939), and Marcel Proust's *A la recherche du temps perdu* (1913–27). Proust's text is also not alone in recasting assumptions about heterosexuality for the period. A particular version of the argument over gender and language is made for women's writing, where different experiences may derive from the developmental process, in Freud's terms a product of the 'family romance' which conditions males and females in gender-specific ways. Or they may be the result of a female author's agonistic relation to an essentially male tradition of writing, or from psychological processes thought to be specific to women as a gender (DuPlessis 1985: 2–3). Virginia Woolf participated very actively in these arguments, sometimes making a case for a specific 'female sentence', at other times arguing for a writing that transcended gendered differentiation through a kind of androgynous perspective. Her very particular contribution to modernist writerly practice was to construct novels where psychological identity, the experience of temporality and textual innovation are completely inter-dependent.

The impact of war

The twentieth century's two World Wars inevitably made decisive contributions to the development and subsequent fate of modernism. The Second World War and the succeeding period of nuclear confrontation – the Cold War – can be said to have re-located and consolidated modernism within a new, American context, whereas at the heart of the earlier period of west European modernism was the cataclysmic experience of the First World War. Painting, writing, music and film were all inevitably further transformed in the process of responding to the events of 1914–18, and their aftermath. The conflict itself became another engine of social change, rivalling the experience of the metropolises as a motive for recasting forms of expression.

The First World War also demonstrates some of the profound contradictions in definitions that attempt to map a single modernist movement or cultural formation. Some modernist movements in the pre-war period celebrated the potential for vigorous transformation which technology offered. The dynamism of speed and power derived from machines was seen as an extension of human capacity which could be turned against the moribund structures and values of late nineteenth-century society. Artists of this persuasion could welcome the onset of conflict in 1914 as the supreme expression of technological mastery, and their painting, collages and syntax articulated the excited disruptions which were expressive of this dynamism. This was an aspect of modernism which celebrated modernity's violence, and welcomed the accelerated rhythms and anonymities of mass-urban living. In endorsing the *Futurism* great European war, these avant-garde artists joined with the variety of sections of public opinion and the political establishment which gave their assent to the conflict as a 'cleansing' or 'heroic nationalist' enterprise. This kind of techno-utopianism was developed to catastrophic effect in Germany during the 1930s, when Joseph Goebbels called for a *stählernde Romantik* – a 'steel-like romanticism' (Herf 1984: 3).

Rationality or the unconscious?

In complete contradiction to this celebratory tendency within some of the new art forms, a more widespread response to the New Age was motivated by pessimism and despair. This articulated an anguished individualism, where the human essence was felt to be threatened by the inhumanity and destructive capacity of the new technologies. Throughout the nineteenth century a pervasive unease had grown up in response to the consequences of industrialism, and all kinds of reaction against the oppressions of the machine age had been expressed. Often this rejection of contemporary material development went along with a profound nostalgia for pre-industrial, certainly for pre-modern forms of society and belief, a generalized attitude which is described as 'romantic anti-industrialism'. While modernist artists and writers often rejected the socially-endorsed forms of religion, such as Christianity, many of them explored substitutive forms of belief, drawn eclectically from a wide range of sources – New Paganism, anthropological texts, religions of the Far

[23]

Hardy's "paganism"

East, world mythology, the classical religions of Greece and Rome. These perspectives which drew on mysticism, reaction and despair also tended to view modernity's development as a movement towards imminent apocalypse, and the experiences of the First World War could only confirm this analysis in the minds of many artists, writers and intellectuals.

utilitarianism

Here then is a complete contradiction within the paradigm which is offered as modernism: one tendency within it can be described as a rationalist, modernizing ambition which endorses technological progress and the renovation of society through aggressive administration and directed change. Simultaneously, and supposedly within the same para-digm, there is a reaction against nearly everything that is to be under-stood as modernity – rejection of the metropolis, of technology, of the scientific administration of life and the social sphere – though this rejection is articulated through modernist styles in writing, painting, or music. And if a rationalist, calculative attitude characterizes one aspect of modernist culture, then the reactive tendency explored irrationalism

Dadaism

and unconscious experience as pre-modern resources within the psyche which were to be called on as a form of resistance to the tyranny of bureaucratic renovation in modernity. And of course, more confusing still, both strains could be at work within the same individual simul-taneously, or at different moments of their development. These con-flicting tendencies are clearly present in the work of arch-modernists such as Lawrence and H.D., Pound and Eliot. As we shall see, this flagrant contradiction within modernism can be extended into positions taken over the meaning of the postmodern.

Formal experiment or conventional form?

Artistic responses to the First World War also demonstrate another major difficulty within the generalized definition of early twentieth-century culture as modernist: how precisely can we differentiate between works which are thoroughly modern in their form and content, and those which appear to be conventional, but somehow do contain elements of the new because they address similar issues within their period? A major artistic movement in Germany that developed immediately before the First World War was identified at the time as Expressionism, and it was characterized by many of those aspects of pessimism, anguished indi-vidualism and apocalyptic despair which have been described as the anti-modern tendency within modernism. Painters and poets working

[24]

within the Expressionist mode in Germany inevitably adopted an anti-
militarist stance, which was in part a criticism of German nationalist
policies; the poets Georg Trakl (1887–1914), August Stramm (1874–1915)
and Alfred Lichtenstein (1889–1914), and the artists Käthe Kollwitz
(1867–1945) and Otto Dix (1891–1969) took this position. Consequently
much of the poetry written in German against the war was extremely
Expressionist in form, and drew on an established culture of political
resistance to German militarism (Cardinal 1984).

England, needless to say, had no comparable sub-culture which
combined vigorous artistic and political activity, and in complete contrast the predominant movement in English poetry during the period was
that of Georgianism. This style of writing sought to continue the virtues
of late nineteenth-century elegy, based in celebration of English pastoral
conventions and ruralist attitudes (Symons 1987: 15–20; Timms 1987). The
best-known Georgian poets include Rupert Brooke (1887–1915), W. H.
Davies (1871–1940), and Walter de la Mare (1873–1956). Both Expressionism
and Georgianism were successful movements in market terms, but
clearly were appealing to quite different kinds of taste and readership.
The movement known as Expressionism can be confidently assigned to
modernism, but what about the English Georgians? Even though they
articulated conservative taste and views in their highly successful antho-
logies, aspects of Georgianism were also drawn upon by the most
outspoken of the British war poets as they parodied or negated Georgian
convention within their writings about the horrors of the trenches.
Therefore the poems in English which we all know as the most eloquent
denunciations of the horrors of trench warfare and the fiascos of set-piece
'battles' in the First War present a problem in terms of aesthetic category:
are Wilfred Owen, Siegfried Sassoon, Robert Graves, and Ivor Gurney
modernist or conservative in their form (Featherstone 1995: 18–24)? Or
are these formal questions completely beside the point, given the urgency
of the poems' material content (Yeats 1936: xxxiv)?

Elite modernism versus popular taste

> I have seen the forces of death with Mr Chesterton at their head
> upon a white horse. Mr Pound, Mr Joyce, and Mr Lewis write living
> English; one does not realize the awfulness of death until one meets
> with the living language.
>
> (T. S. Eliot, 'Observations', *The Egoist*, May 1918)

[25]

Early twentieth-century modernism encouraged artistic styles (or man-nerisms) which made its artefacts both challenging and enigmatic, and therefore it can be said to have restricted the kind of appeal which they might make to a wider audience. It is always possible to be nostalgic for a period when the best writing and the most accomplished art circulated widely among all sections of the public, but it is certainly the case that there was a considerable degree of consensus during the mid-nineteenth century as to who were the foremost contemporary novelists and poets. Distribution of this work was also enviably widespread, both among the established middle-class readership, and among a significant section of the aspiring, labouring classes. During the period of modernism, this consensus over literary and cultural value became fragmented, and the readership broke into different constituencies.

The most popular authors during the high modernist period in Britain were dramatists such as J. M. Barrie and George Bernard Shaw, novelists like Marie Corelli, John Buchan, Arnold Bennett and John Galsworthy, novelist-essayists such as G. K. Chesterton, poets such as A. E. Housman and Sir John Squire, and the extraordinarily energetic H. G. Wells, a category all on his own. The Poets Laureate of the time were Alfred Austin, in post from 1890, and Robert Bridges (1913) who was succeeded by John Masefield in 1930. Critical-theoretical accounts which give an adequate sense of the contemporaneity of these popular works together with the now more celebrated, but then distinctly 'minority' modernist writers such as Joyce, Eliot and Woolf are only just beginning to be written (Trotter 1993). Good literary biography is still more helpful than most theoretical writing in giving a specific sense of how writing was made in the period, and how different groupings interacted with each other (for example, Glendinning 1987). The relation between popular culture and high cultural values is a central part of the discussions of postmodernism, but has not yet adequately been extended to the earlier period.

Because modernist works demand interpretive ingenuity and a substan-tial range of cultural reference on the part of their audience or readers, they provoked the need for commentary and contextual information by way of research. As a result, though they were often conceived in the spirit of critique of their period, modernist works now seem inevitably to have precipitated an extensive institutional framework which categorizes them and attempts to explain them. This relationship between intellectually demanding or recondite cultural production, museums as institutions which legitimize this difficulty, and a consequent industry of explanation, academic and otherwise, also becomes a part of the supposed rejection of modernism as elitist art by the postmodern populists.

Modernism – a limiting paradigm

The construction and perpetuation of syllabuses and curricula in the Humanities can be a dispiritingly selective process, confirming and circulating only a choice grouping of names, works, or movements, and therefore creating damaging distortions and misrepresentation. At the edges of every syllabus are a host of excluded names, careers and agendas, and to study these reveals the nature of the selections that are at work in the dominant accounts. Teachers and students should always be questioning these limits, aware of the values that are being silently endorsed in the selective span of attention which academic institutions allow, and we should be careful of the works, practices and values which are silenced through these processes of selection. And if we are to take the paradigm of cosmopolitan modernism at its word, then we should also be prepared to read in several languages, and develop adequate inter-disciplinary approaches which are able to evaluate works in the range of media exploited by modernist practice, relating these to an adequate sense of complex historical development.

For these kinds of reason, we can make three objections to the reductive use of the term modernism:

1 That there was a profound transformation in all artistic and cultural practices during the first three decades of this century cannot be denied, but categorizing it as a single phenomenon is unhelpful. Modernism as a sophisticated paradigm is only established in the mid-century as a retrospective rationalization for the array of artistic and cultural practices of the earlier period. Modernism was not a word which was used in this way during the period itself; the earliest citations in *OED* show 'modernism' being used in a denigrating sense – from 1929, describing New York, 'A city whose "modernism" consists in copying the poorest French models of the New Tradition.'

2 The notion of a monolithic modernism creates false dichotomies between 'formalist-progressive' art and 'conventional-realist' work in the period, imposing categories that exclude, or lead to the denigration of, un-modernist works, and which are unhelpful in thinking about the complex liaisons between works and their social contexts. And too

[27]

often the period immediately prior to the heroic phase of experimental cultural production is vilified, as false dichotomies are created between nineteenth-century and early twentieth-century production, leaving significant figures stranded as 'transitional' or 'failed' formalists. Works by women may be particularly subject to this kind of selectivity.

3 If modernism faded in the course of the 1920s, how are we to describe what came after? As a failure of nerve, or a return to the true path of nineteenth-century naturalism/realism? Just as the transitional period before modernism is over-shadowed, there is a similar failure to construct compelling accounts of the developments and continuities, the new agendas of the 1930s and 1940s. Much of the cultural activity of this period was responding in panic, trauma or outrage to the long, unfolding political crisis in Europe. Economic slump, the brutalizations of National Socialism and Stalin's centralization programmes required artists and writers to respond to their depredations. But the diverse developments of writing, painting, and film in this phase are not installed as worthy of study in the same way as those of the heroic modernist phase. This inattention derives from the failure to notice work which is more socially engaged, more directly politically troubled, than the individualist-expressivist ethic encouraged by the paradigm of modernism.

For these reasons it is useful to consider some of the ways in which writers' and artists' careers either developed, or failed to respond to the changing conditions between the early 1920s and the late 1930s. The painter-novelist-polemicist Percy Wyndham Lewis (1884–1957) was a noisy participant in much of the artistic innovation of the classic modernist period, but when he reviewed developments from the vantage of 1937 in his autobiography, *Blasting and Bombardiering,* he felt that the heroic experiments of the avant-garde to which he belonged had in effect been wasted on the world:

> *We are the first men of a Future that has not materialized.* We belong to a 'great age' that has not 'come off'. We moved too quickly for the world. We set too sharp a pace. And, more and more exhausted by War, Slump, and Revolution, the world has *fallen back.* Its ambition has withered: it has declined into a listless compromise – half 'modern', half Cavalcade!
>
> (Lewis 1937: 258)

Lewis was only one of many commentators during the 1930s who tried to account for the very different cultural styles of the two decades after 1918. Another, the essayist Cyril Connolly, divided authors into Mandarin or Vernacular/Colloquial, corresponding to their modernist or naturalist/realist styles (Connolly [1938] 1961: 57–84). But the most ambitious survey of this kind was by Eric Blair (better known as 'George Orwell') whose 'Inside the Whale', written during the first months of the Second World War, took a different view of Lewis's generation and their achievements: 'When one looks back at the twenties, nothing is queerer than the way in which every important event in Europe escaped the notice of the English intelligentsia' (Orwell [1940] 1970: 557).

Orwell was one of a number of writers in the first post-modernist generation who felt uneasy about the political content or implications of high-modernist culture. Many modernist works betrayed an ambiguous relationship with colonialism; there was often a surface rejection of European imperial pretensions, for example, in Ezra Pound's *Homage to Sextus Propertius* (1917), but latent colonialist attitudes such as viewing non-white races as Other, as primordial and authentic, were even more prevalent. The extreme utopianism of many authors from the 1920s gradually mutated into more pragmatic political extremisms by the early 1930s, as in the case of Ezra Pound and T. S. Eliot. By contrast, the German novelist Thomas Mann (1875–1955), born in the generation previous to that of Wyndham Lewis, sustained a unique consistency of achievement across the cataclysmic disruptions of the first half-century. From the family chronicle *Buddenbrooks* (1901), to the analysis of a diseased Europe in *The Magic Mountain* (1924), to the dark allegory of *Doctor Faustus* (1947), his realist fiction did not cut itself off from the actual conditions of the contemporary world. Mann's *Diaries 1918–1939* are an extraordinary record of his struggle to sustain forms of fiction which could seriously address the personal and political tragedies of the mid-century, and the continuity of his production throughout the modernist period and beyond is a remarkable feat (Mann [1977] 1984). No British or American authors of the same period produced poetry or fiction which so successfully explored the major events in texts that remained access-ible to a relatively wide audience. As a consequence, Mann's work also produced some of the most thoughtful critical debate during the 1930s between politically committed writers such as Bertolt Brecht, Georg Lukács, Walter Benjamin and Theodor Adorno (Jameson 1977). This was again a level of critical and philosophical debate unavailable to Britain in the period.

[handwritten margin note: Modernism's avante-garde styles made it distant and elitist]

[29]

Modernism's aftermath

Charles Harrison, an influential historian and theorist of modern painting, develops a compelling analysis of the transition from modernist to
postmodern art production. His account does not accept the common
view of mid-century modernist painting as the heroic achievement of an
expressive-individualist creativity. Harrison cites the consensus of critical opinion which was formed around the paintings of Jackson Pollock,
Willem de Kooning, Arshile Gorky and the sculptures of David Smith
in the early 1950s as a defining moment in the establishment of post-war
cultural norms. What is crucial, in his view, is the collaboration of art
criticism and commentary in the period with the art works themselves,
a complicity which resulted in the establishment of a new aesthetic. In
this regime of taste, particular kinds of art production and value were
'talked up', and other agendas were effectively marginalized (Harrison
and Orton 1984). For Harrison, the consequences of this Cold War
settlement of the cultural landscape are momentous: 'What is at issue ...
is no less than the moral content of our history' (Harrison 1991: 6).

This argument, which derives specifically from the history of art
criticism and theory, can be usefully generalized for all culture of the
period. Modernism on this view is not a particular repertoire of formal
artistic devices – use of collage, abstraction, the supreme valuation of
individual expressiveness – so much as the climate of expectations and
definitions which is created, and within which one kind of artistic agenda
is promoted at the expense of all others. The way in which Henry
Moore's monumental abstract sculpture was consistently championed
during the post-war period as a peculiarly British achievement is one
example of this art-politics at work. Harrison's analysis is also useful
because it extends the period of modernist art into the second half of the
century, observing that there is a kind of hiatus for modernism during
the 1930s and 1940s, followed by a globalizing of a certain view of 'the
modern' in the post-war period. Since the late 1960s the Art & Language
group (of which Harrison is a leading member) has responded to this
analysis of the condition of modern art production by co-ordinating their
art-making activity with systematic critical-theoretical exposition, in an
attempt to change the terms within which artistic production is understood. This kind of project seeks a new expressivity within a revised
paradigm for cultural meanings, one which engages with the political
blindnesses and occlusions of prevailing assumptions: 'To engage in a

critique of modernism as a culture of art was thus to propose a form of work emancipated from the constituting power of modernism as a discourse' (Harrison 1991: 13).

For Harrison, what is taken to be postmodernism in art of the 1960s and subsequently may better be seen as the revival of genuinely challenging and conceptually alert aspects of the earlier 'classical' modernist tradition that had been effaced by the 'establishment' modernism of the 1950s. The incorporation of criticism and theory to artistic practices produced a 'writerly' modernism, miscalled 'postmodern', much of which was only of academic interest, and which should be distinguished from the work which was genuinely posing new questions and exploiting new strategies in relation to the prevailing assumptions about value in art (Harrison 1991: 22, 30–1).

There are therefore major problems in thinking about the transition from modernism to postmodernism, not least the elision of the catastrophic experience of three decades, from the 1930s to the late 1950s (Lindey 1990). It is tempting to see this as another conspiracy contrived to suppress knowledge of social conflict, political crisis and the forms of cultural response which these provoked. But the elision is more likely to be an amnesia which authoritative institutions and their functionaries have been happy to encourage. Misha Glenny is the Eastern Europe correspondent for the BBC, and he is a resourceful reporter. He called his account of the European revolutions which occurred during 1989 and 1990 *The Rebirth of History* (Glenny 1993). His title takes issue with Francis Fukuyama's modish success, *The End of History and the Last Man* (1992), which was influential among commentators and policy makers in the United States after the end of the Cold War. 'Rebirth' suggests that a period of stagnation is now at an end with the collapse of the Cold-War stalemate, but it also implies the discovery of aspects of the past, the reawakening of old traumas, which still have to be understood and resolved. Reviewing the subsequent development of European modernism is certainly a part of this urgent revaluation.

What are the formal qualities that we admire in paintings, films, poems and novels? How do we reconcile the different kinds of attention that we give to works which are directly pleasurable, and those which make more complex kinds of demands? What are the ethical values, extending into political agendas, which cultural texts and objects imply for us? All of the central arguments over the scope and meaning of postmodernism can be referred back to these fundamental questions inherited from the difficult break-up and reformation of classic modernism. Walter Benjamin's writing is often quoted in discussions about the nature of modernity, but he insisted on attending to particular texts rather than fashionable generalities: 'he had little use for catchwords in general [such as Expressionism] and was less attached to schools than to specific phenomena' (Scholem [1975] 1982: 65). If we can critically review the competing definitions of modernity and postmodernity by referring them to specific works, then we may be in a better position to contextualize and evaluate the culture of our own dynamic and confusing moment.

Postmodernism: from Elite to Mass Culture?

> For a multitude of causes unknown to former times are now
> acting with a combined force to blunt the discriminating
> powers of the mind, and unfitting it for all voluntary exertion
> to reduce it to a state of almost savage torpor.
>
> (*Who wrote this and when?*)

We have briefly reviewed some of the influential descriptions of modernity and modernism, and also the material conditions which are said to
create postmodernity. We can now consider key elements of what is
described as the new culture of postmodernism. The fundamental issues
here are concerned with the definition of culture itself and the uses to
which it is put in the new times of the 1990s.

Who might be a good example of a postmodern artist? Eiko Ishioka is
one of Japan's foremost graphic designers (Eiko 1990). As a supremely
talented art director she has designed promotional imagery for film
director Akira Kurosawa and for films such as Francis Ford Coppola's
Apocalypse Now. She has also produced artwork for the American minimal-
ist composer Philip Glass and jazz trumpeter Miles Davis. But Eiko
Ishioka is not a bland commercial artist because in much of her imagery
she has been concerned to affront Japanese notions of women's subservi-
ence. In the mid-1970s for example she designed a series of posters to
promote dresses by the leading couturier Issey Miyake, adding text from
traditional Japanese haiku poems to emphasize her images of strong,
independent women: 'The nightingale sings for no one but herself.' But
she also creates more enigmatic work; in 1978 she directed a one-minute
TV commercial to promote Parco, a new Japanese department store. The
ad showed Faye Dunaway wearing a black dress against a black background, peeling and eating a hard-boiled egg. The department store
name was faded up for the last few seconds of the action, and a low-key
voice-over uttered a sentence in broken English : 'This is film for Parco.'
The ad was highly successful, and Eiko rationalized its effects in terms

of performance art: eating an egg was a totally 'global act' done by rich and poor, advanced and developing peoples:

> Through art direction and acting, eating a hard-boiled egg became an act that was sensuous and intellectual, sophisticated and raw, funny and serious, masculine and feminine, artistic and commercial.
>
> (Jackson 1990: 7)

Eiko Ishioka is an excellent example of a creative individual who might be categorized as a postmodern. Having grown up in the poverty of post-war Japan, she now works with world-class film-makers and musicians. She uses a profound knowledge of traditional Japanese culture in her work as a commercial artist, but she also brings a critical edge to her designs. She draws voraciously on imagery from all periods and cultures, but has a troubled awareness of how her national culture is becoming homogenized. Working in the midst of the design and entertainment industries which are a major cause of this confusion, Eiko can still be critical of the process, and reflect on it in her imagery:

> Our culture has become confused. It's like a *makunouchi-bento* — the traditional Japanese box-lunch, full of little portions of different dishes ... It's creative chaos: humorous, erotic, vulgar, intelligent ... but I think perhaps Japan has become too westernised — too *whitenised.*
>
> (Jackson 1990: 8)

Conventional aesthetics would not recognize Eiko Ishioka's ads and posters as art at all because they are highly successful commercial design, but it is exactly in her eclectic fusion of art and advertising that she demonstrates new forms of contemporary artistic production.

Postmodernity is often described as blurring or destroying distinctions between established cultural hierarchies, and it is said to do this by introducing themes and images from mass/popular/consumer culture into the prestige forms of high culture, such as literature and the fine arts. The terms in which 'the cultural' is described here — high against low, mass against elite, consumer-popular as opposed to educated — are not value-free, but are intrinsic to the debate. Put in this hierarchical form, the crisis posed by postmodern culture repeats confrontations which have been staged from the early eighteenth century. Since that time social elites have been concerned to defend and consolidate their supremacy through regulation of their hard-won cultural capital. They have felt threatened by the growth of new classes which represent audiences with different needs and interests, and who are perceived to endanger refined values. The quotation at the beginning of this section lamenting the growth of a vicious and degrading common culture which acts to blunt the mind's discriminations was written by William Wordsworth as long ago as 1800 (Wordsworth and Coleridge [1798, 1800] 1991). Wordsworth intended that the effects of his poetry should actively work against this torpor induced by the distracting and stupefying effects of contemporary, late eighteenth-century culture (and see Porter 1993: 9).

Refinement, taste, discrimination and evaluation are some of the key terms in this social history of cultural regulation. The possession and exercise of these skills by an individual demonstrates their command of privileged knowledge which is related to social status. The act of giving cultural value to particular texts or objects requires the exercise of aesthetic judgement, and the social history of aesthetics can be traced in the rise of these new classes seeking expression for their status and fulfilment through cultural competence (Bourdieu [1979] 1984). Therefore on this view there is no intrinsic value to the content of cultural categories; *King Lear* is not intrinsically better than *King Kong*. Shakespeare's play is only maintained in a privileged place as a pre-eminent cultural text through an elaborate history of aesthetic evaluation which is expressive of complex social differentiation. And maintaining the cultural supremacy of *King Lear* also sustains the system of social differences which endorses its position. *King Lear* has a more powerful interpretive community maintaining its status, and against which the arguments in favour of *King Kong* can make little headway. This will only happen when popular culture is taken as seriously as Shakespeare's tragedy, not in moral-aesthetic terms, but in terms of its history as a social text. One of the great virtues of the debate over postmodern culture is that it has carried forward this new kind of evaluation of the function of common culture in the modern period exactly by refusing traditional moral-aesthetic valuations (Ross 1989; Varnedoe and Gopnik 1990).

This kind of new cultural history can also alert us to qualities which are in fact shared by high art forms and everyday culture. For example in the midst of the disruptions of the Bolshevik revolution, the Russian Formalist critic Victor Shklovsky wrote a celebrated and influential analysis of the effects which, he claimed, are specific to works of literature. What novels and poems do best, Shklovsky argued, is de-familiarize their readers' perceptions so that they have a heightened awareness of life, people and objects around them. Shklovsky's most famous essay, 'Art and Technique', defines the process like this:

> I personally feel that defamiliarization is found almost everywhere form is found ... An image ... creates a 'vision' of the object instead of serving as a means for knowing it.
>
> (Lemon and Reis 1965: 18)

Because we recognize it as a representation of a thing, and not the thing itself?

    Aesthetic form therefore draws attention to itself as a poem or novel, actually regardless of the content which it is expressing. At the same period in France, the leading radical theorist of shop window dressing, H. Glévéo, was promoting a new way of displaying commodities in the smart Parisian department stores. In his article 'Modern display: the power of suggestion of the object' (*La Publicité* 21, November 1923) Glévéo advocated isolating single items in the display window, rather than piles of multiple examples of commodities. The displayed item in this way 'becomes somehow suggestive, silently but surely, to the brain of the public drawn to the window' (Varnedoe and Gopnik 1990: 280). Such a display defamiliarizes the hat/vase/tennis racket, and in Shklovsky's terms, creates a 'vision' of the object. High-cultural perception and advertising perception are closely allied here, and their closeness offered possibilities which Dadaist artists such as Marcel Duchamp were quick to exploit. When Duchamp submitted a porcelain urinal signed 'R. Mutt' and entitled 'Fountain' to the Society of Independent Artists' show in New York in 1917 he was playing with these ambiguities, among others. By contextualizing the ceramic object in an exhibition à la Glévéo, Duchamp added art-value to the functional object. But he was also drawing attention to the aesthetic success of the urinal's form, which as a modernist he endorsed.

Can an ordinary object be made into art when we are presented with a "vision" of it?

    Twentieth-century common culture has been viewed as a threat to refined and enlightened minds by many different groups. In England the work of F. R. Leavis and the journal *Scrutiny* saw literary discrimination as a means of sustaining intelligent thought against the mediocrity of 'admass civilization' (Mulhern 1979). In Germany Theodor Adorno, Max Horkheimer and the Frankfurt Institute of Social Research, influenced by the bitter European experiences of the period from the First to the Second World War, developed a deeply pessimistic view of the effects of the culture industry on modern populations (Horkheimer and Adorno [1947] 1972). The powerful combination of the advertising and entertainment industries was seen as the main threat to individual freedom of thought and expression. In America during the 1950s the concept of mass

[36]

culture was fiercely debated within the context of the need to define a pluralist democratic consensus able to defend itself against the supposed threat of mass totalitarianism presented by world communism (Ross 1989: 42–64). This social history of culture therefore also intersects with the history of national identities, since nation states in the modern period have increasingly asserted political power and control through forms of cultural nationalism, that is through the creation and manipulation of particular cultural traditions in order to create definitions of supposedly true nationality and citizenship. All of these criteria were put to the test in the immediate post-war period by new social conditions and the creative responses which they produced.

By the early 1950s an aesthetic derived from modernism was being installed at the level of high culture in the form of Abstract Expressionist painting and Existentialist literature, and then in consumer culture through the adoption of design mannerisms taken from modernist art. But advertising was once more the focus for an agitated debate over the nature of its influence on the general population. Authors such as Vance Packard attacked Madison Avenue ad agencies and accused them of being no better than the communists who indoctrinated their captive peoples: 'brain-washing' is first recorded by *OED* in this sense from October 1950. A post-war culture was beginning to develop which was organized around mass consumption and the need to create endless new markets (Packard 1962). For the first time young people became a significant economic group, and fashion-music-style coalesced to form the new phenomenon of an aggressively confident youth culture.

A cluster of London-based artists and writers in the early 1950s were the first to make active use of this new phenomenon in their work. The British Pop artists were excited by the brash vigour of American advertising imagery, and drew on it in reaction to the staid and insular versions of modernism then current in the British arts establishment. In London, architects Alison and Peter Smithson, sculptor Eduardo Paolozzi, architectural historian Reyner Banham, novelist J. G. Ballard and the painter Richard Hamilton formed a loose association known as the Independent Group. They vigorously researched aspects of mass culture while also revising definitions of classical modernism (Hebdige 1988: 45–116; Varnedoe and Gopnik 1990: 314–25). Richard Hamilton's collage *Just What Is It That Makes Today's Homes So Different, So Appealing?* was made in 1956 as a poster image for the influential exhibition 'This Is Tomorrow'. A male figure works out with an oversized Tootsie Pop lollipop; a female nude figure pouts on the sofa and poses in a lampshade-hat. In the distant background a woman hoovers the stairs with a new-style spherical vacuum cleaner. The interior is a cosily inept British version of contemporary decor, the furnishings still a little starved by austerity. But the time of the interior is an eclectic time. The view from the window is filled with a 1930s cinema frontage advertising the first talkie, Al Jolson's *The Jazz Singer* from 1927. There is no ceiling to the lounge, only a black inter-stellar sky and a huge planet surface which anticipates special effects from *2001* or *Star Wars*. The room is in fact between-times: outside is the media-driven past, and above is a space future – unless, of course, the planet is just a wallpaper effect.

The Pop artists of the 1950s worked to overcome the division between the two meanings of the word 'culture': on the one hand, 'specialized, prestige art', and on the other 'the way we live'. The most useful cultural studies now build on this kind of initiative to break down the stark opposition between high and low cultural production, and reach these conclusions:

> Prestige art forms have consistently taken over materials from popular commodity culture, sometimes in a critical spirit, but often more neutrally as subjects for enquiry – the hero of Joyce's *Ulysses*, Leopold Bloom, earns a very modern living, for example, by selling advertising space in the Dublin press.

> Mass commodity culture increasingly incorporates elements from minority forms for its own uses: Eiko Ishioka's career demonstrates this, as do all mass-media adaptations from literature and the visual arts.

> The audiences for all the kinds of culture are highly diversified, each audience receiving and constructing meanings for their particular purposes. Crudely reductive and dismissive attitudes to the 'mass' and the 'popular', or to 'elite' cultures are not constructive.

Richard Hamilton's *Just What Is It ...?* serves as a useful waymark between modernism and postmodernism. It is a restaging, in popular format, of Marcel Duchamp's scandalously enigmatic *The Bride Stripped Bare by her Bachelors, Even (The Large Glass)* (1915–23) and it parodies the new life of commodities which was burgeoning in the mid-1950s. The man and woman are camp and kitsch, their objects are cute. The new is desirable, but desire objectifies men and women alike as 'ham', which presides over the picture as a large tin on the 'coffee table' (first quoted use *OED* 1959). The collage's original function as a poster advertising an excited exploration of the new commodity culture should also be remembered: the image affectionately plays with the decor, the parody is humorous. We can now go on to review the techniques associated with postmodern arts as they developed from the 1960s onwards. Are they continuous with modernist practices, or do they represent a quite new form of cultural production?

Architecture, mother of the arts

The earliest systematic use of postmodernism and the postmodern as functional categories occurred in arguments over the direction which architecture and urban planning might take in the mid-1970s. The terms were applied to the work of architects who were reacting against the so-called International Style, which they took to be the characteristic architecture created by modernism. This was the supremely functional and aggressively novel approach to building developed during the 1920s by architects such as 'Le Corbusier' (Charles Edouard Jeanneret, 1887–1965), Walter Gropius (1883–1969) and Ludwig Mies van der Rohe (1886–1969). The International Style in building and planning can be allied with the rationalist-progressive tendencies of European modernism, since it celebrated a positive break with ossified traditions by harnessing the technological possibilities created by new materials and attitudes (Frampton 1992: 248–61). Gropius and the Bauhaus architect/designers embraced rationalization as a 'purifying agency' which would strip away meaningless ornament in order to construct buildings which would be effective because of their functional simplicity: 'We have had enough and to spare of the arbitrary reproduction of historic styles' (Gropius [1935] 1965: 44). Steel, concrete and glass enabled a new mastery of space which was to be modernity's contribution to 'the aesthetic satisfaction of the human soul' (ibid.: 24) – notions of a spiritual holism still infused even the Bauhaus's project of aggressive modernization. With the ever-greater refinement in the use of these new materials, voids would triumph over solids, space over substance.

The New Architecture of the 1920s also welcomed standardization, prefabrication and mechanization, again not as ends in themselves, but in order to free people from the laborious work which inevitably accompanied artisan skills, so as to be able to release them for 'some higher order of activity' (ibid.: 33). Standardization could be applied from

[39]

absolutely
chilling

the smallest detail of domestic design, through to the overall organization of entire cities, creating the homogeneity which was characteristic of 'a superior urban culture' (ibid.: 38). Gropius and his associates were utterly convinced of the functional beauty of modern, delicate structures poised lightly on the ground, and of the informing unity which good design could bring to all buildings and objects. By the late 1930s the International Style had become true to its name through the constructions of enthusiastic exponents in every continent.

Faced with the urgent need to reconstruct cities as effective new communities after the wholesale destruction of the Second World War, the International Style and many of its assumptions about the shaping of metropolitan space were put to work throughout Europe and America. The postmodern architects and theorists of the early 1970s were responding to the widely perceived failures of this urban redevelopment, but it is important to recognize the achievements and successes of Bauhaus modernism when it was applied to the demands of post-war reconstruction. As David Harvey argues, the scale of the task was formidable, and urban planning had to resolve housing shortages and the need to provide civic amenities, as well as recreating industrial and commercial infrastructures (Harvey 1989: 70; and more critically Frampton 1992: 262–8). By contrast, many of the buildings ascribed to the postmodern phase of the 1970s and 1980s are commercial developments, speculative office constructions or corporate headquarters which are symbols of the economic power of multinational business. Ricardo Bofill's public housing projects such as Les Espaces d'Abraxas in Marne-la-Vallée (1979–83) give little emphasis to the provision of shared facilities such as nurseries or leisure areas, and would seem to be expressive of postmodernism's privatization of the urban space [see illustration p. 142].

Effective reaction against the failures (and successes) of Bauhaus formalism is dated to the early 1970s, and was fuelled by exactly the kind of resentments which Gropius himself had tried to forestall: 'The fear that individuality will be crushed out by the growing "tyranny" of standardization is the sort of myth which cannot sustain the briefest examination' (Gropius [1935] 1965: 36–7). Architectural postmodernism claimed to be responsive to the immediate urban contexts in which its buildings were situated, entering into dialogue with the vernacular localisms of material and style, and also with the opinions and needs of the buildings' occupants. By contrast, international modernism was criticized for being unresponsive to both, a criticism that had been made

subjectivism

early in the day, for example in the person of Professor Silenus in Evelyn Waugh's *Decline and Fall*: 'I suppose there ought to be a staircase,' he said gloomily. 'Why can't the creatures stay in one place? Up and down, in and out, round and round! Why can't they sit still and work? Do dynamos require staircases?' (Waugh [1928] 1937: 120).

Postmodernism in architecture was reactionary (like Waugh) in rejecting the modernist project; it proposed to revive pre-modernist manners such as eclecticism, the playful collaging of diverse styles within one building or development, a return to the use of Graeco-Roman pillars and capitals, and the entire ornamental vocabulary of classicism. This was described by Charles Jencks, the best-known theorist of postmodern architecture, as a return to linguistic relativism within the language of building, as against the monolingual purism of the international modern (Jencks 1977). According to Jencks, architects such as Ralph Erskine, Robert Venturi, and Lucien Kroll were to be identified as a coherent grouping by the mid-1970s because their buildings were 'double coded': that is, they were happy to use contemporary building materials and technique but they combined these with elements from earlier traditional, classical or vernacular architectures. This introduced a playfulness, a parodic dialogue, into the fabric of their constructions: the buildings could appeal to the citizen in the street, and simultaneously – in a different way – to the critical audience of fellow-architects, theorists and journalists (Jencks 1987: 14).

In 1980 Michael Graves' design for a Public Services Building won the competition to provide an annex to Portland city hall and court house, so becoming the first major commission for a public building in the new postmodern style [illustration p. 134]. His proposal was recommended by Philip Johnson and John Burgee, and immediately aroused fierce controversy, being opposed in the city by an alliance of ordinary citizens and late-modernist practitioners such as Pietro Belluschi who attacked the building in these terms: 'Discipline, the back-bone of architecture as a civic art, is ridiculed ... So they demolish the hated glass box and erect the enlarged juke box or the oversized beribboned Christmas package, well knowing that on completion it will be out-of-date' (Jencks 1980: 134).

Supporters of the building argue that it is responsive to the Beaux Arts public buildings in its vicinity, and that it is in fact based on the classical skyscraper structure of an accentuated street-level base surmounted by a shaft and capital. The interior successfully combines public space on the first two floors together with low-cost office accommodation in the thirteen

[41]

floors above. The decorative polychrome exterior quotes wittily from the tradition of public building in Europe and America, and is consequently in active dialogue with the other pre-modernist buildings in Portland, and certainly more so than the mirror-glass skylumps erected in the city by late modernists such as Pietro Belluschi. Critics of the building argue that its detailing is bizarre and incongruous – Graves withdrew some of the most contentious detailing on his original design, which included swags of fibreglass garlands and a monumental allegorical representation of 'Portlandia'. Some local responses labelled the building a 'temple for bureaucrats', a response which seemed to perpetuate the International Style's alienation from people in the street. The architectural historian Kenneth Frampton also criticizes the building's incongruity and the lack of relation between its facades and interiors: Graves, he concludes, 'is more of a designer of *objets d'art* than an architect' (Frampton 1992: 308).

Architecture, of all cultural practices, is the most expensive and the most implicated in the new internationalism of commodity culture. Therefore the reaction against the standardization of classical modernism could quickly degenerate into a new set of conventions, just as insensitively replicated throughout the world as that of the modernism which it had claimed to displace. The standardization and prefabrication welcomed in the 1920s by the Bauhaus designers threatens by the 1990s to make the profession of architect virtually redundant, since unit construction only requires a pre-designed building-carcass which can then be masked with designer cladding (Frampton 1992: 307).

However, in his essay below (Part II, Section Two) Julian Roberts reaches back to another invigorating element in modernist architectural theory, that of constructivism, and argues that most of the buildings and arguments created in the name of postmodernism are bogus, and have failed to understand the true potential of modernist practice (see also Harvey 1989: 97–8).

Representation in crisis? A lexicon of postmodern technique

A definable group of strategies and forms recur in the description of postmodern arts and this lexicon orders them into a hierarchy. An all-purpose postmodern item might be constructed like this: it uses eclecticism to generate parody and irony; its style may owe something to schlock, kitsch or camp taste. It may be partly allegorical, certainly self-reflexive and contain some kind of list. It will not be realistic. Now

[42]

construct your own project to meet these demands. Here is a helpful (slightly parodic) example: Julian Clary is to make a party-political TV advert on behalf of the Liberal Democrats. He is dressed as The Spirit of Choice, and represents the 1980s by shopping in Sainsbury's (with a list) for a range of period dog-accessories. He fails to find what he wants and buys a video of *Super Dogs* instead.

• **Eclecticism** The word was first used in the late classical period to describe a school of Greek philosophers who claimed to think no thoughts of their own, but rather selected ideas from existing schools. Eclecticism as a picking-and-mixing of styles and themes is obviously endemic to all cultures, but some periods combine materials more wilfully and more self-consciously than others. A comparable word from the history of religious thought is syncretism, which is the mixing of opposed or apparently irreconcilable traditions into a unified theology. During the renaissance the combination of Christian and classical materials was a common, sometimes dangerous practice: Edmund Spenser's *Faerie Queene* is a radically syncretist epic; John Milton had difficulty subjugating the pagan classical mythology which he mixed with the Christian Genesis myth in *Paradise Lost*.

Both eclecticism and syncretism offend decorum, which is the observation of regulated taste. But the mixing of conventions in order to produce novel effects is obviously endemic to all art forms. It has been argued that the new print-based culture of the renaissance enabled writers and artists to piece together more quotations more rapidly than ever before, through use of indices and printed editions; this induced all kinds of change, from the appropriation of formerly anonymous popular 'folklore' by named authors, to the more complex organization of dramatic narratives (Woodbridge 1993). It may also be that as individual careers or particular periods come to an end they recombine elements from their earlier phases in search of new effects: Shakespeare's last plays are eclectic, self-conscious, parodic, high-tech (for their period), and perhaps even *camp* (see below). *Prospero's Books*, Peter Greenaway's film of *The Tempest* (1992), explores this pomo-potential very adroitly.

Modernism intensified the use of eclectic practices through the exploitation of collage and related strategies such as montage and photomontage. But postmodernism is often characterized as a radically eclectic mode, whether in architecture, writing, fashion and design, visual arts or media production. In this way it also challenges if not offends decorum by contravening ideas about the regulated hierarchy of cultural values.

[43]

Vast repertoires of disparate materials are scanned and selected, and this is enabled by the imaging abilities of contemporary technology.

• **Parody** In classical Greek the verb meant 'to sing beside', that is to make a version of an original where the copy was not necessarily satirical. But from the sixteenth century in English parody has usually implied a mocking, burlesque version which ridicules by exaggerating qualities in the original which it distorts, producing a pastiche, or a patching together of pieces. Salman Rushdie wrote a parody of the founding of Islam in *The Satanic Verses* which he intended seriously, but which was taken to be only offensively satirical. Parody in the original sense of 'a song beside' also produces the postmodern genre of the hybrid work, where one part comments upon another, as in Alasdair Gray's *Lanark. A Life in Four Books* (1981), where the 'Epilogue' to Book Four is an extensive index of the plagiarisms committed in the novel. Here, as with the use of *allegory* (see below) postmodern works revert to pre-modern conventions, and behave more like medieval texts. In the visual arts words 'sing beside' pictures, so that text-and-image combinations are a characteristic postmodern genre. Works which run two columns of text simultaneously in parallel are a particularly scandalous kind of postmodern 'singing-beside'. By presenting their material in this way they prevent the reader from ever being able to conclude a reading, and are a clear example of postmodern indecidability. Jacques Derrida's *Glas* (1974) and John Ashbery's poem 'Litany' (1979) are two good examples of this kind of (deliberately) infuriating text.

Parody is a mode which reproduces a previous form, and therefore implicitly involves questions of derivation and re-presentation: what has happened to the original in this process of transition? A parody is therefore a deviant *simulacrum* (see entry below, and Krauss 1986B). Weak postmodernist works could be said simply to parody and ironize to no purpose, in a frantic picking-and-mixing. Television endlessly recirculates its own materials in the form of repeated series which are re-badged as 'archive nostalgia', and then trades the same personnel between programmes in the use of stars and personalities performing in ads, appearing on chat shows, doing guest spots. This process very quickly becomes self-parodic. Strong postmodernism would claim to combine materials to induce particular effects. Cindy Sherman's unnerving photo-graphs are staged as stills from movies that were never made, but whose narrative we can deduce from the single image. Sherman is herself the 'talent' in her images, but she is so radically remodelled from picture to picture that there is no apparent continuity of the person. She therefore parodies the power of images that demand our submission (Owens [1980] 1992: 84). But there is a persistent problem with parodic forms reproducing questionable materials in order to make the audience reflect on them, because no text can control the ways in which it will be read, or mis-read. The parodic text might itself become implicated with those materials in the process of reproducing them. This also is a traditional aesthetic difficulty: is Shakespeare's *Merchant of Venice* an anti-semitic play, or does it present a critique of anti-semitism?

same thing with Nietzsche [handwritten annotation]

• **Irony** Eclecticism and parody imply irony. The original Greek meaning of the word was 'dissimulation, pretended ignorance', for example when Socrates feigned ignorance in order to trap his opponents in argument. Irony is therefore disingenuous, saying one thing, but implying its opposite through sarcasm and ridicule. Irony is a knowing, self-conscious process, implying an unstated meaning in the text to which the reader/audience is alert. Postmodern representation is said to be peculiarly ironic because it is ungrounded, not appealing for validation from truths or mandates which are external to the work, such as a real world or an ethical regimen. Weak postmodernism plays endlessly with unresolved possibilities of meaning, like a hyperactive music-video which simply shuffles images at high speed to no particular effect. More decisive forms of postmodern text can be said to rehearse the reader/viewer in the possible consequences of options on meaning which they might take up as their particular interpretation. An early example of this tactic is the conclusion to John Fowles' novel *The French Lieutenant's Woman* (1969) which offers two quite distinct possibilities of plot development. In Part II, Section Three below I argue that John Ashbery's *Three Poems* is characteristic of the way in which his poetry offers the reader various perspectives for consideration. Works which do this might be described as propaedeutic texts, that is, introductory or preliminary works, because they prepare us for subsequent kinds of decision, offering the *simulacrum* (see below) of ethical choice.

The genre-bending of *Twin Peaks* at its best chills and amuses because, for example, we empathetically join with the pure horror of Laura Palmer's mother as she screams to excess, utters a surplus of screams, screams embarrassingly, in reaction to news of her daughter's murder. But then how many screams would be appropriate for such a situation? In the slippery-soap format of the series, the shot is held too long, and the tragedy of the murder breaks through the conventionality of routine TV-grief, which should be more contained and managed. At moments like this the nearly all-pervasive irony of the series is suspended in favour of unironized sympathy, which makes the game-playing of the fiction more welcome when it returns.

• **Allegory** When one narrative is read as covertly representing one or more other meanings, then it is described as being allegorical. Many parts of the Old Testament were traditionally read as allegorical foretellings of the New Testament. The Authorized Version of 1611 provides elaborate cross-referencing between the two parts of the Bible, allowing the reader to see how the Christian revelation was foreshadowed by the ancient text: for example, Moses despairing of being delivered out of Egypt (Exodus 5.23) allegorically foretells Peter's lack of faith in Jesus when he walked on water (Matthew 14.31). Allegory therefore was one of the most influential conventions in reading and writing until the romantic period beginning in the late eighteenth century, when it was increasingly dismissed as outmoded.

The reasons for this change and its consequences are explored in the piece on Tom Phillips and Peter Greenaway's *TV Dante* in Part II, Section Two, below. But for the moment we can follow Craig Owens' influential articles on allegory where he identified postmodern artistic practice closely with allegorical procedures because it is a genre which allows the proliferation of irony and parody through eclecticism (Owens [1980] 1992). Allegory is inherently appropriative, it 'confiscates' its materials; it is a model of the way in which texts are read through each other; allegory often chooses fragmentary and incomplete materials for its speculation – think of the critical commentary added to Coleridge's *Kubla Khan* which attempts to explain its purported buried meanings, or the marginal prose glosses which Coleridge himself added to *The Rime of the Ancient Mariner* 20 years after he had first written it, as a way of complicating and ironizing his original text (McGann 1985). Medieval and renaissance allegory was often 'paratactic', that is to say, it added one detail or narrative to another in a seemingly disorganized way, with no thought for 'organic' structure, it reproduced material in a mechanical fashion. And crucially, allegory turns images into verbal meaning and regards words as pictures, demonstrating the mutual interdependence of meaning which is so particular to postmodern works.

Lists Lists are a venerable convention in epic literature, for example the genealogical tables in the Old Testament, or the list of ships in Homer's *Iliad*. Medieval literature used lists to impress, or as in Chaucer's *Franklin's Tale* lines 1367–1466, as a cruel satire on the sexual pieties of courtly love. Milton's lists in *Paradise Lost* are formidable mood music, building tone and reference. Lists in authors such as Swift or Defoe accumulate material goods and commodities, as an indication of the rising tide of Things which becomes so pervasive in twentieth-century writing. So despite the apparently unpromising nature of a mere list of items, many different effects can be generated by them, from satire to forceful tonality. Viewed linguistically a list is an undermotivated statement, paratactically adding pure names, and offering the reader minimum help in subordinating one item to another. Lists therefore dramatize our reading response through their intransigence, and they accord with postmodern interests through their repetition and formality which challenge our interpretive skill. Herman Melville's *Moby Dick* (1851) presents as a kind of gigantic epigraph a list of 82 extracts describing whales; this is a surplus of materials which obscures the nature of the beast and mystifies it, just as the white whale itself is allegorized in the process of Ishmael's ironized narrative. James Joyce exploited the list for modernism in *Ulysses*, where as the style of the episodes becomes more intransigent, lists break out as a disorder of the text, or as the random noise of language combining and ceasing to cohere when Leopold Bloom finally drifts into sleep: 'Sinbad the Sailor and Tinbad the Taylor and Jinbad the Jailer and Whinbad the Whaler ... and Linbad the Yailer and Xinbad the Phthailer' (Joyce [1922] 1986: 607).

Lists often feature in postmodern texts because they represent the proliferation of items in the late capitalist world, the rubble of commodity through which choice has to be exercised. Lists do not prioritize their contents, they represent blank information which matches the blank regard of a postmodern consumer. The American communication-artist Jenny Holzer moved from painting to compiling provocative slogans and lists because she felt the postmodern need to work with language in a visual way. From 1977 she began to construct a list of several dozen 'mock clichés' titled *Truisms*, which she displayed on billboards, T-shirts, and eventually on LED (light-emitting diode) machines:

HUMANISM IS OBSOLETE
IDEALS ARE EVENTUALLY REPLACED BY CONVENTIONAL GOALS
INHERITANCE MUST BE ABOLISHED
KILLING IS UNAVOIDABLE BUT IS NOTHING TO BE PROUD OF
LABOR IS A LIFE-DESTROYING ACTIVITY
MONEY CREATES TASTE
MORALS ARE FOR LITTLE PEOPLE

She describes how difficult it was to invent folksy generalities which sounded as if they might be authentic. And when displayed in public spaces like Times Square the list of *Truisms* confronted the viewer with an uninflected list of banal statements, each of which required a different response, but the alphabetical listing revealed no priorities.

All of the strategies listed so far are as old as hills, and can be found in all kinds of work. The next four elements of postmodern culture may be more specific to the twentieth century because they are created by the new kinds of material culture and taste specific to modern times. This discussion of schlock, kitsch and camp is very dependent on Andrew Ross's *No Respect. Intellectuals and Popular Culture* (Ross 1989: 135–70).

• **Schlock** A yiddish word for 'cheap, shoddy or defective goods' and first listed by *OED* from the *New York Tribune* for 1915, it is applied to the decorative trivia that we buy or give to each other, meaningless objects that have sentimental value as gifts or mementoes: what we put on the mantelpiece, what kids keep in the toy box, or on the rear parcel shelf in the car: a model dog with a nodding head whose eyes light up when you apply the brakes. Or a Garfield that you stick to a window. Jeff Koons, '*poète maudit* of American adolescence' (Varnedoe and Gopnik 1990: 396) perfectly captured schlock values in his porcelain and polychrome wood sculptures during the late 1980s.

• **Kitsch** Schlock is harmless, unpretentious, sentimental rubble. A step up from this is kitsch, which might be defined as rubbish-with-attitude. Kitsch is bad taste with pretensions, stuff bought by people who *think* they know, but don't really; so those of us who *do* know, can get a rise out of their pitiful ignorance. Kitsch implied 'bad taste' from the mid-1920s in English, and was used by the influential art critic Clement Greenberg in 1939 to define the antithesis of modernist aesthetic value: 'Kitsch is mechanical and operates by formulas. Kitsch is vicarious experience and faked sensations. Kitsch changes according to style, but remains always the same. Kitsch is the epitome of all that is spurious in the life of our times' (Greenberg [1939] 1986: 12).

Kitsch taste is therefore what other people have, as identified by you and your knowing friends who naturally share a privileged community of taste. Fibreglass wainscot panels on garage doors are kitsch; so were reproductions of paintings by Vladimir Tretchikoff (but see the next entry too); and so are Merchant-Ivory filmizations of novels by E. M. Forster. This last example may have shocked you. Has it revealed *you* as an unknowing style-victim of kitsch? The point here is that these categories are an active demonstration of the manufacture and exercise of taste as a social regulator, described above (pp. 34–5). Kitsch is now therefore one of the crucial categories used to define individuals and classes who are to be excluded – by the regulation of genuine good taste – from the cultural capital which defines its possessors as intrinsically in-the-know.

• **Camp** Theorists of camp behaviour define it as the culture and taste of marginal groups who celebrate the fact of their marginality through parody and self-mockery. Although it is most often associated with homosexuality, camp in this broader definition can be practised by other kinds of outsider group, for example by the dandy, the declassed intellectual, or ethnic minorities. The prehistory of homosexual camp taste is necessarily obscure. In 1725 Samuel Stevens, a moral crusader, visited the house of Margaret Clap in Holborn, London. There he saw 'between 40 and 50 men making love to one another, as they called it ... Then they would get up, dance and make curtsies, and mimic the voices of women.' Was this camp behaviour? It was certainly dangerous. As a result of subsequent prosecutions several men were hanged and others died in prison (Bray 1988: 81–91), so the culture of homosexual behaviours had good reason for discretion. Camp style therefore originates as a private language, shared by a group as part of a common identity and a protection from outsiders; it is a perverse elitism, taking pleasure in tastes and values which are conventionally scorned. Camp in this sense can also be applied to the valuation of normally despised objects, where a taste is developed and shared among a cult following. A carefully cultivated bad taste is camp, for example a refined pleasure taken in late-night TV shows such as *Cell Block H*, or in the 1960s spoof mystery *The Prisoner*. Vladimir Tretchikoff's *Chinese Girl* was a popular print bought by tens of thousands of people in the 1960s for 76/6d from department stores. The print in its original period was kitsch, but to value Tretchikoff now is camp (or else just plain unreconstructed).

Camp tastes and enthusiasms spread beyond their specific audiences during the late 1960s and throughout the 1970s in all kinds of genres. An early British example from the 1960s was the camp humour of the BBC radio comedy *Round the Horn*, and later the television series *Are You Being Served?* These were characteristic examples of very British social comedy, playing the new frankness about sexuality against comic stereotypes of old-fashioned class attitudes. During the same period American camp taste for particular movie stars such as Bette Davis and Mae West, or chanteuses such as Judy Garland and Barbara Streisand either revived interest in old film careers, or contributed significantly to the artistes' success. Stars such as Davis or Garland were valued by gay audiences partly because they succeeded in spite of the conventions of appearance and performance expected of film stars and singers. Bette Davis's histrionic acting style was a parody of screen femininity, acting out the artifice of sexual identity which was deeply sympathetic to homosexual experience. As both feminists and gay activists increasingly questioned routine assumptions about gendered identity and behaviour, a performance by an artist such as Davis could be viewed as a critique of any idea of an intrinsic sexual identity. By contrast, some stars can never be celebrated by camp taste, because they are 'only' male or female, and are, as it were, dumb-struck by the weight of their inescapable gender: Jean Gabin, for example, the French heart-throb of the 1930s and 1940s, is a stupefied victim of his masculinism, from a camp *point de vue*.

What do schlock, kitsch and camp have to do with postmodernism? They are all invaluable categories for works which play games with the history and conventions of taste. They are also inseparable from the excess, exploitation and trivia of mass-commodity culture, and they are unavoidable when we are thinking about our idea-of-America (even if we are also American). Watching *Pee-Wee's Big Adventure* (1985) may take us closer to the postmodern heart than almost anything else.

• **Simulacrum** In a world of commodities that are endlessly reproducible, the process of serial replication takes on a logic and momentum of its own, to the point where it becomes impossible to distinguish between the original and the facsimile. We may simulate images, objects, environments, the past, other people, our selves. There is even a disease that looks suspiciously like a postmodern affliction: the unfortunate victims of Capgras' Syndrome believe that their acquaintances have been replaced by identical substitutes. Jean Baudrillard is responsible for the theoretical development of this fantasy where the all-pervasive nature of imagery in the contemporary world 'de-realizes' reality itself, to the extent that truth and falsity cannot be distinguished. Notoriously, for Baudrillard, the Gulf War did not take place, only a mediatized simulation which 'we' all watched. But better than this charlatan theory are the science-fiction versions of the idea. Philip K. Dick's fiction is full of nightmarish replication as in *Do Androids Dream of Electric Sheep?*, filmed by Ridley Scott as *Blade Runner* (see below Part II, Section Two). Primo Levi, the memorialist of the holocaust, wrote a haunting variant on the idea of human duplication in his short story 'Some Applications of the Mimer' (Levi [1966] 1990), in which Gilberto, 'a child of the century', replicates first his wife, and then himself.

In postmodern theory, re-presentation is intrinsically factitious, and should be displayed in its artificiality (Krauss 1986B). In this way mimesis can be read as delusive, and known to be not-the-thing-which-it-presents (which can never be known). Representation offers the reader/viewer an imitation where the simulacrum stands in the place of the authentic. Because the simulacrum is indistinguishable from the original, all confidence in authenticity and uniqueness of the object has to be abandoned, and what is celebrated is the success of artifice. Therefore postmodern works refer by layerings of reference within their own systems, by parody, and by eclecticism. The vehicle has priority over the message, and primary meaning as such is suspended, because there is nowhere to refer for meaning-closure.

• **Realism** The antithesis of postmodern practice. From the postmodern position realism is inadequate because it implies an unexamined relationship with some prior reality, as in a painting or photograph which so convincingly represents its subject that all questions about the possible selectivity of the image or the distortions which it may introduce are simply not raised. In so far as realism pretends to offer an unproblematic representation, it is in fact the most deceptive form of representation, reproducing its assumptions through the audience's unexamined response to an apparently natural image or text. In the early 1980s Sherrie Levine rephotographed a selection of famous photographs of victims of rural poverty which had originally been taken by Walker Evans in the 1930s. One effect of Levine's appropriation of Evans' moral realism was to emphasize the un-reality of the original images, suggesting that they were reliant on period-specific expectations to do with the representation of poverty and stoical resignation (Singerman 1994).

Another kind of difficulty is presented by the tradition of socialist realism, which is art containing an explicitly political or broadly ethical purpose. The crudest version of this might be Stalin's description of writers as 'engineers of men's souls', an authoritarian definition which then required the subjugation of all artistic conventions to the demands of state propaganda, as in Soviet socialist realism (Jameson 1977). For the postmodern, realist works have not been subject to an adequate epistemological critique: that is, how do you know that you mean what you think you mean? They are doctrinaire, insufficiently knowing, and (most acatastrophic) boring. A realist aesthetics for a postmodern critic abbreviates crucial issues of representation by imposing social or moral imperatives which suppress the most urgent questions: what is being imaged, by whom and on whose behalf? These concerns are directly addressed in the contributions in Part II by Gayatri Spivak and Trinh T. Minh-ha.

Subjectivity and subjection, history and nature

One of the most compelling and sinister propositions in all of the literature defining postmodernity is the claim that even our subjectivity has been changed as a result of the conditions described so far. The definition of historical psychologies, that is, the kinds of subjectivity experienced in past times, has always been central to study in the humanities. Personality in past times seems to have been significantly different to our own, owing to material circumstances, social expectations, and belief systems. Scholars therefore speculate about the nature of subjective experience in, for example, classical times, the middle ages, or the early modern period. Recent influential theorists such as Michel Foucault or Stephen Greenblatt have attempted to describe fundamental shifts in psychology which have been brought about during periods of rapid social transition (Foucault [1966] 1970; Greenblatt 1980). They argue that large-scale changes in assumptions concerning, for example, the categorization of knowledge, or attitudes to presentation of the self and experience, can produce radical discontinuities in fundamental beliefs about the relation of private experience and social conventions. Historiography inspired by women's studies has also contributed massively to this analysis of the kinds of subjectivity induced by evolving social context and ideology; generalizations about past experience, they argue, have often ignored or significantly distorted women's perspectives (Brant and Purkiss 1992).

The pace of global economic change today is almost certainly faster than it has ever been, and so might be expected to produce new modes of experience in, for example, a villager from rural Thailand who is forced to move to Bangkok as an economic migrant (Harvey 1989: 132–44). But it is not only in the pre-industrial, developing world that subjectivity is undergoing change, according to some postmodern theorists. They argue that there is an equally radical mutation at work in our selves, the citizens of the post-industrial, information- and leisure-based economies.

The mutation in subjectivity induced by postmodernity is described

[52]

in several ways. The distracting, invasive effects of media culture are said to make us more responsive to visual imagery than to writing; the habit of reading is in decline, whether the texts are newspapers, novels, poetry, or children's fiction. Television, video and film all distract from the page; in advertising the visual image now predominates over written copy, where until the 1940s the picture served the text. Postmodernity also, it is argued, induces different kinds of predatory looking: the cinema screen fixates its audience via the hypnotic gaze, but the TV screen encourages a distracted glance via compulsive channel-hopping on the remote button. This visual attention is a superficial and intermittent concentration, not sustainable beyond a few minutes. Television flow is carefully segmented to cope with this wandering focus, and in turn reinforces a habitual distraction. One of the latest moral panics in the United States concerns 'dumbing down', a phenomenon where the lack of verbal facility in college students is said to reflect a lowering of I.Q. compared to the scores attained by their parents at the same age. This generation, the argument goes, is the first in America which will be not only poorer but also more stupid than its parents.

But these image-inflected changes are superficial compared to the claims made for deeper kinds of mutation. Where the characteristic neurosis of the early twentieth century was hysteria, the projection of profound, displaced trauma, postmodernity is said to induce narcissistic, schizoid illness. The culture of modernism expressed a psychology organized through ideas of depth and authentic emotion, as for example in D. H. Lawrence's fiction discussed earlier. Freud's model of the unconscious and preconscious proposed that the largest area of our personality is hidden from us, and that this alien presence actively influences our conscious life in ways that we are unable to recognize. But the postmodern psyche has been sublimated through commodity and image so that there is no profundity, there are no depths, because everything occurs at surface level. An early totem for this new subjectivity was the enigmatic, blank monolith discovered by the apes and astronauts in Stanley Kubrick's *2001: A Space Odyssey* (and made in the totemic year 1968). An impenetrable reflective surface shields technological power of magical complexity; activity is transacted at the micro-level, silicon wafers mimic and outstrip the synapses of a human brain.

This blank power induces a blank response. Where modernist emotion was authentic exactly because it was only expressed at nearly total cost, as in Edvard Munch's painting *The Scream*, postmodern emotion has

[53]

no cost because there is no authenticity (Jameson 1991: 10–16; Taylor 1987: 16–39). A more impersonal, floating response to multiple and evenly accented stimuli is said to occur in the context of our experience of the postmodern sensorium. This can be the high-reflective walls of contemporary architecture, the roving spread of our attention as we hunt for commodity, the channel-grazing of multiple television stations via the infra-red remote, the technicized stroke of house music within its utterly managed environment where we feel the pulse along our heart, or the sublimed and floating intervals of a neo-medieval composer like Arvo Pärt.

This new kind of affectivity is a response to the invasive power of contemporary stimuli, and is a reversion to earlier forms of emotion, goes the argument, because it is more generalized, more awe-struck, than the earlier modernist affectivity. The postmodern subject has moved from agonistic, individualist meaning, organized around 'depth' models of emotionality, back to the sublimity of pre-romantic feeling, which was supposedly less nuanced, more communal, and not committed, for example, to Freudian notions of personal developmental history. Postmodern subjectivity is peculiarly the response of persons in crowds in the shopping mall: emerge from the subway station at the Lexington and Fifth Avenue intersection, and take your first walk down into Manhattan to know what this means. Be awed like a peasant as you pass – no, are passed – in front of the Trump Tower, knowing that somewhere in the sublimity of its highest apartments Sophia Loren leases a whole floor! Be abolished by the appalling wall of the General Motors Building! Then compare this unforgettable passage with your first pigeon-scattering stroll into Saint Mark's Square, Venice: how there the crowds taking their coffee under Florian's arcades sounded like Thomas Mann, making a human murmur of joyful sadness under old buildings.

These alarming distortions of subjectivity are then also related to an oppressive sense of subjection, that is, a reduction of human autonomy in postmodern times. We suffer subjection, the argument goes, because of the way in which the desire for commodities has become so completely invasive, taking away any other dimension of personal desire or action. Personal affectivity, the way in which we feel and express emotion, is only articulated in language which is already compromised by the advertising which has so thoroughly colonized all human needs (Williamson 1978: 40–70). Subjection also implies that there is large-scale disaffection with the public institutions which formerly spoke for

Individual aspirations. This is most obvious in the failure of political arguments to address the accumulating, threatening problems such as unemployment, inter-communal hatreds, and progressive degradation of the environment, urban and rural. If the grand narratives inherited from the Enlightenment period which promised to facilitate progress have failed, then the individual suffers comprehensive sub-jection, being 'thrown under' the domination of institutions and events which are otherwise irresistible, and kept there by the randomizing image-flow of contemporary cultural events.

These postmodern catastrophic descriptions therefore maintain that the possibility of effective, reasoned action in the public sphere is now so far removed from individual access that the political has become another completely managed and mediated language:

> only images exist and are produced and are consumed ... pleasure passes through the image: here is the great mutation. Such a reversal necessarily raises the ethical question: not that the image is immoral, irreligious, or diabolic ... but because, when generalized, it completely de-realizes the human world of conflicts and desires, under cover of illustrating it. What characterizes the so-called advanced societies is that they today consume images and no longer, like those of the past, beliefs; they are therefore more liberal, less fanatical, but also more 'false' (less 'authentic') – something we translate, in ordinary consciousness, by the avowal of an impression of nauseated boredom, as if the universalized image were producing a world that is without difference (indifferent).
>
> (Barthes [1980] 1982: 118–19)

The ways in which history is understood and represented are con-nected to these grim theories of contemporary subjectivity as pure subjection. The key term here is the idea of human agency, or the capacity to act and influence events in any meaningful way – even, in any way at all. If subjection is so complete and inescapable, then there is no scope for individual or collective activity which might affect social development. This completely passive conception combines with the postmodern ability to reproduce experience in facsimile, and produces history and the past as simple spectacle.

What is at issue here is the nature of the narratives that are constructed to describe the past, and the kinds of conclusion drawn from them (Samuel 1991, 1992; Stone 1991). Postmodern representations of history, it is argued, simply commodify past experience as nostalgia or escapism, rather than framing historical narrative and historical research as critical reflection on the present. The compelling need in the post-industrial world to create new forms of economic activity in the regions and cities which are no longer productive has produced the characteristic post-modern ambience of the heritage centre and tourist trail. The urban environment is themed through a selective presentation of its past, in order to maintain present economic activity (Hewison 1987). Disney is currently proposing a themepark of American history, to be built outside Washington (the role of Mickey Mouse, a spokesman says, is at this point unclear). In England there are plans for a 280-acre Shakespeare World to be developed outside Stratford-on-Avon: the venture-capitalists en-visioning these attractions style themselves 'imagineers'.

Many of the components of postmodernity can be seen as posing a formidable threat to their obvious antithesis, which is the 'natural'. This is true in the socio-economic descriptions, and also consequently in the cultural paradigms. The sense we all share of ecological systems stressed and threatened derive from the ever more intense demands made on the natural environment as a consequence of over-development, or mis-managed development. Nature ceases to provide an imaginative recourse as the pastoral alternative to over-sophisticated urban life, because it no longer represents a self-sufficient, endlessly renewing provision. Within postmodernity the natural is another category of commodity, interesting only because of its increasing scarcity value.

Conclusion: Resisting the Postmodern

Having reviewed with maximum compression a range of definitions of postmodernism, it may now be useful briefly to compare this analysis of a broad period and its characteristics with any similar descriptions of periods and their culture, in order to gain a longer perspective.

Postmodernism is often given the hard sell as being uniquely transfiguring, epochal, and even apocalyptic. It is, we are told, the Angel of the New whose like has not been seen before. But there are numerous definitions of particular periods which are also characterized by specific cultural practices and sometimes also by particular social organization. They too have attracted dramatic claims in their time. European historiography and art history for instance discuss the middle ages, the renaissance, mannerist, baroque, and romantic periods, each with its specific qualities. Descriptions of postmodernity at one level are only another attempt at periodization, that is, the analytic description of a particular moment and its defining characteristics, and it deserves as much if not more scepticism as similar labels. What are the weaknesses of period descriptions like these? Let's return to St Mark's Square in Venice, which was the postmodern Tokyo of the sixteenth century, and stage a comparison between renaissance and postmodernism, in terms of the kind of paradigmatic description which they offer.

The use of paradigms: renaissance and postmodernity

Definitions by period in cultural history are established through differentiation: renaissance against middle ages, mannerism succeeding to renaissance (Gombrich 1971). As characterizations they are reliant on a rejection of, or contrast with, the description of their adjacent periods. This is true of postmodernism, which is deeply implicated with the prior moment of modernism, as we have seen. What can succeed to postmodernity is unclear (though 'new modernism' is being canvassed fairly widely at time of writing, and 'transmodernism' is also a whisper in the

[57]

control galleries; 'new medievalism' is an interesting possibility). Postmodernism is also a label which is current in its own time, evidently, and so it can be promoted, opposed, or conformed with, by people and their works: to this extent it may also be a self-confirming prophecy – here I am, do as I say. This was also true of the renaissance, but was not true of modernism, which is a subsequent rationalization and labelling (Williams 1989).

As with postmodernity, many definitions of the renaissance as a cultural moment were also linked to economic descriptions of the period: as the first European expansion and establishment of colonial dependencies, as the period which established cash economy, inflation, and integrated trade-currency networks. The emergent international order sought its own supervision through the protocols of diplomacy, a new set of regulative behaviours within international relations. Innovations in the reception and expression of space/time during the renaissance can be linked to the period's material innovations in mensuration and commodity exchange, just as for postmodernity (Harvey 1989: Part III). The arguments around postmodern expressive forms and their production through new media are also paralleled in the critical literature on the rise of new reader- and writerships during the renaissance period, directly attributable to the innovation of moveable type technology (Woodbridge 1993).

Renaissance cultural and philosophical forms are also in many ways analogous to those described by postmodernism. The systematic scepticism of postmodern philosophical critique reproduces in significant ways the sceptical forms of Montaigne's *Essais*, where radical doubt was named Pyrrhonism:

> Pyrrho, who framed so pleasant a Science of ignorance ... forasmuch as he maintained the weaknesse of mans judgement, to be so extreame, as it could take nor resolution, nor inclination: and would perpetually suspend it, ballancing, beholding and receiving all things, as indifferent.
> (Montaigne [1580–95, translated 1603] 1897: IV 247–8, and see III 303)

We considered the 'indifferent beholding and receiving' which *Twin Peaks* demands as a teletext of postmodern indifferentism. It affectively engages us, and then mocks the convention which we had been foolish enough momentarily to take seriously. And if parodic reflexivity is a defining quality of postmodern art, then all of the sixteenth-century works praised for their 'maniera' or style, and subsequently categorized as Mannerist, certainly possess a comparable quality. A celebrated poem by John Ashbery, 'Self-Portrait in a Convex Mirror', makes this kind of connection quite explicit. The 552 lines of the poem are a meditation on the layerings of reality and illusion in Francesco il Parmigianino's self-portrait of 1524, and comment simultaneously on the processes of representation within the poem itself. But perhaps a truly processual renaissance painting would have had to be even more radically self-consuming to be genuinely postmodern: as if a misbehaving Caravaggio had eaten all the fruit before he had actually finished his Still Lives.

Period definitions are also often motivated by the desire to promote a particular ethos in the interpretation of the chosen time, an ethos which in fact also has a particular agenda in the present. Jacob Burckhardt's *The Civilization of the Renaissance in Italy* ([1860] 1945) sought to define the renaissance as 'the history of early modern individualism' (Kerrigan and Braden 1989: xi), and this progressive humanistic reading of the period controlled scholarly assumptions for over a century. It was also very evidently a reading characteristic of the mid-nineteenth century, looking for justification of its own assumptions in an earlier time. Literary-critical methodology describes a period description such as this as an example of the 'hermeneutic circle': that is to say, the scholar describes qualities in general terms which s/he then proceeds to discover, ignoring evidence to the contrary, in a self-confirming circle. A covert historiography, or philosophy of history, therefore motivated the established descriptions of renaissance: Burckhardt and his successors were in fact arguing a version of Hegel's philosophy of history, which sought for a particular developmental logic at work in historical events as a way of addressing the present.

Contemporary scholarship therefore tends to discuss the 'renaissance' in more neutrally descriptive terms such as the 'early modern' period, exactly because the older historiography is felt to prejudge and foreclose questions about the epoch which are more usefully left open. It would be ironic if the theorists of postmodernity were busy creating a limiting paradigm for our own period at the same time as new historicists and cultural materialists are discarding paradigmatic descriptions of earlier movements because they are too prescriptive.

Culture and the debt bomb

During the last 30 years, the era of hyper-modernity, the proportion of the world population living in countries which enjoyed the highest GDP

(Gross Domestic Product) fell from 28.5 to 22.6 per cent. Conversely in the same period the populations of countries suffering relative decline of GDP in relation to the developed world rose from 43.3 to 51 per cent. And nearly one quarter of the world's population actually became poorer in absolute terms during the same period, at 23.7 per cent (Socialist Economic Briefing 1990). In 1985, Africa's debt repayments 'were roughly double what it received in emergency aid for the famines: three billion dollars went into Africa and six [billion] went out' (Harding 1993: xiv). This brutal conclusion can be drawn: new modernism is bought at the expense of old misery.

But even within the social economies of the supposedly post-industrial leisure world, the postmodern regime is constructed at enormous and divisive cost. Ronald Reagan's administration invested in the military-industrial complex at the expense of social programmes developed during the 1960s. Traditional blue-collar institutions were weakened through de-industrialization and anti-union legislation, and the poorest sections of the population became progressively poorer. By the mid-1980s more than half of the children of metropolises such as New York, Chicago, Baltimore and New Orleans were being raised on incomes officially rated as below the poverty line (Harvey 1989: 331; 1993: 92). Similar divisive tendencies were followed by Margaret Thatcher's successive administrations in England, where the failure to modernize national institutions and economic structures had become chronically evident by the end of the decade (Hutton 1995). If we accept the argument that the nuclear confrontation of the Cold War period was broken and 'won' by Western insistence on progressively increasing arms expenditure for science-fictional defence programmes such as the Strategic Defence Initiative, then we might ask why a similar expenditure cannot now be committed to the reconstruction of the former Warsaw Pact economies that were so successfully crippled. If there are no medicines available in the Moscow Children's Hospital, exactly whose fault is this?

There is no single process of 'postmodernity' at work in the socio-economic and political dimensions which inevitably produces a particular cultural form of the 'postmodern'. Labelling global economic trends with the technocratic, post-industrial glamour of postmodernity provides a distorting framework for cultural analysis: the over-development of the societies which might consider themselves post-industrial is achieved at the expense of the structural under-development of the remainder of the globe (George 1989). The idea of postmodernity in this view is a parochialism of the first world entertained at the expense of everyone else. The cultural paradigm of the postmodern also fails to describe one single cultural formation which is produced by a specific economic mode: cultural production is more complicated than this. Categories such as the postmodern which claim to explain everything, and which are therefore themselves inescapable, are authoritarian abstractions. The varieties of people, processes and audiences involved in the range of arts and media are too diverse to be usefully described in one terminology. New forms of eclecticism, new combinations of genre and textured meaning can as well be described as the continuation of earlier practices, intensified via technological manipulation.

Many aspects of the debates over postmodernity do however encourage analysis of contemporary artistic innovation, as represented in this collection. The intensely imaged nature of our culture produces quantities of information that has to be tended and managed, an intellectual livestock with its own commodity market. In the course of the last two decades postmodernism as a term became taken up and circulated on the international networks of academic exchange, part of the increasing theorization of culture that has been a major development in the period. But beyond this professional franchise of readers and writers, postmodernism also became a more generally circulated idea, through the nexus of universities, conferences, publishers, journals and magazines, galleries, and television channels. These channels are not simply carriers of the message, but also promoters and refiners of the word. A severe view of this development has it that with this new order the social-radical distance formerly maintained by the academy and its intellectuals from the institutions of power and oppression suffered collapse, and that the para-intellectuals of postmodernity are no more than shepherds of style. They have lost the kind of critical acuity possessed by generalist intellectuals of previous generations such as Antonio Gramsci, Simone de Beauvoir, Lionel Trilling or Raymond Williams. A more optimistic version of the argument proposes that the intelligentsia can still serve as gate-keepers of the informatic flow, and intervene critically in the dissemination of knowledge by defining and promoting particular versions of critique within postmodernity.

Postmodernity exists if at all only within a corner of the symbolic economy that has burgeoned as part of the new information industries, constructed at the cost of particular populations and for the benefit of social management. The informatic revolution delivers complex consequences; it allows new kinds of textured work in graphics and writing, but of itself it is not a transparent medium which gives utopian access to an ideal plenum of information. This has to be fought for, as it always did:

> It is as if the very notion of the journalist as a teller of truths unpalatable to ruling elites, as whistle-blower in the public interest, has been fatally eroded in recent years. This is in great part the result of the 'communications revolution' (to quote Rupert Murdoch) that has produced not an information society but a media society in which vast amounts of repetitive information are confined to a narrow spectrum of 'thinkable thought', and the vocabulary of state and vested-interest manipulation is increasingly elevated above that of free journalism. In the Gulf [War] coverage, the effect is that many people are overwhelmed and immobilised, their misgivings not reflected in the opinion polls, only their compliance.
>
> (Pilger 1991)

On the other hand we should resist the arguments of pomo-theorists who wish to reduce all our experience to the thinness of the television screen. Those versions of postmodernity which claim that we are enveloped by an inescapable plasma of consumerist values are vicious, and should be refused – don't buy it. Boycott Baudrillard. It is not necessarily the case that we are purely passive victims of a mediatized information flow. There are televisual versions of events which the audience watches, and which inflect behaviour beyond reception as passive spectacle. Audiences make donations, write letters in anger; children receive a version of the world with astonishment.

Postmodernism as a description of our culture makes us alert to long-range continuities in the arts, as well as to disruption and discontinuity of forms. It certainly provokes a reconsideration of value judgements about supposed high- and low-cultural differentials; its debates are producing brilliant new histories of the cultures that we have in common, and their relation to contemporary history, contemporary politics. Postmodernity as a category does encourage us to think critically about the relations between local and global cultures. It prompts ideas about the rise of defensive nationalisms which are seeking to define themselves against a trans-national order of economic and cultural domination which they perceive to be a threat. Postmodernism moves in the direction of encouraging the analysis of the active differentials at work between cultures, and syllabuses in future need to encourage the possibilities of understanding the emergent global interdependencies, and their tensions, together with agendas for the appreciation of regional and supranational cultures (Bhabha 1990, 1994). It is asking a good deal of national curricula that they stop promoting exclusively national cultural values in the Humanities. But to propose this is only to take the Humanities at their word: as genuinely the study of human works, but this time with the added material awareness of gendered experience and specific locality.

Further reading

One of the most effective ways of following the arguments about postmodernism during the last 15 years is to scan the contents pages of the academic journals which published significant articles. The changing emphases and terms of reference are clearly demonstrated from year to year as authors respond to each other or initiate new areas for research. The titles of journals which are worth browsing are listed in the 'Further Reading' at the beginning of each section.

Journals *Boundary 2. An International Journal of Literature and Culture*, 19/2 Summer 1992 'Feminism and Postmodernism', 20/3 Fall 1993 'The Postmodern Debate in Latin America'; *New German Critique; New Left Review; Telos; Zone.* A journal which takes full advantage of ultramodern technology is *Postmodern Culture*, founded in 1990 and published three times yearly in electronic format. The journal is hosted by North Carolina State University and is available free via email, access Listserv@listserv. ncsu.edu. *Postmodern Culture* also offers pmc-moo, a 'real-time, text-based, virtual reality environment in which you can interact with other subscribers ... and participate in live conferences' via the Internet. For information: pmc@unity.ncsu.edu (source: *On Internet 94* (1994) Tony Abbott (ed.), 276, Westport and London: Mecklemedia).

The philosophy of modernity

Peter Hulme and Ludmilla Jordanova (eds), *The Enlightenment and its Shadows* (1989) surveys the legacies of the Enlightenment. Jean-François Lyotard's *The Postmodern Condition. A Report on Knowledge* ([1979] 1984) is an infuential analysis of the contemporary 'failure of grand narratives'. Jurgen Habermas's 'Modernity: An Unfinished Project' is reprinted in Hal Foster's *Anti-Aesthetic: Essays on Postmodern Culture* (1983), an often-quoted anthology, retitled *Postmodern Culture* (1985). Marshall Berman,

All That is Solid Melts into Air (1983) describes transitions from nineteenth-to twentieth-century modernity. Christoph Asendorf, *Batteries of Life. On the History of Things and their Perception in Modernity* ([1984] 1993) is a brilliant and stimulating discussion, using an innovative page format. A vigorous critique of postmodernist relativism is Ernest Gellner, *Post-modernism, Reason and Religion* (1992) which argues in defence of an 'Enlightenment rationalist fundamentalism'. The essays by Kate Soper, David Harvey and Jeffrey Weeks in *Principled Positions. Postmodernism and the Rediscovery of Value* (1993), edited by Judith Squires, are excellent discussions of the possibility of new ethical and political agendas in pluralist societies. Postmodern debates have even invaded theological writing: an interesting example is Rebecca Clouse, 'A postmodern look at the "mystical body"', *Mystics Quarterly* 20/1 March 1994. John Frow, *What Was Postmodernism?* (1991) is a well-focused criticism of the whole idea.

Postmodernism as cultural dominant

The article which set the agenda for much subsequent discussion is Fredric Jameson's 'Postmodernism, or the cultural logic of late capital-ism', *New Left Review* 146 (July/August 1984). Jameson elaborates his marxist-derived theory of postmodernism as a mode of cultural pro-duction in *Postmodernism, or the Cultural Logic of Late Capitalism* (1991), one of the most ambitious general accounts. But Jameson is criticized for failing to modify his position in the light of objections, and for writing too theoretically and without convincing reference to specific examples of film, music, literature, popular culture and architecture. Raymond Williams's *Towards 2000* (1983) was a prescient discussion of many of the global issues. A more firmly contextualized account of the transforma-tion of the global economy and urban landscapes is David Harvey, *The Condition of Postmodernity* (1989). Steven Connor, *Postmodernist Culture. An Introduction to Theories of the Contemporary* (1989) reviews a range of cultural forms in relation to postmodern theory. Nicholas Zurbrugg, *Parameters of Postmodernism* (1993) is an original, aphoristic survey of particular writers' and artists' contributions. A representative selection of essays and extracts are *Postmodernism. A Reader* (1992) edited by Thomas Docherty; Patricia Waugh, *Postmodernism. A Reader* (1992) and Peter Brooker, *Modernism/Postmodernism* (1992). Andrew Ross edited *Universal Abandon? The Politics of Postmodernism* (1989) for the Social Text collective.

References

[Square brackets indicate date of first publication.]

ADORNO, Theodor (1991) *The Culture Industry: Selected Essays on Mass Culture*, edited by J. M. Bernstein, London: Routledge.

ASENDORF, Christoph ([1984] 1993) *Batteries of Life. On the History of Things and their Perception in Modernity*, translated by Don Reneau, Berkeley, Los Angeles and London: University of California Press.

BAKER, Houston A. Jr. (1987) *Modernism and the Harlem Renaissance*, Chicago and London: University of Chicago Press.

BALL, F. C. (1973) *One of the Damned. The Life and Times of Robert Tressell, Author of 'The Ragged Trousered Philanthropists'*, London: Weidenfeld and Nicolson.

BARTHES, Roland ([1980] 1982) *Camera Lucida. Reflections on Photography*, translated by Richard Howard, London: Cape.

BAUDRILLARD, Jean (1989) *Selected Writings*, edited by Mark Poster, Cambridge: Polity Press.

—— (1990) *Revenge of the Crystal. Selected Writings on the Modern Object and Its Destiny, 1968–1983*, edited and translated by Paul Foss and Julian Pefanis, London and Concord, Massachusetts: Pluto Press, in association with the Power Institute of Fine Arts, University of Sidney.

BENJAMIN, Walter (1973A) *Charles Baudelaire: A Lyric Poet in the Era of High Capitalism*, London: New Left Books.

—— (1973B) *Illuminations*, edited with an introduction by Hannah Arendt, translated by Harry Zohn, Glasgow: Fontana/Collins.

BENSTOCK, Shari (1987) *Women of the Left Bank. Paris, 1900–1940*, London: Virago.

BHABHA, Homi K. (ed.) (1990) *Nation and Narration*, London and New York: Routledge.

—— (1994) *The Location of Culture*, London and New York: Routledge.

BLAIN, Virginia, Patricia CLEMENTS and Isobel GRUNDY (eds) (1990) *The Feminist Companion to Literature in English. Women Writers from the Middle Ages to the Present*, London: B. T. Batsford Ltd.

BOURDIEU, Pierre ([1979] 1984) *Distinction: A Social Critique of the Judgement of Taste*, translated by Richard Nice, London: Routledge and Kegan Paul.

BRANT, Clare, and Diane PURKISS (eds) (1992) *Women, Texts and Histories 1575–1760*, London and New York: Routledge.

BRAY, Alan (1988) *Homosexuality in Renaissance England*, London: GMP Publishers Ltd.

BUCHLOH, H. D. (1982) 'Allegorical procedures: appropriation and montage in contemporary art', in *Artforum*, September.

BURCKHARDT, Jacob ([1860] 1945) *The Civilization of the Renaissance in Italy*, translated by S. G. C. Middlemore, Oxford and London: Phaidon.

CALLINICOS, Alex (1989) *Against Postmodernism. A Marxist Critique*, Cambridge: Polity Press.

CARDINAL, Roger (1984) *Expressionism*, London: Granada Publishing Ltd.

CONNOLLY, Cyril ([1938] 1961) *Enemies of Promise*, Harmondsworth: Penguin.

DUPLESSIS, Rachel Blau (1985) *Writing beyond the Ending: Narrative Strategies of Twentieth-Century Women Writers*, Bloomington: Indiana University Press.

EIKO, Ishioka (1990) *Eiko by Eiko: Eiko Ishioka – Japan's Ultimate Designer*, London: Jonathan Cape.

ELDERFIELD, John (1985) *Kurt Schwitters*, London: Thames and Hudson.

FEATHERSTONE, Mike (1991) *Consumer Culture and Postmodernism*, London, Newbury Park, New Delhi: Sage Publications.

FEATHERSTONE, Simon (1995) *War Poetry: An introductory reader*, London: Routledge.

FOSTER, Hal (ed.) (1983) *The Anti-Aesthetic: Essays on Postmodern Culture*, Port Townsend, Washington: Bay Press.

FOUCAULT, Michel ([1966] 1970) *The Order of Things. An Archaeology of the Human Sciences*, translated from the French, London: Tavistock Publications.

FRAMPTON, Kenneth (1992; 1st edn 1980) *Modern Architecture. A Critical History*, London: Thames and Hudson.

FREEMAN, Michael (1990) 'Human rights and the corruption of governments, 1789–1989', in Peter Hulme and Ludmilla Jordanova (eds) *The Enlightenment and Its Shadows*, London and New York: Routledge.

FRISBY, David (1986) *Fragments of Modernity: Theories of Modernity in the Work of Simmel, Kracauer and Benjamin*, Cambridge: Polity Press; Cambridge, Mass.: MIT Press.

—— (1992) *Simmel and Since. Essays on Georg Simmel's Social Theory*, London and New York: Routledge.

FUKUYAMA, Francis (1992) *The End of History and the Last Man*, London: Hamish Hamilton.

GELLNER, Ernst (1992) *Postmodernism, Reason and Religion*, London: Routledge.

GEORGE, Susan (1989) *A Fate Worse than Debt*, Harmondsworth: Penguin.

GLENDINNING, Victoria (1987) *Rebecca West. A Life*, London: Weidenfeld and Nicolson.

GLENNY, Misha (1993; 1st edn 1990) *The Rebirth of History. Eastern Europe in the Age of Democracy*, Harmondsworth: Penguin.

GOMBRICH, E. H. (1971) 'The origins of stylistic terminology', in *Norm and Form*, London: Phaidon.

GREENBERG, Clement ([1939] 1986) 'Avant-Garde and Kitsch', in *The Collected Essays and Criticism, Volume 1: Perceptions and Judgements, 1939–1944*, edited by John O'Brian, Chicago and London: University of Chicago Press.

GREENBLATT, Stephen (1980) *Renaissance Self-Fashioning: from More to Shakespeare*, Chicago, Illinois: University of Chicago Press.

GROPIUS, Walter ([1935] 1965) *The New Architecture and the Bauhaus*, translated by P. Morton Shand, introduction by Frank Pick, London: Faber and Faber.

GUILBAUT, Serge (1983) *How New York Stole the Idea of Modern Art: Abstract Expressionism, Freedom and the Cold War*, translated by Arthur Goldhammer, Chicago and London: University of Chicago Press.

HABERMAS, Jurgen (1983) 'Modernity – an incomplete project', translated by Seyla Ben-Habib, in Hal Foster (ed.).

HARDING, Jeremy (1993) *Small Wars, Small Mercies. Journeys in Africa's Disputed Nations*, London: Viking Penguin.

HARRISON, Charles (1991) *Essays on Art & Language*, Oxford: Basil Blackwell.

HARRISON, Charles, and Fred ORTON (eds) (1984) *Modernism, Criticism, Realism*, London: Harper and Row.

HARVEY, David (1989) *The Condition of Postmodernity. An Enquiry into the Origins of Cultural Change*, Oxford: Basil Blackwell.

—— (1993) 'Class relations, social justice and the politics of difference', 85–120 in Judith Squires (ed.).

HEBDIGE, Dick (1988) *Hiding in the Light. On Images and Things*, London and New York: Routledge.

HERF, Jeffrey (1984) *Reactionary Modernism: Technology, Culture and Politics in Weimar and the Third Reich*, Cambridge: Cambridge University Press.

HEWISON, Robert (1987) *The Heritage Industry*, London: Methuen.

HOLLIS, Patricia (ed.) (1979) *Women in Public, 1850–1900: Documents of the Victorian Women's Movement*, London: George Allen and Unwin.

HORKHEIMER, Max, and Theodor ADORNO ([1947] 1972) *The Dialectic of Enlightenment*, translated by John Cumming, London: Allen Lane.

HULL, Gloria T. (1987) *Color, Sex and Poetry: Three Women Writers of the Harlem Renaissance*, Bloomington: Indiana University Press.

HUTTON, Will (1995) *The State We're In*, London: Jonathan Cape.

IVERSEN, Margaret (1989) 'The positions of postmodernism', *The Oxford Art Journal* 12/1: 31–4.

JACKSON, Tim (1990) 'Out to box-lunch', the *Independent on Sunday*, 18 November: 7–8.

JAMESON, Fredric (1977) 'Reflections in conclusion', 196–213 in *Aesthetics and Politics. Ernst Bloch, Georg Lukács, Bertolt Brecht, Walter Benjamin, Theodor Adorno*, translation editor Ronald Taylor, London: Verso.

—— (1983) 'Postmodernism and consumer society', in Hal Foster (ed.).

—— (1984) 'Postmodernism, or the cultural logic of late capitalism', *New Left Review* 146: 53–92.

—— (1991) *Postmodernism, or The Cultural Logic of Late Capitalism*, London: Verso.

JENCKS, Charles (1977, 6th revised edn 1991) *The Language of Post-Modern Architecture*, London: Academy Editions.

—— (1980) *Architectural Design* 5/6, 'Post-Modern Classicism', guest editor, London.

—— (1987, 3rd edn 1989) *What is Post-Modernism?*, London and New York: Academy Editions and St Martin's Press.

JOANNOU, Maroula (1995) 'Ladies, please don't smash these windows', *Women's Writing, Feminist Consciousness and Social Change 1918–38*, Oxford and Providence: Berg Publishers.

JOYCE, James ([1922] 1986) *Ulysses*, student's edition. The corrected text edited by Hans Walter Gabler with Wolfhard Steppe and Claus Melchior and with a new preface by Richard Ellmann, Harmondsworth: Penguin Books in association with The Bodley Head.

KERRIGAN, William, and Gordon BRADEN (1989) *The Idea of the Renaissance*, Baltimore and London: Johns Hopkins University Press.

KINGS, Susan (1987) *Sex and Suffrage in Britain 1860–1914*, Princeton: Princeton University Press.

KRAUSS, Rosalind E. (1985A) *The Originality of the Avant-Garde and Other Modernist Myths*, Cambridge, Mass.: MIT Press.

—— (1985B) 'Corpus Delicti', *October* 33: 31–72.

—— (1986A) 'Anti-vision', *October* 36: 147–54.

—— (1986B) 'Originality as repetition: introduction', *October* 37: 35–40.

LAWRENCE, D. H. ([1913] 1992) *Sons and Lovers*, edited by Helen Baron and Carl Baron, Cambridge: Cambridge University Press.

—— ([1920] 1988) *Women in Love*, edited by David Farmer, Lindeth Vasey and John Worthen. Introduction by Melvyn Bragg. London and Glasgow: Grafton Books.

LEIGHTEN, Patricia (1989) *Re-Ordering the Universe: Picasso and Anarchism, 1897–1914*, New Jersey: Princeton University Press.

LEMON, Lee T., and Marion J. REIS (1965) translation and introduction, *Russian Formalist Criticism. Four Essays*, Lincoln and London: University of Nebraska Press.

LEVI, Primo ([1966] 1990) *The Sixth Day and Other Tales*, translated by Raymond Rosenthal, London: Michael Joseph.

LEWIS, Wyndham (1937) *Blasting and Bombardiering*, London: Eyre and Spottiswoode.

LINDEY, Christine (1990) 'The hidden tradition: western popular prints', 109–39 in *Art in the Cold War. From Vladivostok to Kalamazoo, 1945–1962*, London: The Herbert Press.

LYOTARD, Jean-François ([1979] 1984) *The Postmodern Condition: A Report on Knowledge*, translated by Geoff Bennington and Brian Massumi with a foreword by Fredric Jameson, Minneapolis, Minn.: University of Minnesota Press.

—— (1986) 'Defining the postmodern', in *Postmodernism*, ICA Documents 4, Lisa Appignanesi (ed.), London: Institute of Contemporary Arts.

MANN, Thomas ([1977] 1984) *Diaries 1918–1939*, selection and foreword by Hermann Kesten. Translated from the German by Richard and Clara Winston. London: Robin Clark Ltd.

MCGANN, Jerome (1985) '*The Ancient Mariner*: the meaning of the meanings', 135–72 in *The Beauty of Inflections. Literary Investigations in Historical Method and Theory*, Oxford: Clarendon Press.

MIYOSHI, Masao (1989) 'Against the native grain: the Japanese novel and the "postmodern" West', in Masao Miyoshi and H. D. Harootunian (eds) *Postmodernism and Japan*, Durham and London: Duke University Press.

MONTAIGNE, Michael, Lord of ([1580–95, translated 1603] 1897) *The Essayes, or Moral, Politic, and Military Discourses*, translated by John Florio, six volumes, London: J. M. Dent.

MORRIS, Meaghan (1988) 'Room 101 or a few worst things in the world', in André Frankovits (ed.) *Seduced and Abandoned: The Baudrillard Scene*, Glebe, Australia: Stonemoss.

MULHERN, Francis (1979) *The Moment of 'Scrutiny'*, London: New Left Books.

MULVEY, Laura (1989) *Visual and Other Pleasures*, Basingstoke: Macmillan.

'ORWELL, George' [Eric Blair] ([1940] 1970) 'Inside the whale', in *An Age Like This. The Collected Essays, Journalism and Letters*, volume 1, edited by Sonia Orwell and Ian Angus, Harmondsworth: Penguin Books, in association with Martin Secker and Warburg.

OWENS, Craig ([1980] 1992) 'The allegorical impulse: toward a theory of postmodernism' parts one and two, 52–87 in *Beyond Recognition. Representation, Power and Culture*, edited by Scott Bryson, Barbara Kruger, Lynne Tillman, and Jane Weinstock, with an introduction by Simon Watney, Berkeley, Los Angeles, Oxford: University of California Press.

PACKARD, Vance (1962) *The Hidden Persuaders*, Harmondsworth: Penguin.

PAZ, Octavio (1970) *Marcel Duchamp or The Castle of Purity*, London: Cape Goliard Press.

PENLEY, Constance (1989) *The Future of an Illusion. Film, Feminism and Psychoanalysis*, London: Routledge.

PILGER, John (1991) 'Myth-makers of the Gulf war', the *Guardian*, January 7.

POLLOCK, Griselda (1988) *Vision and Difference. Femininity, Feminism and the Histories of Art*, London and New York: Routledge.

PORTER, Roy (1992) 'Pre-modernism and the art of shopping', 3–14 in *Critical Quarterly* 34/4, Winter.

—— (1993) 'Baudrillard: history, hysteria and consumption', 1–21 in Chris Rojek and Bryan S. Turner (eds) *Forget Baudrillard?*, London and New York: Routledge.

RILKE, Rainer Maria ([1922] 1963) *The Duino Elegies*, German text with an English translation, introduction and commentary by J. B. Leishman and Stephen Spender, 4th (revised) edn. London: The Hogarth Press.

RORTY, Richard (1984) 'Habermas and Lyotard on postmodernity', in Richard J. Bernstein (ed.) (1985) *Habermas and Modernity*, Cambridge: Polity Press in association with Basil Blackwell, Oxford.

ROSS, Andrew (1989) *No Respect. Intellectuals and Popular Culture*, New York and London: Routledge

—— (1991) *Strange Weather. Culture, Science and Technology in the Age of Limits*, London and New York: Verso.

SAMUEL, Raphael (1991) 'Reading the signs' Part One, 88–109 in *History Workshop Journal* 32.

—— (1992) 'Reading the signs' Part Two, 220–31 in *History Workshop Journal* 33.

SCHOLEM, Gershom ([1975] 1982) *Walter Benjamin. The Story of a Friend-*

ship, translation by the Jewish Publication Society of America, London: Faber.

SCOTT, Bonnie Kime (ed.) (1990) *The Gender of Modernism. A Critical Anthology*, Bloomington and Indianapolis: Indiana University Press.

SEGAL, Naomi (1988) 'Sexual politics and the avant-garde: from Apollinaire to Woolf', 235–51 in Edward Timms and Peter Collier (eds) *Visions and Blueprints. Avant-Garde Culture and Radical Politics in Early Twentieth-Century Europe*, Manchester: Manchester University Press.

SHOWALTER, Elaine (1987) *The Female Malady. Women, Madness, and English Culture, 1830–1980*, London: Virago.

SINGERMAN, Howard (1994) 'Seeing Sherry Levine', *October* 67 Winter: 79–107.

SOCIALIST ECONOMIC BRIEFING (1990) *The Rise of World Poverty*, London: House of Commons.

SONTAG, Susan (1966) 'Notes on "camp"', in *Against Interpretation and Other Essays*, New York: Delta.

SOPER, Kate (1993) 'Postmodernism, subjectivity and the question of value', 17–30 in Judith Squires (ed.).

SQUIRES, Judith (ed.) (1993) *Principled Positions. Postmodernism and the Rediscovery of Value*, London: Lawrence and Wishart.

STEEL, D. A. (1990) 'DADA-ADAD. Kurt Schwitters, poetry, collage, typography and the advert', *Word and Image* 6/2 April–June: 198–209.

STONE, Lawrence (1991) 'History and postmodernism', *Past and Present* CXXXI, May. And see the subsequent debate in volume CXXXIII, November 1991, and CXXXV, May 1992.

SYMONS, Julian (1987) *Makers of the New. The Revolution in Literature, 1912–1939*, London: Andre Deutsch.

TAYLOR, Brandon (1987) 'Beyond post-modern aesthetics', 'Is collage a test-case for post-modernism?' 53–70 in *Modernism, Post-modernism, Realism. A Critical Perspective for Art*, Winchester: Winchester School of Art Press.

TIMMS, Edward (1987) 'Expressionists and Georgians: demonic city and enchanted village', 111–27 in Edward Timms and Peter Collier (eds) *Visions and Blueprints. Avant-Garde Culture and Radical Politics in Early Twentieth-Century Europe*, Manchester: Manchester University Press.

TODD, Janet (ed.) (1989) *Dictionary of British Women Writers*, London: Routledge.

'TRESSELL, Robert' [Robert Noonan] ([1914] 1965) *The Ragged Trousered*

Philanthropists, with an introduction by Alan Sillitoe, London: Granada Publishing Ltd.

TROTTER, David (1993) *The English Novel in History 1895–1920*, London: Routledge.

VARNEDOE, Kirk, and Adam GOPNIK (1990) *High & Low. Modern Art and Popular Culture*, New York: Museum of Modern Art.

VENTURI, Robert, Denise Scott BROWN and Steven IZENOUR (1972, revised 1977) *Learning from Las Vegas: The Forgotten Symbolism of Architectural Form*, Cambridge, Mass., and London: MIT Press.

WALDMAN, Diane (1989) *Jenny Holzer*, New York: Solomon R. Guggenheim Museum and Harry N. Abrams, Inc.

WAUGH, Evelyn ([1928] 1937) *Decline and Fall*, Harmondsworth: Penguin.

WHIMSTER, Sam, and Scott LASH (eds) (1987) *Max Weber, Rationality and Modernity*, London: Allen & Unwin.

WILLIAMS, Raymond (1983) *Towards 2000*, London: Chatto & Windus, The Hogarth Press.

—— (1989) *The Politics of Modernism. Against the New Conformists*, edited and introduced by Tony Pinkney, London and New York: Verso.

WILLIAMSON, Judith (1978) *Decoding Advertisements. Ideology and Meaning in Advertising*, London and New York: Marion Boyars.

WOODBRIDGE, Linda (1993) 'Patchwork: piecing the early modern mind in England's first century of print culture', *English Literary Renaissance* 23/1, Winter.

WORDSWORTH, William, and Samuel Taylor COLERIDGE ([1798, 1800] 1991) *Lyrical Ballads*. The text of the 1798 edition with the additional 1800 poems and the Prefaces edited with introduction, notes and appendices by R. L. Brett and A. R. Jones, 2nd edn, London and New York: Routledge.

YEATS, William Butler (1936) 'Introduction' to *The Oxford Book of Modern Verse 1892–1935*, Oxford: Clarendon Press.

PART II
Essays on Postmodernism

One: Popular Culture

Introduction

I argued in Part I that it is difficult, if not impossible, to locate an absolutely new kind of aesthetic by defining specific forms and practices in the contemporary arts. The repertoire of devices which are described as postmodern can be found in works from earlier periods, or else they were elaborated during the innovations of classical modernism. But the paradigm of postmodernity seems to be more persuasive when it is describing the absolutely novel kinds of leisure economy and consumerist taste which have developed in the so-called post-industrial societies since the 1950s. These economies and societies are without any genuine precedents in the scale of their consumption, the organization of their workforces, and perhaps in some aspects of the mentality which they induce. The idea of the postmodern might therefore be most appropriate when it is used to define these patterns of consumption and the kinds of taste and expectation which regulate them.

Postmodernity, on this argument, is only an attitude of mind promoted by the lifestyles of advanced economies. The critical literature about postmodernism is therefore often most interesting and original when it is configuring these issues which are only just being brought into focus. At its best, this kind of study combines contemporary history and sociology in order to map the relationships between popular taste and cultural elites, simultaneously referring these 'structures of feeling' to the political agendas of the post-war period (Hebdige 1988; Ross 1989). Popular music is central to the widely-shared culture of the advanced economies, and is now heavily promoted in post-communist societies, Africa, Asia and the Pacific. If theories of postmodernity are to have any validity at all then they should apply to the range of contemporary pop/rock and the ways in which it is disseminated.

Rock on: the popular front against postmodernism

During the mid-1980s a number of theorists were quick to single out MTV and music television as obvious examples of postmodern cultural practice. The fragmented presentation of the programmes seemed to parody institutionalized television scheduling; the music and the videos incorporated elite cultural reference in their mass-market forms via parody and pastiche; the new sublime affectivity of the postmodern viewer was invoked on behalf of an audience which was thought to be watching in new ways (Wollen 1986; Kaplan 1987). Meanwhile the sampling techniques of rap and hip-hop were also cited to prove that technology was promoting a radical eclecticism down on the dance floor. Finally the emergence of 'postmodern rock' as a promotional category seemed to prove the case that postmodernity had really arrived over the airwaves, and therefore in our hearts.

Rock music has been the world's dominant popular musical form since the 1950s, promoted and enjoyed through the construction of a youth culture which was formed about the exploitation of taste via fashion and music. Rock certainly is an extraordinarily eclectic form, initially combining disparate materials from American culture, and then adapting and drawing from the localities of every country where it is enjoyed. But as I have already argued, eclecticism alone is not enough to define postmodernism; any successful cultural movement that crosses national boundaries will behave eclectically, like the major religions in the past. The extraordinary diversity of styles in rock music over the last 30 years also works against high-level theoretical descriptions which try to impose a unity on popular music. Andrew Goodwin's piece begins this section because he argues against the usefulness of postmodernism as a way of understanding current developments in the popular music industry. He points out that MTV has increasingly conformed to established scheduling patterns which deny the supposedly uninflected flow-effect of the ideal postmodern signal. Goodwin also argues that the eclectic quotation of styles through sampling is often used to establish a particular sense of period and development, and is not simply a pick-'n-mix effect, or a 'blank parody' with no precise meaning. Most telling of all, Goodwin rejects the notion that there is a levelling of cultural hierarchies of taste, which is supposedly being brought about on the one hand by the homogenizing effect of mass/popular music as it samples elite forms, and on the other by composers working in the orchestral and operatic traditions who have achieved significant sales to a mass audience.

Goodwin argues that the popular-music scene is in fact highly diversified, with any number of competing audiences who define themselves against each other, and who routinely maintain distinctions

[76]

between artistic-elite forms of their preferred music and mainstream commercial performers in the same genre: Prince against Michael Jackson, Public Enemy rather than MC Hammer. It is surely part of the buzz of following many forms of indie or hip-hop to know that you are more discerning than the ordinary punter; rap, reggae and ragga styles spread beyond the inner-city communities where they began partly because they have the cred and charisma of minority forms. Which is to say that arguments about relative cultural value are just as fierce within the constituencies for rock and other popular musics as they are among high-cultural aficionados.

Musicians such as Philip Glass, Steve Reich, Laurie Anderson, and Brian Eno are sometimes categorized as being a new kind of art/popular composer because they appear to combine successfully some attributes of rock form with high-cultural traits: mass-popular and elite-traditional distinctions are supposed to have been overcome through consumer eclecticism. But, Goodwin argues, none of these composers sell significantly in the mass market, and they remain a sub-genre of the 'serious' music industry. Therefore theorists of postmodernism who confidently claim that there is a real integration of popular and elite cultural forms ignore the social and economic differentiations which are still articulated through hierarchies of taste. Postmodernism as the cultural paradigm which claims to be alert to the new formations of modernity in fact may be blindly perpetuating the political structures which it hopes to have wished away. It is therefore vital that the paradigm of postmodernity is tested – if necessary, to destruction – by detailed reference to actual musical and other artistic practices, to ensure that we have an accurate and not just a seductive theoretical model for relating cultural production to social change. Goodwin's 'Popular Music and Postmodern Theory' asks:

> Does postmodernism as a cultural category give an accurate account of contemporary pop and rock music?

> How is the idea of the postmodern qualified by detailed, empirical assessments of contemporary music and its audiences?

> How can criticism of contemporary culture combine analysis of specific works with an adequate understanding of their audiences?

LA: the city as postmodern futureshock

The second essay in this section discusses Ridley Scott's *Blade Runner* as the film which established many postmodern themes for the visual language of the 1980s. Scott's film is a careful, sophisticated adaptation of Philip K. Dick's novel *Do Androids Dream of Electric Sheep?* (1968), and both works use the idea of the Californian dream in order to create a nightmarish future world. Their dark versions of a decaying mega-city – San Francisco for Dick, Los Angeles for Scott – are only the latest in a long series of novels and films which have been inspired by the region, including the 1930s detective fiction of Raymond Chandler and James M. Cain, and their *film noir* adaptations made during the 1940s. Mike Davis's *City of Quartz. Excavating the Future of Los Angeles* (1990) is a fine example of the new genre of academic studies which combines a complex urban history together with the forms of popular culture which it has produced. Davis's book provides an ideal introduction to the cultural projections about city life which Philip K. Dick and Ridley Scott construct.

what about Nathaniel West?

'Recognizing a "human-Thing": cyborgs, robots and replicants in Philip K. Dick's *Do Androids Dream of Electric Sheep?* and Ridley Scott's *Blade Runner*' asks the following questions:

> What is it in the content and form of a film such as *Blade Runner* that establishes it as a contemporary classic?

> What changes are made to popular fiction when it is revisioned as a feature film?

> How do commercially successful films articulate the current obsessions and anxieties which are often taken to be characteristic of postmodernism?

Further reading and viewing

Journals *Cultural Critique*; *Cultural Studies*; *New Formations*; *Popular Music*; *Theory, Culture and Society*. For film: *Sight and Sound*; *Screen*.

The most innovative kind of critical history which contributes to the debate over postmodernity and consumption is establishing the connections between popular culture and national-popular history, for example, Andrew Ross, *No Respect. Intellectuals and Popular Culture* (1989), and Mike Davis, *City of Quartz. Excavating the Future in Los Angeles* (1990). Dick Hebdige, *Hiding in the Light. On Images and Things* (1988) maps the creation of a youth culture in Great Britain from the early 1950s. Roland Barthes, *Mythologies* ([1957] 1973) inspired a lot of this kind of attention;

Umberto Eco, *Travels in Hyperreality* (1986) is very accessible. Andreas Huyssen, *After the Great Divide: Modernism, Mass Culture, Postmodernism* (1986) is an influential account. Judith Williamson, *Consuming Passions. The Dynamics of Popular Culture* (1986) and Griel Marcus, *Lipstick Traces. A Secret History of the Twentieth Century* (1989) are lively discussions. Andrew Goodwin, *Dancing in the Distraction Factory. Music Television and Popular Culture* (1993) extends his arguments made here.

Blade Runner is usefully contextualized among other science fiction films such as *Alien* in *Alien Zone. Cultural Theory and Contemporary Science Fiction*, edited by Annette Kuhn (1990). Umberto Eco's '*Casablanca*: cult movies and intertextual collage' in David Lodge (ed.), *Modern Criticism and Theory: A Reader* (1988) explores the ways in which films achieve cult status. David Lynch and Mark Frost's *Twin Peaks* is available as ten videocassettes (1991), 15-rated. Jim Collins, 'Television and postmodernism' in Robert C. Allen, *Channels of Discourse, Reassembled. Television and Contemporary Criticism* (1992) discusses *Twin Peaks* (1990) as a watershed in American TV scheduling. Rick Instrell, 'Life after "Twin Peaks"' in *Media Education Journal (AIMS: Media Education in Scotland)* (1991) 11: 328, is an excellent discussion of the series as postmodern text.

References

DAVIS, Mike (1990) *City of Quartz. Excavating the Future of Los Angeles*, photographs by Robert Morrow, London and New York: Verso.

HEBDIGE, Dick (1988) *Hiding in the Light. On Images and Things*, London and New York: Routledge.

KAPLAN A. (1987) *Rocking Around the Clock: Music Television, Postmodernisn and Consumer Culture*, New York: Methuen.

PENLEY, Constance (1989) *The Future of an Illusion. Feminism and Psychoanalysis*, London: Routledge.

PFEIL F. (1988) 'Postmodernism as a "structure of feeling"', in C. Nelson and L. Grossberg (eds) *Marxism and the Interpretation of Literature*, London: Macmillan.

ROSS, Andrew (1989) *No Respect. Intellectuals and Popular Culture*, New York and London: Routledge.

WOLLEN, P. (1986) 'Ways of thinking about music video (and postmodernism)', *Critical Quarterly* 28: 1 and 2.

I
Popular Music and Postmodern Theory

ANDREW GOODWIN

The debate about postmodernism now intersects popular music at a number of distinct levels:

1 *MTV/music television* In the work of Tetzlaff (1986), Fiske (1986), Aufderheide (1986), Wollen (1986), and Kaplan (1987), the postmodern nature of MTV and music television is identified through diverse criteria such as: the fusion of modernist high art and more popular cultural discourses; the abandonment of grand narrative structures, including the deconstruction of both realist and modernist regimes of representation, and the deconstruction of the TV schedule itself; the presence of intertextuality and pastiche; and in what Kaplan sees as a 'schizophrenic' posthumanist address.

I have criticized these ideas elsewhere (Goodwin, 1987a), and do not wish to take up much space here to repeat my argument. The objections to the postmodern interpretation of music television can engage with its reading of the relation between film theory and music videos, its near-total neglect of the music itself, its failure to locate the clips adequately within the context of pop-music culture, or its superficial understanding of pastiche. Here I will just note one of the major *empirical* problems: MTV itself has spent the years since the emergence of postmodern theory blatantly defying the terms of postmodernity. While there are superficial parallels, such as the creation of a category of 'postmodern video' (which I will discuss later), the organization of both the video clips and the MTV text itself has been increasingly traditional and convention-bound. Most notably, it is strange to discover that a media form whose postmodernity was supposedly secured partly through its 24-hour 'flow' and abandonment of traditional scheduling practices, has – over the last five years – progressively established rigid programme slots and begun utilizing the routine practices of TV scheduling, often around the deployment of conventional broadcast-TV genres.

2 *The music itself* Pop music artists and texts have also been employed as textual 'examples' which are used to illustrate theories of the

postmodern (Jameson, 1984 and 1988). In relation to the music itself, I will try to show later in this essay that while it is possible to discover categories of postmodern music and perhaps practices of postmodern consumption, the grand claims of postmodern theory remain insubstantial as an account of the current state of popular music.

3 *Technology*   Technological developments within the popular music industry suggest interesting parallels with some postmodern theses, although these correspondences have only been taken up by advocates of postmodern theory in passing. Specifically, these critical strategies miss both the historicizing function of sampling technologies in contemporary pop (Goodwin, 1988) and the ways in which textual incorporation cannot be adequately understood as 'blank parody'. We need other categories to add to pastiche, which demonstrate how contemporary pop opposes, celebrates and promotes the texts it steals from (see Goodwin, 1987b). I have also noted that the technologies of sampling and musical theft are not used only to construct images that speak of fakery and forgery (McRobbie, 1986); they are also used to invoke history and authenticity – the most obvious recent example being the collaboration between sixties soul star James Brown and eighties rappers Full Force, in making a record significantly titled *I'm Real*.[1] We need to know how pastiche actually relates to the blurring of historical periodization, where it has often been overlooked that the 'quoting' of sounds and styles acts to historicize contemporary culture (although Lipsitz, 1986/7 and Straw, 1988 are atypically careful on that question).

4 *Structures of Feeling*   Postmodern theory has provided one interesting entry point for understanding the consumption of popular music, and this lies in Fred Pfeil's (1985 and 1988) deployment of Raymond Williams' notion of 'structures of feeling'. Pfeil argues from a sociological and psychoanalytic point of view, delineating the material base of the post-war American 'PMC' (professional-managerial class) in the break-up of urban centres, the (related) decline of patriarchal authority, the rise of television at the core of a public sphere, and the growing importance of leisure consumption in the construction of identity. This sociological account of a structure of feeling suggests rich possibilities for a historical materialist account of postmodern culture (see Grossberg, 1988) ... although it also alerts us to what may be its limited social purchase.

This, ultimately sociological, project remains underdeveloped empirically but suggests a mode of analysis that is less concerned with identifying postmodern texts, in favour of looking at the emergence of

[81]

reading formations which celebrate pastiche, and ahistorical modes of consumption. (The account has the merit of also explaining the popularity of postmodern theory amongst those American academics who hail from precisely that reading formation.)

5 *'Postmodern rock'* 'Postmodern rock' has itself emerged as a sales category within the music industry, and within music television (for instance, in MTV's programme *Post Modern MTV*).

This essay confronts these developments with the aim of clarifying what is at stake. Here I share Hebdige's (1988) carefully qualified view that the term 'postmodernism', while hampered by its incoherence, is so wide-ranging that it must be describing something. (Other, more cynical, observers have suggested that the label is the fanciful creation of critics and scholars, but that this process brings into being a 'real' cultural category, through its effects on producers, critics and consumers.) My central argument is that the debate is currently confused by the presentation of binary polarities within limited fields of reference, and through the mixing up of two categories that need to be distinguished – cultural capital and aesthetic form. I will begin by examining two aspects of the debate about postmodernism and pop music, which have their roots respectively in arguments about aesthetic form (see Lukács *et al.*, 1977) and in the analysis of cultural capital most eloquently developed by Pierre Bourdieu (1980 and 1984). I will proceed to show that confusion between these two debates has led to incoherence in the postmodern analysis of pop and rock music. Finally, this chapter will consider the emergence of 'postmodern rock' as a generic category within the music industry.

In search of the postmodern text

Confronted by the divergent nature of postmodern accounts of culture, scholars have tended to work very ineffectively with the specific empirical demands of understanding popular music. The debate about postmodernism is certainly not notable for the precision of its definitions; as many commentators have observed, it is often unclear whether postmodernism is a cultural condition or new theoretical paradigm. There is also confusion around the question of whether postmodernism deploys irony, or a post-ironic discourse of 'blank parody'. And in the analysis of cultural capital, postmodernists have often confused *intertextuality* with the mere blurring of generic categories, and then gone on to read the collapse of aesthetic distinctions into these processes, as if they necessarily imply the latter, which they do not.

Some writers argue that rock music is postmodern by virtue of its eclecticism, through its foundations in interracial, intercultural and intertextual practices (e.g., McRobbie, 1986; Hebdige, 1988; Weinstein, 1989). Lipsitz (1986/7) provides the most fully empirical version of this position. His argument is acute and important, although in my opinion its references to postmodernism are largely redundant. Empirically, Lipsitz cannot be faulted for his observation that rock music is characterized by extraordinary eclecticism and intertextuality: specifically, his argument relates postmodern concepts to Mexican-American musics developed by musicians in East Los Angeles, including the internationally popular band Los Lobos. But, like all accounts which use eclecticism as their founding postmodern motif, it is hard to see what is being *explained* here. The logic that one typically finds is this: postmodernism employs eclecticism and intertextuality; rock music is eclectic and intertextual; *ergo*, rock music is postmodern. But what does this tell us about rock music or postmodernism, other than that they might explain *each other*? (In other words, postmodernism might as well be a parasite *description* of post-war pop, rather than an explanatory paradigm.)

If the textual specifics of pop's genres are merely redundant (if, in fact, one believes that rock, pop and contemporary music *tout court* are postmodern in some more general sense), then what is the point of analyzing them? There is an urgent need to clarify the terms of this debate. Unsurprisingly, given the confusion of its terms, the identification of postmodern texts has ranged across an extraordinarily divergent, and incoherent, profusion of textual instances: John Cage, Steve Reich, Laurie Anderson, Philip Glass, Brian Eno, Talking Heads, Prince, punk rock, Madonna, Bruce Springsteen, the British 'New Pop' (Thompson Twins, Scritti Politti, Duran Duran, Thomas Dolby, etc.), Sigue Sigue Sputnik, rap, hip-hop, Los Lobos, and World Beat music have all been cited as quintessentially postmodern.

This *eclecticism of theory* is extremely unhelpful. It stems in part from an initial confusion of two debates, which postmodern theory fails to distinguish. Firstly, there is a debate within 'serious' avant-garde circles about the trajectory of modernist music in the age of Philip Glass, Steve Reich and Terry Riley (see, for a brief and accessible account, Jones, 1987). Secondly, there are debates within popular music about pastiche and authenticity. 'Modernism' means something quite different within each of these two fields, for in the first area it has been the dominant aesthetic strategy, while in the latter it remains – within different genres

[83]

– everything from utterly marginal to coexistent with older, realist forms. Hence the term 'postmodern' not only describes different musical (and extra-musical) strategies, it also relates quite differently to the field of cultural power, and to the possession of cultural and economic capital in each area.

This confusion is obvious in an early formative attempt to understand rock music in postmodern terms – Fredric Jameson's (1984) deployment of rock and roll in the initial moment of bringing postmodernism into the cultural studies academy (a position which has recently been restated without revision in Jameson, 1988).[2] Commenting on Jameson's analysis of architecture, Mike Davis has recently written that 'Jameson's post-modernism tends to homogenize the details of the contemporary land-scape, to subsume under a master concept too many contradictory phenomena which, though undoubtedly visible in the same chrono-logical moment, are none the less separated in their true temporalities' (Davis, 1988: 80). The same can be said of Jameson's analysis of music, which offers a reading of rock history that places The Beatles and The Rolling Stones, on the one hand, as examples of 'high modernism' and The Clash, Talking Heads and The Gang of Four, on the other, as 'postmodern'. What this broad classification of music elides, however, is the necessity of identifying musical differences within the two historical moments which suggest more specific, if still crude, parameters of rock 'realism' (The Clash) and rock 'modernism' (Talking Heads, Gang of Four), and of rock 'authenticity' (The Stones) versus pop artifice (The Beatles).

Historically, the music of The Beatles and The Rolling Stones articulated the social and political currents of the 1960s counter-culture. The Clash and The Gang of Four (the latter being explicitly Marxist in orientation) addressed political questions from a standpoint associated with the emergence of punk rock – a quite different counter-cultural form which eschewed the love and peace message of The Beatles or the nihilistic hedonism of The Stones in favour of blunt left-wing critiques of life in Britain in the late 1970s.

Looked at from the point of view of aesthetic form, The Beatles and The Rolling Stones need to be differentiated: if the development of modernism is at issue here, the increasingly artificial (up until the last, posthumous 1970 LP *Let It Be*) of The Beatles is modernist (self-conscious, ironic, knowingly artificial), in contrast with the 'authentic' rough-edged blues inflections of The Stones and their lyrical themes of sexuality and

[84]

violence. The Beatles, it might be argued, typified a notion of musical 'progress', where The Rolling Stones (with the exception of their Beatles-influenced album *Their Satanic Majesties Request*) simply repeated a rhythm and blues formula which typifies a form of rock realism (e.g., in both the social content of their lyrics, and in the transparent, unself-conscious nature of the music itself). That The Stones have mined this groove almost unrelentingly is apparent in the critical responses and marketing strategies which framed their 1989 LP *Steel Wheels* – an album that was reviewed and discussed in terms of its 'truth' to an older rhythm and blues aesthetic. (Paul McCartney, in contrast, spent 1989 and 1990 on tour with a band who play extracts from The Beatles' inaugural art-rock album *Sgt Pepper.*)

When we move on to the music of the late 1970s, there is another very clear distinction to be made between realist and modernist musics. The Clash are, in this context (and in many other ways) the Rolling Stones of the punk era with their 'realist' raw sound, their incorporation of 'black' musical genres (R&B for The Stones, reggae for The Clash), and in the effort to be transparent in their musical and lyrical communication with the audience. Talking Heads[3] and The Gang of Four are explicitly modernist in orientation – offering such classic modernist techniques as ambiguity, self-reflexivity, use of shock effects and deconstructions of song structure and tonal rationality.

Jameson's first efforts to grapple with rock music from within an account of the postmodern condition remain, then, empirically quite unconvincing – a criticism that has often been made of the *detail* of the textual illustration deployed in what must now be considered the founding essays of a Marxist postmodernism. But while later efforts to work with this theory in relation to popular music are certainly better informed about the music, there is a noticeable shift in orientation, away from Jameson's concern with the relation between social formation and aesthetic form, in favour of an emphasis upon cultural capital and the apparent dismantling of distinctions between art and mass culture.

But is it Art?

In recent debates about postmodernism, it is often quite casually assumed that we are now living in an era where distinctions between art and mass culture have collapsed. Popular music is sometimes used to establish this argument, and in postmodern writing on pop the elision of high art and pop culture is usually taken for granted. A central problem in these accounts, as I will show, is the conceptual tension that exists between postmodernism's insistence on eclecticism in contemporary culture, and its focus on the apparent conflation of art and mass culture.

Much of this work suffers from two debilitating limitations. Firstly, it often misreads the argument about cultural capital as though the presence or absence of particular aesthetic discourses could be discerned through the identification of timeless historical features, instead of undertaking a conjunctural analysis of the mobilizing categories of cultural power. As Andrew Ross has reminded us, via Bourdieu: 'Cultural power does not inhere in the contents of categories of taste. On the contrary, it is exercised through the capacity to draw the line between and around categories of taste; it is the power to define where each relational category begins and ends, and the power to determine what it contains at any one time' (Ross 1989: 61). Within the field of contemporary popular music, the processes of selection, exclusion, celebration and denigration are used by critics, fans and the musicians themselves in ways that continue to sustain the operation of forms of cultural capital. In particular there remains a tendency to identify as 'serious' those acts who subvert and undermine the conventions of the pop song, often in ways that are classically modernist. This process operates *within* generic categories as well as across the whole field of pop, so that art/pop distinctions can be made (and *are* made, by fans and critics), respectively, in mainstream pop (Pet Shop Boys/New Kids on the Block), soul (Prince/Michael Jackson), rock (Sonic Youth/U2), heavy metal (Metallica/Def Leppard), and rap (Public Enemy/MC Hammer). The briefest of conversations with almost any fan of one of the above acts would confirm that arguments about art versus trash remain rampant within today's pop.

Secondly, postmodern theory establishes its categories too easily, by defining discourses of art and mass culture through the use of extremely limited terms of reference. A standard strategy is the presentation of two bi-polar opposites which are held to signify art, on the one hand, and mass culture, on the other. The writer will then show how they have increasingly converged, thus magically bringing the truth of postmodernism to light. What is usually missing are all the various genres of pop music which lie *outside* the binary opposition, and which may run counter to the analysis.

Jon Stratton's (1989) account of three key moments in rock history and their relation to aesthetic categories pays much closer attention to musical meanings and is more historically specific in its arguments than Jameson's early typology. Yet it, too, contains a curious flaw. Stratton identifies a convergence of popular and high cultural discourses in rock's third 'moment', *circa* 1975–9, when a 'postmodern' aesthetic (Stratton's description) of minimalism in form, combined with excessive affect, straddles both popular culture (the punk rock of The Sex Pistols, for instance) and the art-music of Brian Eno, Laurie Anderson and Philip Glass. This makes sound musicological sense, but its usefulness is diminished by the sociological realities of pop consumption. Eno, Anderson, and Glass *are* consumed as high-art, with the exception of Eno's work with the pop group Roxy Music (and even there he was portrayed as the freakish, arty boffin, to Brian Ferry's populist neo-Sinatra), and Anderson's freakish 1983 hit single 'O Superman'. For many pop fans, Eno is known as someone who helps to produce the rock group U2 (and perhaps Talking Heads), not as an avant-garde or postmodern composer. In that area his work is closely associated with art-rock; so much so that a recent musicological account of Eno places his solo work firmly in a tradition of 'progressive rock' (Tamm, 1989) – a category which should be (as I will demonstrate later) anathema to post-modernism. Musicologically, Stratton's account is persuasive; socio-logically it demonstrates the limits of text analysis (however well-grounded historically) when confronted with the actual practices of pop consumption.

What the postmodernists frequently miss in their accounts of popular music are the continuing presence of the categories of the popular and the artistic. There are, in a sense, two Brian Enos: Eno the avant-garde musician and Eno the popular record producer – and the audience for *both* Enos is probably infinitesimal. Scholars accustomed to listening to Laurie Anderson, Philip Glass and even Talking Heads run the danger of greatly overestimating their impact in pop culture, and – most importantly – the crucial elements of cultural capital that attach to them.

It seems to me almost redundant to have to point out the sociological specifics that place, say, Philip Glass in the category of art-pop, but in this context it seems important to spell out the details: Glass does not produce music which is recognizably like a pop song; lyrics, where they are used, deviate from the conventional modes of address of pop[4] and the structural and (poly)rhythmic content of his pieces deviates from rock convention. For instance, while much has been made of the superficial resemblance between the music of Philip Glass and rock through their shared emphasis on *repetition*, this misses the point that Glass's music takes this technique to extremes that are rarely deployed in pop. Because he defies the recognized forms of rock and pop music, Philip Glass albums are usually found in record stores under headings such as 'Classical', 'Jazz' and (a telling insult) 'New Age'. His concerts take place in halls associated with classical and modern music performances, rather than rock clubs or stadia. In solo performance, the staging of his music reflects the 'serious' conventions of the venue (e.g., the absence of dramatic use of lighting, stage set or visual effects). When the Philip Glass Ensemble performs its operatic works, the staging is highly visual – but the conventions are those of the art-rock 'concept' performance (Pink Floyd, Genesis, etc.), not a rock and roll show. Glass (1987: 3–26) himself makes the influence of modernist artists like Beckett, Brecht, Pinter and Godard quite explicit here – influences that are also very clearly at work in the performances of Laurie Anderson.[5] The behaviour of the audience is in either case reverential and distanced, listening attentively to the music, rather than moving, cheering or singing along.[6] Artists like Glass, Eno and Laurie Anderson in fact occupy a space within contemporary pop that reproduces the position of progressive rock and art-rock in the 1960s and 1970s. It is music for college students and middle-class graduates who have the cultural capital to decode the significance of its heightened use of repetition, its minimalism, and its shifting of attention away from the pop star and towards multi-media contextualization. The music may share an abstract principle with rock and roll (a basis in the use of repetitive structures), but its sound and staging hardly resemble that world at all.

I want now to develop these criticisms, by making two points, which operate at discrete levels. First, empirically speaking, each of the different attempts to substantiate the legitimacy of postmodern theory operates by bracketing out vast areas of contemporary pop that contradict the theory. Secondly, and more fundamentally, each of these approaches establishes the category of postmodernism by setting up binary oppositions from within extremely limited (and quite divergent) fields of reference. Categories of the postmodern which are constructed around oppositions such as punk/pop, authenticity/artifice, rock/New Pop, modernist rock/postmodern pop and so forth each leave out too much – indeed, the *absences* are precisely what allows each account to seem coherent. (This problem in its turn derives partially from the fact that analysts have tended to focus on just one or two aspects of the debate about postmodernism, thus generating entirely different, and sometimes contradictory, positions using the same conceptual field. The problem, in other words, is that the conceptual field is itself unstable.)

A way out of this confusion is suggested, in my view, by Susan McClary's (1989) careful analysis of avant-garde and postmodern musics. McClary's definition of the postmodern is tight and focused, centering on art-music which abandons the 'difficulty' of high modernism (e.g., Schoenberg) in favour of popular, pleasurable devices such as tonality, melody and simpler rhythms. It thus represents an account of the postmodern which (reasonably, if unusually) relates that category to modernism itself. For McClary, the quintessential postmodern composers are Philip Glass, Steve Reich and Laurie Anderson. Her account offers a definition of postmodern music which has the merit of being clearly argued and coherent. However, in revealing the limited appeal of postmodern music (none of these artists are mass sellers) amongst audiences for 'serious music', McClary's arguments undermine a central tenet of postmodern theory – the notion of a convergence of art and mass culture.

The confusion arises because postmodern theory has mixed up two different issues – the identification of eclecticism (which pervades rock and pop) and the collapse of distinctions based on cultural capital (which remain pervasive, especially *within* the field of rock music, as Frith and Horne (1987) have shown). When this mistake is laid over the misapprehension that modernism operates in the field of pop music just as it does in 'serious' modern music, the result is conceptual chaos. Whatever its inroads in the visual codes of television (Brechtian devices in prime-time programming, modernist jump cuts in soap-powder commercials, etc.), the much neglected *aural* codes of music are a different matter. While modernist techniques are accepted by the gatekeepers of high culture, in the market-place of commerce the sounds of dissonance are not so welcome. Today's rap music, like punk rock before it, encounters extraordinary difficulty in gaining airplay and media exposure precisely because its *sounds*, as much as its sentiments, are not conducive to a commercial environment. The music is, in classic modernist tradition, *disruptive*. It would be interesting to consider further the reasons for this disjuncture between visual and aural modernism in the market-place. For my purpose here, I simply wish to note the pertinence of Georgina Born's comments:

[89]

It is odd and significant that music is so often cited as the success story of postmodern reintegration ... Effectively, these cultural theorists collude in asserting that the postmodern *rapprochement* has been achieved ... It is not only by ignoring the hegemonic 'other' of powerful, contemporary high culture, and failing to deconstruct its rhetoric of *rapprochement*, that writers have arrived at their optimistic and utopian postmodern perspectives. The assertion that modern music culture is moving beyond the modernist/populist divide to achieve a postmodern synthesis or reintegration must be based on empirical study ... rather than making facile assertions, it is necessary to analyse real socio-economic and aesthetic differences that exist.

(Born, 1987: 70)

This seems to me to be the problem, for instance, with Lawrence Levine's (1988) tendency to see the collapse of cultural categories in the work of The Kronos Quartet (a San Francisco act who have worked with Philip Glass, and whose repertoire includes string quartet arrangements of Jimi Hendrix songs) as an example, along with numerous instances where jazz has been incorporated into high cultural institutions. It might be possible to cite The Kronos Quartet as postmodern, but as with Philip Glass, they clearly have very little to do with popular culture as it is actually lived by fans of rock and pop. And the argument about jazz was countered in the late 1970s by Roger Taylor (1978), in an essay written against what he saw as the *incorporation* of a radical musical form via its integration into the category of 'Art'.

There is a parallel with Taylor's account of jazz within rock music itself. It is noticeable, for instance, that postmodern accounts do not, as they might be tempted to do, invoke the development of art-rock following the 1967 release of The Beatles LP *Sgt Pepper,* or the subsequent flowering of 'progressive rock', which had both modernist (Velvet Underground, Henry Cow, Soft Machine, Hatfield and the North) and neo-classical (Emerson, Lake & Palmer, Genesis, Pink Floyd, Yes) aspirations. There is evidence for an art/mass culture fusion in a variety of elements here: the specific use of texts from high culture (beginning with Procul Harum's appropriation of Bach's Suite No. 3 in D major in 'A Whiter Shade Of Pale' and continuing with pieces such as Emerson, Lake & Palmer's versions of Aaron Copland's 'Hoedown', Ravel's 'Bolero' – which in structure significantly parallels the later work of Philip Glass – and Mussorgsky's *Pictures From An Exhibition*); neo-classical performances featuring rock bands with symphony orchestras (Deep Purple, Rick

Wakeman); the use of poetry and prose rendered outside the context of a rock lyric (Henry Cow, Rick Wakeman, David Bowie's use of 'cut-ups'); attempts to expand the pop song to twenty-minute pieces, sometimes linked across more than one side of an album (e.g., Yes's *Tales From Topographic Oceans*, Jethro Tull's *Thick As A Brick*) – a trend which reached a peak in ELP's pretentiously titled double album *Works*; the rejection of the gestures of rock performance, in favour of a neo-operatic 'acting out' of the songs (David Bowie, Genesis) or 'serious' strategies, such as having the lead guitarist seated on a stool (King Crimson, Genesis); performances in neo-classical settings (Pink Floyd's album/movie *Live At Pompeii*); and instances of rock musicians citing and using classical and modern symphonic works to 'educate' the rock audience – employing an extract from Stravinsky's *Firebird Suite*, for instance, as an introductory theme to a rock concert (e.g., *Yessongs*).

These instances are not generally cited, of course, because they work against a central premise of postmodernism. Art-music in the pop context confirms the vague notion of eclecticism, and buttresses superficial descriptions of intertextuality, while it *undermines* the postmodern thesis of cultural fusion, in its explicit effort to preserve a bourgeois notion of Art in opposition to mainstream, 'commercial' rock and pop. The genre of progressive rock is clearly a declining (albeit a persistent) one, but my example is none the less instructive, since it is a discourse which persists. Following the emergence of punk rock (which had its own art wing, typified by bands like Devo, Talking Heads, Cabaret Voltaire, 23 Skidoo and Wire), a number of New Wave bands have effectively replaced the progressive rock acts as favourites amongst students and college-educated consumers (Hüsker Dü, New Order, The Sugarcubes, The Replacements, Public Image Limited). This is particularly so in the United States, where the most important ideological component of punk rock (a progressive sweeping away of the rock establishment) has had very little lasting effect. Three of the acts mentioned above toured North America in 1989 under a 'Monsters of *Art*' rubric – a slogan which marks itself out from the 'Monsters Of Rock' label used to promote heavy metal bands. (As I will show in the final section of this paper, that particular definition of art-rock is almost co-terminous with one understanding of the term 'postmodern rock'.)

Indeed, the progressive rock/postmodern rock connection is, as I write, about to be institutionalized in British broadcasting, in a forthcoming programme on the BBC's art-music service, Radio 3:

PROG ROCK

Radio 3 chiefs have agreed to roll over Beethoven to make way for a new programme which will bring rock to the classical station. The BBC's hitherto conservative network have enlisted the help of two young(ish) rocking fellows to boost their listenership on a new show *Mixing It.*

From next month you can tune in to a meaty musical stew which includes Peter Gabriel, Laurie Anderson, Brian Eno, Philip Glass and the godfather of minimalism, Steve Reich.

(*New Musical Express*, 29 September 1990)

Far from constituting a crossover phenomenon, yesterday's prog rockers, like today's postmodernists, explicitly marked themselves out from the field of 'pop' in rejection of the structural form of the pop song, their use of complex, dissonant, forms of tonality, and in the absence of lyrical themes centered on romance, escape or 'the street'. Progressive rock bands aspired to a cultural capital of Art, and anyone who doubts that Steve Reich still does this should read his programme notes, which unambiguously locate the music within institutional contexts of serious music, and which describe the music itself with a reverence which is, to my rock fan's sensibility, rather comic:

> *Sextet* for four percussionists and two keyboard players is scored for three marimbas, two vibraphones, two bass drums, crotales, sticks, tam-tam, two pianos and two synthesisers.
>
> The work is in five movements played without pause. The relationship of the five movements is that of an arch form A-B-C-B-A. The first and last movements are fast, the second and fourth moderate, and the third, slow. Changes of tempo are made abruptly at the beginning of new movements by metric modulation to either get slower or faster ... The harmonies used are largely dominant chords with added tones creating a somewhat darker, chromatic, and more varied harmonic language than in my earlier works.[7]

My point is *not* that this description of the music intrinsically establishes Reich's work as art-music. Pop and rock can also be described in these ways; and it frequently is, in musician's magazines like *Guitar Player,* and in the occasional forays made by 'serious' critics into pop (see, for example, Mellers, 1973). My point is rather that this critical discourse illustrates a manner of promoting the music and assumes a mode of listening both of which are the antithesis of popular music.

Another way of arguing for Reich as a postmodernist is in his use of

[92]

Third World musics. Weinstein (1989), among others, has implied that the phenomenon of World Beat music is postmodern by virtue of its generic conflations. (As I have already suggested, if this is true, then the whole of rock music must also be postmodern.) A problem here, for the art-pop fusion argument, is that African percussion techniques played in a Western concert hall (Reich's 1971 composition *Drumming*, for instance) where the audience is immobile and the performers enact the music with the gestures and costume of the 'serious' musician can no longer be heard as 'popular' or 'folk' music. (Furthermore, it seems to me it might also be objected that Reich's use of Third World folk music is, in the concert hall environment in which it is usually performed, no more postmodern than is, for instance, Haydn's use of European folk.)

More pertinently, there persists a modernist strand in pop music which continues to draw on masculinist traditions of noise, *music concrète* and Futurism, in both the sounds and the (sometimes neo-fascist or proto-Soviet) iconography used to promote the music. This music has thus taken up the modernist strand of progressive rock; a fact that is made biographically concrete in the career of drummer Chris Cutler, who played with art-rock acts Henry Cow and The Art Bears in the 1970s, and who now performs with one of punk's original art-groups, Pere Ubu. The continuity is apparent in this comment from rock musician Billy Bragg, concerning the transparent connection between Russian constructivism and British electro-pop: 'If Mayakovsky had been alive today he'd have been in Depeche Mode.'[8] Here I would cite the 'industrial' bands like Nitzer Ebb, Front 242, Laibach and Ministry, and avant-garde rock noise-makers like Sonic Youth (who defy pop codes in part by using a variety of unconventional guitar tunings) as the most obvious examples. There is also the use of politicized *bricolage* and dissonance in American rap music (mobilized around images of drugs, gangs and crime), and a heavy metal/thrash metal wing articulating this same discourse (but with a different iconography – horror and Satanism). Crucially, many of these acts display an unrelenting hostility to mass culture, especially television (Beatnigs, Negativland, Wire, Metallica, Megadeth, Public Enemy, NWA, Ice-T). Their perceived authenticity derives in no small measure from their *antipathy to popular culture*, and this remains a crucial nuance of contemporary pop that postmodern critics consistently overlook.

The music of Public Enemy, for instance (*It Takes A Nation of Millions to Hold Us Back, Fear Of A Black Planet*), can be seen as postmodern in its use of a modernist dissonance within the framework of mass popularity (via

CBS Records). But the debate about rap (which is so often cited as a postmodern musical form, because of the pervasive intertextuality implied by its use of 'sampling') routinely overlooks the continuing presence of an art/mass culture discourse located in resistance to it; i.e., the continuing arguments (which precisely reproduce debates about rock and roll in the 1950s, and punk rock in the 1970s) about whether or not rap 'really' is *music*. These debates can be followed in arenas as diverse as conversations between rock and rap fans, published rock criticism, music-business institutions such as the Grammy awards, and in the arts pages of the élite press. If postmodernist critics paid the slightest attention to these accounts of popular music they would know that the battle against bourgeois notions of culture is waged, every day, by acts like Public Enemy, whose 'postmodernism' (if it is such) exists in a totally different environment from the music of Philip Glass *et al.*, and where the struggle for *modernism* (let alone *post*modernism) cannot yet be taken for granted.

Just as social divisions persist and underlie the construction of supposedly postmodern buildings (Davis, 1988; Jacoby, 1987: 169–72), so they are also replicated in the market-place for contemporary music. Postmodern music, whether defined tightly as a form which develops in opposition to the difficulty of the avant-garde (McClary's usage, which in my view remains the only meaningful sense in which postmodern *texts* can be identified, since it is the only approach which shows how music might be related to a dominant modernism), or more loosely as an intertextual movement in more mainstream pop, often erases itself on the terrain of cultural capital. The abolition of the art/mass culture distinction is not apparent in either instance, for postmodern pop remains in most cases either an explicitly high cultural form, or a pop form constructed in at least partial opposition to 'inauthentic' popular culture (TV, advertising, mainstream pop).

Coda: hyper-marketing postmodernism

It is not possible to provide a neat 'conclusion' to this discussion. Since I maintain that the premises of postmodern theory are incoherent and that its aesthetic is a grab-bag of interesting observations which do not necessarily belong together, it follows that conclusions about the nature of postmodern music will depend on which part of the postmodern condition we choose to stress. Arguments about *aesthetic form* produce one way of looking at pop music. The concept of *cultural capital* produces quite different results. The relationship between the two is extremely complex. Looked at from the point of view of tonality or narrative structure, it can be argued quite convincingly that modernism persists as an art-rock form within pop, amongst those acts who defy the description of popular music set out in Adorno's classic (1941) article. (Indeed, one good reason for arguing for the continued distinction between pop music and art-rock lies in the fact that the 'postmodern' artists precisely subvert the conventions of pop that Adorno described so well, but failed to understand.) If, however, the focus were on *timbre*, then the noise of rock music (especially in the use of distorted electric guitar sounds) would be modernist in a much more general sense,[9] and the relation between aesthetic form and cultural capital would have to be thought through differently. The notion of *pastiche*, on the other hand, would generate entirely different conclusions — it might form a basis for seeing postmodernism in contemporary acts as diverse as Prince, Transvision Vamp and The Mekons, where it *does* seem that 'blank parody' is an accurate term for the self-referential deployment of 'found' music.

Unless we are committed to demonstrating the coherence or explanatory purpose of postmodern theory (which I am not), there is no need to construct rational order from these confusions. In order to grapple adequately with these issues, we need both a better theory of pop music (which would include, for example, some investigation of the relation between *timbre* and modernism) and more empirical work on today's pop audience. 'More work needs to be done' is however a boring conclusion, even where it is true. I will finish instead by noting one of the most bizarre developments in the brief history of media and cultural studies, in which abstruse French theory has 'trickled down' into the popular consciousness, via the cultural industries, so that the word 'postmodern' reached record stores, magazines and television programmes just a few years after it entered the academy: proponents of postmodernism will no doubt feel that this phenomenon is itself hugely postmodern.

As if to confuse the debate further still, the music industry has now pitched in with its own effort to define the terms of our debate, with the emergence (around 1988) of the new category of 'postmodern rock'. MTV was a pioneer in this trend, labelling its 'alternative' rock programme *Post Modern MTV*, in August 1988. Record companies then began to adopt the term, using it to promote records by Thrashing Doves, Pere Ubu and

Peter Case. Pop stars like Elvis Costello and Bono (of U2) began to use the term in media interviews. Across these usages, from French theorist Jean Baudrillard (the subject of 1988 articles in both *The Face* and *Rolling Stone*)[10] to the musings of a Christian rock vocalist, there is of course little coherence.

Talking to students about the term 'postmodern rock' I have been able to discover three distinct usages. For some consumers it seems to correspond roughly with categories like 'art rock', 'indie pop' or 'college radio' music – that is to say, acts who define themselves as existing outside the mainstream of the charts, and whose music is supposed to be taken more seriously than the supposedly disposable sounds of pop. (This interpretation buttresses my argument above, of course, since it implies the conventional division between rock and pop, with the former having artistic pretensions not deemed appropriate for the latter.) This seems to be the understanding employed in the music industry itself. For instance, in the 1989 MTV *Video Music Awards* programme, host Arsenio Hall framed college-radio favourites The Cure thus: 'They're nominees for one of our next categories. That is, postmodern video. In other words, the best video by a performer or a group that's brought an alternative music [sic].'[11] This understanding of postmodernity has also leaked into the musical press. The Los Angeles-based magazine *Hits* now publishes a 'Post Modern' chart and airplay listing (Jane's Addiction, Living Colour, Bob Mould, Sonic Youth, World Party, Depeche Mode), a 'PoMo Picks' review section (Prefab Sprout, Los Lobos, An Emotional Fish, The Cure) and a 'Post Toasted' gossip column! Interviewed in *Hits*, Arista Records Senior Vice-President of Sales and Distribution Rick Bleiweiss offers his defini- tion of a Post-Modern act: 'Post Modern or alternative are wide-ranging terms. The acts I'm talking about are Urban Dance Squad, Kris McKay, the Church … We're treating Jimmy Ryser in a similar manner. While you couldn't call him alternative like some of the groups I've mentioned, the plan is the same.'[12]

A second definition takes a more literal approach, defining the category in relation to 'modern rock' – a catch-all category used by radio stations in the United States (such as KITS in San Francisco) to promote 1980s music, including the straightforward rock of bands like U2, but with special emphasis on the electro-pop of acts like Erasure and Depeche Mode. Postmodern music, here, refers to those acts who, chronologically speaking, come after 'Modern Rock'. This commonsense usage is not routine in the industry, but it is interesting, since it suggests that the

Modern Rock acts have now become established as a genre not unlike 'Classic Rock', in some markets at least, which will generate its own 'alternative'.

Thirdly, postmodern rock can be defined as that music which follows punk, evacuating its articulation of political resistance. Groups like The Smiths, The Cure and New Order can thus be understood as a post-modern response to the 'defeat' of punk and the parallel rise of Thatcherism and Reaganism,[13] which is thus seen to 'explain' what has sometimes half-jokingly been described as this music's 'miserablism'. 'Industrial' music might also fit this pattern. The exact antithesis of what Herbert Marcuse (1968) called 'affirmative culture', this music might constitute a form of postmodern resistance.

The debate about postmodernism in popular music has thus become newly complex in a unique way: since the postmodern is now a sales category/musical genre, in addition to being a theory, cultural condition and artistic practice, further analysis of its relation to music will have to take account of this epistemological feedback loop. But in the dominant usage established by the music industry itself (the first of the three listed above), the term constructs 'postmodern rock' just as I have suggested – as a synonym for 'art-rock'. The debate about postmodernism as it relates to cultural capital therefore continues to chip away at its own conceptual foundations.

Notes

1   On the album *I'm Real* (Scotti Bros./CBS Records, 1988) hip-hop musicians Full Force use samples (including extracts from James Brown's early career) to create the backing for James Brown's performance, which explicitly historicizes and celebrates his work – see, for example, 'Tribute' and 'Godfather'.

2   Jameson (1979) suggests a different parallel between pop and postmodernism, when he locates pop music as a 'simulacrum', in which there is no 'original' textual moment.

3   A strictly modernist reading is given of the David Byrne (of Talking Heads) movie *True Stories*, for instance, when it is read as a social parody, a satirical comment on alienation in a post-industrial society (see Coulson, 1987).

4   Even on *Songs from Liquid Days* (CBS Records, 1986), where Philip Glass collaborates with rock songwriters like David Byrne and Suzanne Vega, the musical setting typically undercuts any connection that the words might have forged with pop culture. Fusing the work of Laurie Anderson and The Kronos Quartet with a performance by Linda Ronstadt (on 'Forgetting') is something of a postmodern landmark – but how many Ronstadt fans will have heard it, let alone *understood* it?

5   A cursory glance at Laurie Anderson's performance video *Home of the Brave* will confirm the presence of alienated, episodic modes of presentation.

6　I am obliged to note, however, that at a Philip Glass concert in Berkeley's Zellerbach Hall in June 1989, two members of the audience were seen playing 'air piano'!

7　These notes are taken from a programme for a concert given at Berkeley's Zellerbach Hall, 3 March 1990.

8　Billy Bragg, quoted *New Musical Express* 23/30 December 1989.

9　I am grateful to Paul Kendall for pointing this out to me. However, pop and rock remain so conventional, and – I would argue – realist/naturalist in form, through elements such as tonality, narrative musical development and song structure, that to elevate timbre to such a position of prominence surely fails to engage with the way that contemporary music is actually heard by its audiences.

10　See, for instance, the interview with Jean Baudrillard in *The Face* (Vol.2, No. 4, January 1989); and the issue of *Rolling Stone* (18 May 1989) in which he is listed as that summer's 'Hot Philosopher King'.

11　*Music Video Awards*, MTV, September 1989. The winners in the postmodern music video category were another 'alternative' rock act, REM (for the clip 'Orange Crush'). The following year, the winning clip was from Sinead O'Connor ('Nothing Compares 2 U' – a cover of a Prince song), the other contenders being Depeche Mode, Red Hot Chili Peppers and Tears for Fears.

12　See *Hits* Vol. 5, No. 209, 17 September 1990. I am grateful to Keith Negus for bringing this material to my attention.

13　I am grateful to Andrew Pogue for an explanation of this use of the term.

References

ADORNO, T. (1941) 'On popular music', *Studies in Philosophy and Social Science* No. 9 reprinted in Frith and Goodwin (1990).

APPIGNANESI, L. (1986) editor, *Postmodernism: ICA Documents 4*, London: Institute for Contemporary Arts.

AUFDERHEIDE, P. (1986) 'Music videos: the look of the sound', in Gitlin (1986).

BORN, G. (1987) 'On modern music: shock, pop and synthesis', *New Formations*, No. 2, Summer.

BOURDIEU, P. (1980) 'A diagram of social position and lifestyle', *Media, Culture & Society*, Vol. 2, No. 3, July.

BOURDIEU, P. (1984) *Distinction: A Social Critique of the Judgement of Taste*, Cambridge, Mass.: Harvard University Press.

COULSON, C. (1987) 'Start making sense', *New Republic*, 23 March.

DAVIS, M., Fred PFEIL and Michael SPRINKER (1985) eds, *The Year Left*, London: Verso.

——— (1988) 'Urban renaissance and the spirit of postmodernism', *New Left Review*, No. 151, May–June 1985. Reprinted in Kaplan (1988).

FISKE, J. (1986) 'MTV: post modern post structural', *Journal of Communication Inquiry*, Vol. 10, No. 1, Winter.

FRITH, S. AND GOODWIN, A. (1990) editors, *On Record: Rock, Pop and the Written Word*, New York: Pantheon; London: Routledge.

FRITH, S. AND HORNE, H. (1987) *Art Into Pop*, London: Methuen.

GITLIN, T. (1986) editor, *Watching Television*, New York: Pantheon.

GLASS, P. (1987) *Music by Philip Glass*, New York: Harper & Row.

GOODWIN, A. (1987a) 'Music video in the (post) modern world', *Screen*, Vol. 28, No. 3, Summer.

—— (1987b) 'From anarchy to Chromakey: music, video, media', *Onetwothreefour: A Rock and Roll Quarterly*, No. 5, Spring.

—— (1988) 'Sample and hold: pop music in the digital age of reproduction', *Critical Quarterly*, Vol. 30, No. 3, Autumn. Reprinted in Frith and Goodwin (1990).

GROSSBERG, L. (1988) *It's A Sin: Postmodernism, Politics and Culture*, with Tony Fry, Ann Curthoys, and Paul Patton. Sydney: Power Publications.

HEBDIGE, D. (1988) *Hiding In The Light: On Images and Things*, London: Comedia/Routledge.

JACOBY, R. (1987) *The Last Intellectuals: American Culture in the Age of Academe*, New York: Basic Books.

JAMESON, F. (1979) 'Reification and Utopia in mass culture', *Social Text*, No. 1, Winter.

—— (1984) 'The politics of theory: ideological positions in the postmodernism debate', *New German Critique*, No. 33, Fall.

—— (1988) 'Postmodernism and consumer society', in Kaplan (1988).

JONES, R. (1987) 'Introduction' to Glass (1987).

KAPLAN, A. (1987) *Rocking Around The Clock: Music Television, Postmodernism and Consumer Culture*, New York: Methuen.

—— (1988) editor, *Postmodernism and its Discontents: Theories, Practices*, London: Verso.

LEVINE, L. (1988) *Highbrow/Lowbrow: The Emergence of Cultural Hierarchy in America*, Berkeley: University of California Press.

LIPSITZ, G. (1986/7), 'Cruising around the historical bloc: postmodernism and popular music in east Los Angeles', *Cultural Critique*, No. 5, Winter. Reprinted in *Time Passages: Collective Memory and American Popular Culture*, Minneapolis: University of Minnesota Press (1990).

LUKÁCS, G. *et al.* (1977) *Aesthetics and Politics*, London: New Left Books.

MARCUSE, H. (1968) *Negations*, London: Allen & Unwin.

MCCLARY, S. (1989) 'Terminal prestige: the case of avant-garde music composition', *Cultural Critique*, No. 12, Spring.

M^CROBBIE, A. (1986) 'Postmodernism and popular culture', in Appignanesi (1986).

MELLERS, W. (1973) *Twilight of the Gods: The Beatles in Retrospect*, London: Faber & Faber.

NELSON, C. AND GROSSBERG, L. (1988) *Marxism and the Interpretation of Culture*, London: Macmillan.

PFEIL, F. (1985) 'Makin' flippy-floppy: postmodernism and the baby-boom PMC', in Davis (1985).

—— (1988) 'Postmodernism as a "structure of feeling"', in Nelson and Grossberg (1988).

ROSS, A. (1989) *No Respect: Intellectuals and Popular Culture*, New York: Routledge.

STRATTON, J. (1989) 'Beyond art: postmodernism and the case of popular music', *Theory, Culture & Society*, Vol. 6, No. 1, February.

STRAW, W. (1988) 'Music video in its contexts: popular music and postmodernism in the 1980s', *Popular Music*, Vol. 7, No. 3.

TAMM, E. (1989) *Brian Eno: His Music and the Vertical Color of Sound*, Winchester, Mass.: Faber & Faber.

TAYLOR, R. (1978) *Art, an Enemy of the People*, Hassocks, Sussex: Harvester Press.

TETZLAFF, D. (1986) 'MTV and the politics of postmodern pop', *Journal of Communication Inquiry*, Vol. 10, No. 1, Winter.

WEINSTEIN, D. (1989) 'The Amnesty International concert tour: trans-nationalism as cultural commodity', *Public Culture* (Bulletin for the Project of Transnational Cultural Studies), Vol. 1, No. 2, Spring.

WOLLEN, P. (1986) 'Ways of thinking about music video (and postmodernism)', *Critical Quarterly*, Vol. 28, Nos. 1 & 2.

2
Recognizing a 'human-Thing': Cyborgs, Robots and Replicants in Philip K. Dick's Do Androids Dream of Electric Sheep? *and Ridley Scott's* Blade Runner

NIGEL WHEALE

Pulp science fiction and cult-status movies are discussed here in terms of their interaction, and the ways in which as popular culture they carry urgent contemporary concerns. Science fiction now forms about ten per cent of paperback fiction sales, and with the continuing success of comics such as *2000 AD* and graphic-novel fiction such as *Watchmen* there's every reason to think that the readership will continue to grow. This chapter explores the writing of one of the most celebrated SF authors, Philip K. Dick, through a discussion of his novel *Do Androids Dream of Electric Sheep?* (Dick 1968: hereafter *DAD* in citation) and its acclaimed film realization as Ridley Scott's *Blade Runner* (Scott 1982, 1991). I concentrate on the central theme of both novel and film: the conflict between authentic and artificial personality, that is, between people and robots. Recent science fiction has perfected the category of the soft robot, combining hints from genetic engineering, cloning and micro-surgery to produce the android, or as *Blade Runner* categorizes them, replicants. The replicant is a convenient being for postmodernity: if the status of representation and image reproduction inflects us so deeply now, and impacts on the nature of knowledge, cultural production and even behaviours, then the notion of the replicant extends the crisis of reproducibility to our selves: what would a human simulacrum be like?

A common reason often given for not paying attention to science fiction is the supposed lack of 'human interest' in the genre: in science fiction, technology by definition dominates to the exclusion of developed personalities or relationships. *Do Androids Dream ... ?* is a special case for this kind of objection because it explicitly plays with confusions between human personality and artificial or machine-derived intelligence. What would be the difference between a physically perfect android kitted out with memories and emotions passably like our own, and a person nurtured through the usual channels? Dick's pulp novel from the late 1960s anticipated issues that have become increasingly pressing 30 years later, and which figure largely in the debates surrounding the idea of postmodernity. Software engineers who are committed to the 'strong' version of belief in the capacity of Artificial Intelligence are confident that there will come a time, perhaps within the next 50 years, when human intelligence will be fully simulated by algorithmic, computational intelligence: computer programs will think like people, and even surpass them in powers of reasoning. Placing such an intelligence within a fleshly body produces a cyborg, a fully integrated flesh-and-metal organism that will be familiar to us from films such as *Terminator*. Level-headed opponents of this speculation do not find it difficult logically to argue against any such development: the best that might be hoped for, they argue, is that computers will only ever be able to simulate the computable aspects of human intelligence, because algorithmic systems by definition can never intuit proofs in the way that ordinary brains do. And since human personality is the result of infinitely complex development and family interaction, no soft-machine could ever be programmed to mimic the depth effects of psychological growth. What would be the point of making babies redundant? This is, however, exactly what cybernetics proposes.

The term 'cyborg' was coined in 1960 as a definition of a 'self-regulating man-machine system' (Tomas 1989: 127) but every period has imagined such 'human-Things', entities which test or define the contemporary sense of intrinsic human value over against its simulacrum: the incubus or succuba in Christian tradition, the Golem in Jewish folklore, Prospero's Ariel and Caliban (and perhaps even Miranda too?), E. T. A. Hoffmann's Sandman, and of course Mary Shelley's Frankenstein (Warrick 1980). The robot also has a long and influential life in film history, beginning with Fritz Lang's eerie adaptation of the Golem legend in *Metropolis* (1926). The Frankenstein popularized in film culture is a figure of pathos as an incompetent replication of the human body, assembled from disjectamenta. Another, more troubling version of the human simulacrum is that of dispossession by alien possession, where original personality is erased by an interloper. Don Siegel's *Invasion of the Body Snatchers* (1956) is a classic narrative of this kind: 'People are being duplicated, and once it's happened to you, you are part of this thing' explains Elizabeth, desperately. Here possession joins with classical paranoid fear of subjugation by alien force, which in the mid-1950s was a synecdoche for the Red Menace.

Closer to postmodern concerns is a possession nightmare such as *The Stepford Wives* (1974) where the menfolk of a small upstate community band together to have their wives replicated by obliging cyborgs (with appalling dress taste). The true dummies in *The Stepford Wives* are of course the men for accepting such feeble substitutes in place of true humanity and personality. Philip K. Dick's androids also belong to their period, the late 1960s, in the ways that they are defined in relation to authentic human emotionality and sanity. But as soon as we have written the glib phrase, we are brought up short, in exactly the manner which the novel provokes: what *is* an authentic human psyche?

Dick's dystopia: the death of species

Do Androids Dream ... ? is set in the late-twentieth-century, decaying megalopolis of San Francisco, a post-holocaust society where the human population has been decimated by the effects of radiation sickness. So far, so conventional; the scenario is one major cliché of pulp SF. This novel's originality, however, is created by the compelling logic to be found in the details of the South Californian world which it evokes. The effects of 'World War Terminus' have induced progressive species death, beginning with birds, then 'foxes one morning, badgers the next, until people had stopped reading the perpetual animal obits' (*DAD* 36). This species-scarcity induces a kind of religion of animal-ownership in the surviving human population, where everyone aspires to possess and care for one of the beast creation. Curating animals is also partly a replacement for child-rearing, because the fear of genetic damage has discouraged human reproduction. The bounty-hunter hero of the novel, Rick Deckard, keeps a black-faced Suffolk ewe on the roof of the apartment block where he lives with his wife Iran. But the sheep is not ideal, in fact it's electric; Deckard can't afford a real one, and he continually checks the list-price of animals in 'his creased, much-studied copy of Sidney's Animal & Fowl Catalogue' (*DAD* 12).

At the verge of its extinction, the natural world becomes a valuable commodity; the process of collecting and buying the living merchandise itself accelerates the destruction, increasing scarcity, and raising prices.

Here the often-praised predictive aspect of good science fiction is very evident. But the keeping of animals in the future world of the novel is an element of a larger belief system: everyone views their own life as part of 'the Ascent', a progress up an increasingly steep incline which they share with the god-like figure of Wilbur Mercer. This religious empathy, or feeling-with, is generated and experienced through technology. By tuning in to an 'empathy box' each individual shares in the Ascent of Mercer, and shares the antagonism directed to their god-figure by some unknown enemies, 'the old antagonists': 'He had crossed over in the usual perplexing fashion; physical merging – accompanied by mental and spiritual identification ... As it did for everyone who at this moment clutched the handles, either here on Earth or on one of the colony planets' (*DAD* 21–2).

'Empathy' joins believers with Mercer, either through use of the black box, or through their empathy which they extend towards the animals they keep, or more rarely, to other individuals. And at the centre of the novel's increasingly tortured attempts to locate absolute differences between androids and human beings we find the linked ideas of empathy and affect. The *Oxford English Dictionary* defines 'empathy' as 'The power of entering into the experience of or understanding objects or emotions outside ourselves'. It is a relatively recent word in English, first recorded by the *OED* in 1912, and imported from the vocabulary of German philosophical aesthetics (Scheler [1913] 1954). Through empathy we know and feel what it is that other people know and feel; it is an experience of (literal) fellow-feeling. 'Compassion' is the medieval word used to designate this sort of emotion (from 1340), and 'sympathy' the renaissance term (1596).

'Affect' is a much older word that has taken on a new lease of life, again in the early twentieth century. It is first recorded by the *OED* from about 1400, conveying a group of related meanings: 'Inward disposition, feeling, as contrasted with external manifestation or action; intent, intention, earnest', and 'Feeling towards or in favour of; kind feeling, affection'. So even in the medieval period 'affect' was already a word with psychological resonances, and it is used for this reason in our own period by psychoanalysts to describe emotional value within the psyche. *Do Androids Dream ... ?* employs this idea of 'affect' to distinguish between a 'person-Thing' and a human entity: humanity experiences affect (and affect-ion), robots don't. But again the novel poses a worrying dilemma: some people suffer from a 'flattening of affect', and in the test situation could be mistaken for robots, on this criterion (Jameson 1984, 1991: 10).

[104]

The androids are organic beings – soft robots – designed by scientific-industrial corporations for use on the planetary colonies to which people from earth are emigrating because of all-pervasive radioactive con-tamination – 'The saying currently blabbed by posters, TV ads, and government junk mail, ran: "Emigrate or degenerate! The choice is yours!"' (*DAD* 11). The robots act as drones for the off-earth colonies where they labour or work as servants. They are modelled as mature individuals who never age, but tragically, they only have a shelf-life of four years: this also gives them a certain desperation. Periodically androids run wild in the colonies and return to earth, hoping not to be recognized.

Because they don't possess empathy, the androids represent a potential threat to the human population; they are physically powerful but completely lacking in conscience, moral sense, guilt and human sym-pathy: 'Now that her initial fear had diminished, something else had begun to emerge from her. Something more strange. And, he thought, deplorable. A coldness. Like, he thought, a breath from the vacuum between inhabited worlds, in fact from nowhere' (*DAD* 54–5). The androids are, potentially, manufactured psychotic killers. And it is only by identifying them through their lack of empathetic response that they can be located and destroyed. Rick Deckard is a bounty hunter, a meaner, twenty-first-century version of Raymond Chandler's Philip Marlowe; he traces androids which illegally return to earth, administers the empathy test, and 'retires' them with a laser gun.

This sounds like a no-nonsense kind of job, but Deckard becomes more and more anguished as the boundaries between android response and humane response are systematically blurred by the action of the novel. Deckard administers the Voigt-Kampff Empathy Test to suspect an-droids; this consists of a series of questions which stimulate minute but measurable reflex responses in the subject being tested. The questions are framed to provoke emotional reaction in the suspect, the logic being that there is an innate, automatic response within the human psyche which is triggered by particularly emotive descriptions. The Voigt-Kampff questions invite responses to practices such as bull-fighting and the use of animal heads mounted as hunting trophies. In the novel's future-world, because of the heightened species-consciousness, these are crimes against animals which universally horrify humanity, and sup-posedly leave androids unaffected. But the latest generation of Nexus-6 'andys' approaches nearer and nearer to human empathetic ability, and these robots cause Deckard particular difficulty.

The first Nexus-6 which – or in her case, perhaps, 'whom' is more appropriate – Deckard meets is Rachael Rosen, and she very nearly passes the empathy-test ordeal; more difficult still, she ceases to be an inanimate object for Deckard, because he finds himself attracted to 'her'. Rachael also turns the tables on Deckard, accusing him of being inhuman because of the instrumental, cold way in which he tries to deal with her. But Deckard does not destroy her because she is 'the property' of the corporation that made her, 'used as a sales device for prospective emigrants' (*DAD* 49). Luba Luft is the next person-Thing which Deckard has to hunt and destroy, and which has become a fine opera singer: 'The Rosen Association built her well, he had to admit. And again he perceived himself *sub specie aeternitatis*, the form-destroyer called forth by what he heard and saw here. Perhaps the better she functions, the better a singer she is, the more I am needed' (*DAD* 77). Luba Luft is a cultured andy: Deckard finds her at an exhibition of Edvard Munch's work, and as a last request before being 'retired' she asks Deckard to buy her a reproduction of Munch's painting *Puberty*. Why this painting? Because it represents a developmental stage which the android never had, and wishes to experience – her name perhaps puns on 'Love of Life'. This aspect of the androids' construction is emphasized in the film adaptation, through different materials. Deckard spends $25.00 on a book containing a print of Munch's painting, and after he has destroyed Luft, 'systematically burned into blurred ash the book of pictures which he had just a few minutes ago bought Luba' (*DAD* 104). Who exactly is exhibiting android behaviour in this situation? 'Luba Luft had seemed genuinely alive; it had not worn the aspect of a simulation' (*DAD* 108).

The debates which this novel provokes by creating 'artificial' people who are effectively indistinguishable from 'authentic' people reproduce in fictional form some elaborate arguments from philosophy. For example, I've taken the phrase 'person-Thing' from Martin Heidegger's *Being and Time*, an influential but now increasingly controversial work, written in Germany during the 1920s. Heidegger's subsequent relations with Hitler and National Socialism cast a long shadow across his philosophical work, but *Being and Time* remains a unique contribution to many questions. What is the quality of our knowledge of other people? How should we avoid treating other people instrumentally, exactly as person-Things? What kinds of criticism can be made of empathy, as a means of understanding others? Are we condemned to treat the world only as an object, and so progressively degrade it (Ronell 1989)? Popular culture carries its own versions of these issues, though they are seen under a different aspect when transposed from writing to the film or video screen.

Visualizing novels, thinking in pictures: *Blade Runner* as optical philosophy

Ridley Scott's *Blade Runner* was released at the same time as Steven Spielberg's *ET.* and was not an immediate success, only just recouping its $15 million costs. *ET.* was much more in tune with the feel-good ethos of President Reagan's inaugural period, and overshadowed Scott's film. But *Blade Runner* – the title is said to be taken from an obscure Victorian term for a private detective, via William Burroughs' novel of that name – became first a 'cult' film, and then a national institution: it is one of only 50 films to be deposited in the Library of Congress, Washington D.C., on account of its contribution to film culture. Perhaps this says little about the value of *Blade Runner* and more about library classification systems, but the film's significance can be more confidently registered in its influence throughout the 1980s, being a major inspiration for William Gibson's celebrated novel *Neuromancer* (1984) and the whole genre of cyberpunk. Scott himself had worked in British TV since the early 1960s, and had directed over 2000 highly successful ads, so he brought the tight visual economy needed in the television ad to every detail of his films. The cityscape of *Blade Runner* – he was trying to give the impression of 'Hong Kong on a very bad day' – has taken on an independent existence in dozens of subsequent films and adverts (and the film moves the action from a dystopic San Francisco to a similarly deranged Los Angeles). *Blade Runner*'s sound-track is as carefully modelled as the image-track, and Vangelis's synthesized score provides a layered and modulated ambient music which again seems to have anticipated subsequent fashions. Ridley Scott's best-known film to date is probably *Alien*, which has obvious connections with *Blade Runner* in style and theme. In terms of literature-to-film transfers, Scott's first feature is also significant, *The Duellists* (1977), because it is a (very fine) adaptation of a short story by Joseph Conrad.

Films adapt novels by making them visual, at the level of meaning as well as of perception. Therefore *Blade Runner* discards Wilbur Mercer and the Cult-of-the-Animal theme from Dick's novel, and concentrates on the visual/narrative compulsion of Rick Deckard's search-and-destroy quest in pursuit of the Nexus-6 androids, who are recategorized

[107]

in the film as 'replicants'. These 'human-Things' are visually compelling, and issues of sight/seeing/interpretation dominate their presence throughout the film: having ditched the quasi-religious framework of *Do Androids Dream . . . ?*, *Blade Runner* can still provoke complicated thoughts, but it does so through visual patterning rather than verbal allegories – though *Blade Runner* still has some very specifically literary moments, as I'll demonstrate. The following discussion analyses four sequences where sight and visual values are coded in complex ways.

1   When Deckard (Harrison Ford) administers the Voigt-Kampff test to Rachael (Sean Young), the screen is filled with the replicant's constricted pupil as we watch with Deckard for the fluctuations of emotional tone which will register the degree of her empathetic response. There is a traditional idea that 'the eye is the window on the soul', and it is as if Deckard is trying to locate the presence/absence of soulfulness in his subject, even as his own emotions become entrained by gazing so deeply into Rachael's magnified pupil. This image may recall two of the earliest shots in the film, one directly after the opening credits and the other a panoramic, establishing view of the megalopolis: intercut with the wideangle cityscape are two brief shots of a pupil reflecting the view and apparently gazing at the Tyrell Corporation headquarter-pyramids. The eye is enigmatic: whose pupil, reacting in what way? His, hers, ours – its? The shots of Rachael's face are breath-taking, and present the female star's features within the long Hollywood tradition of full-face framing shots, at which point we as spectators can also pull back and become aware of how we are entrained via visual pleasure, here addressed to a simulacrum (Mulvey 1989).

The room where Deckard tests out Rachael is a fine example of one of Ridley Scott's elaborate, smokey interiors; Syd Mead was the 'visual futurist' designer for the film, and for the Tyrell executive suite he constructed a fine Aegypto-Fascist decor, a visual domain brilliantly explored seven years later in the sets for *Batman* by designer Anton Furst and director Tim Burton. As we adjust to the interior, an owl flies through the half-light, which might recall Goya's etching 'The Sleep of Reason Brings forth Monsters', itself glancing at the late-Enlightenment motto, 'Minerva's owl flies at dusk'. These allusions, if we care to think of them, raise questions about the misapplication of science as instrumental reason. The Tyrell suite also displays a delicate bonsai tree, another example of biological manipulation, and also perhaps a relic of the Cult of Nature surviving from *Do Androids Dream . . . ?* – Deckard has just such a mini-tree in his own apartment. A magical effect is contrived when Tyrell darkens the room for the Voigt-Kampff test to be administered: at touch of a button the huge windows darken, like a pupil closing down against strong light.

2   In *Blade Runner* the Tyrell Corporation has given its replicants densely modelled memories, complete with photographs and anecdotes from their (non-existent) childhoods. This was done to create some meaning for the emotions which would begin to develop in the robot subjects during their four-year existence. Although the Nexus-6 androids which Deckard hunts are merciless killers, they possess this growing desire for fully human experience, just as in *Do Androids Dream ... ?* Luba Luft wished to possess the image of Munch's painting, so the pathos of *Blade Runner*'s first replicant, Leon (Brion James), is considerable. He is brutal and murderous, but he is also in search of the mother and childhood he never experienced, as if he would like to be better than humanity will allow him to be. The film narrative is brutally established when Leon shoots a psychologist, and just as he begins to reminisce: 'Let me tell you about my mother ...'

Deckard finds some souvenir snap-shots of Leon's 'past' which the replicant has hidden, and he interrogates the photographs in the hope of tracking down the robots. The photograph he chooses to examine records an interior, another of the complex, hazy rooms which are the characteristic domestic spaces of the film. But thanks to technology the photograph possesses three-dimensional depth in the style of a holo-gram, and it becomes a living image which can be inspected via consumer electronics. Deckard has treated Rachael brutally, letting her know that she is not-human, and he morosely drinks through the evening, alone in his haze-ridden apartment. He explores the depth of Leon's photograph through voice-activated computer-enhancement. This technological chic allows him to look around corners into the depth of the image, and in the hidden recesses of the hologram/photo he catches sight of the enigmatic clue that he needs, and orders 'hard copy'. Deckard himself has become a kind of cyborg here, extending his in-sight via the voice-activated computer scan.

3   Seeking for the bio-technological key to 'more life' (and who could disagree?) Roy (Rutger Hauer) and Leon break into the laboratory of Chou, a genetic engineer who manufactures eyes and who contributed to the Nexus-6 range. Roy introduces himself in a pretty obscure way,

by slightly adapting two lines from William Blake's epic poem, *America. A Prophecy* (1791–3). He pronounces:

> Fiery the angels fell, deep thunder rolled around their shores, burning with the fires of Orc.

The lines in Blake are:

> Fiery the Angels rose, and as they rose deep thunder rolled
> Around their shores, indignant burning with the fires of Orc.
>
> (Blake [1793]1971: 199; [1793]1975: 149)

In Blake's prophecy the Angels are the spirits of the American colonies who, inspired by 'the fires of Orc', are revolting against England's tyranny. Blake scholars say that Orc is an anagram for Cor, or Heart, and he is the symbol of youthful rebellion and freedom. It's an obscure, literary moment in the film, beautiful and enigmatic: everyone can see that Roy is one of the colonized who is rebelling against his tyrannical master, but it needs an Explainer to gloss his quotation, and also to add that he alters Blake with a touch of Milton's *Paradise Lost*, because his angels fall, rather than rise. As Chou the genetic engineer gazes terror-stricken into Roy's eyes he recognizes him for what he is, because he made them. Roy quips, 'Chou, if only you could see what I have seen with your eyes' as Leon drapes soft eyeballs trailing their ganglia over Chou's shoulders (and see Fischer 1989).

4   The last example of eye-contact I want to describe is also grisly: Roy gains access to the genius responsible for Nexus design, Tyrell (Joe Turkel), head of the corporation. Tyrell wears huge goggle-specs, he is the image of the 'boy-professor' from ten thousand movies, but now grown old and severe. Some *Blade Runner* experts argue that Tyrell is himself an android, created by the Corporation to act as front-man; there are certainly storylines like this elsewhere in Philip Dick's fiction. In his room Tyrell keeps another owl of Minerva, whose unblinking gaze mirrors his own glasses. 'I've seen things you wouldn't believe', Roy tells his maker, who becomes a literal god-father, because there has been no need for mothering. Mothers are only fictional bodies for the replicants, figures whom they lack and endlessly need. Tyrell is unable to satisfy Roy's desire for More Life: the design problems were insuperable, he says. Failing to gain a lease on life, Roy is effectively condemned to an early death and he is enraged. He takes his revenge by murdering his inadequate father in a gruesome (off-screen) crushing of Tyrell's eyes

and head, dispassionately observed by the owl. 'He that made the eye, shall he not see?' asks Psalm 94; *Blade Runner* says No.

This cancellation of sight as a metaphor of death is also present when the android-beauty Pris (Daryl Hannah) makes up her face, preparing to meet Roy. In a big close-up of her features which fill the screen, Pris sprays horizontally across her closed eyes with black face-paint, laying down a dark war-band which makes a sinister frame for her eyes when she opens them, glaring. This is the war paint in which she dies.

Epilogue: the Director's Cut, the cruellest cut

Blade Runner radically simplifies the plot-line and 'metaphysics' of *Do Androids Dream...?*, but constructs a different logic through visual coding, as all films do. This emphasis on appearance can be said to intensify one of the problems of science fiction as a genre, and this has to do with the representation of gender. Is science fiction inescapably a genre written by men, for boys/men? The loving attention paid to technology, and the flattened portrayal of human character, particularly women's roles, might indicate as much. Authors such as Ursula Le Guin and Doris Lessing have taken up the genre with the explicit intention of creating new kinds of SF narrative and value. A brilliant feminist appropriation of robotics is Donna Haraway's 'Manifesto for Cyborgs' (Haraway 1989). But *Do Androids Dream...?* and *Blade Runner* are not tender-hearted works, they display the routine brutalities and masculinist attitudes of the popular genres to which they owe so many of their conventions. For example: *Do Androids Dream...?* page 145: 'He began hunting through the purse. Like a human woman, Rachael had every class of object conceivable filched and hidden away in her purse; he found himself rooting interminably.' Rick Deckard's infatuation for Rachael is the most troubling instance of this problem. In the novel, bounty hunter and android sleep together, prior to the final shoot-out with the remaining three Nexus-6 robots: Rachael articulates the dilemma: 'You're not going to bed with a woman ... Remember, though: don't think about it, just do it. Don't pause and be philosophical, because from a philosophical standpoint it's dreary. For us both' (*DAD* 146).

That the problem is 'philosophically dreary' is a droll way of putting it, and this goes some way to rescuing the situation. But not all the way. *Blade Runner* opts for a softer option. The closing sequence shows Deckard and Rachael flying at speed to the good green country in the north, and Deckard reveals that Rachael has no 'termination date'. He has an ageless companion for the duration. Is this also tacky? Or is it a witty rewriting of the Greek myth of the dawn goddess Eos and her mortal lover Tithonus? Eos begged Zeus to grant Tithonus immortality, but forgot also to ask for perpetual youth on his own behalf.

Well, that was the finale for popular consumption. In 1992 *Blade Runner – The Director's Cut* was released, following a growing trend of reissuing notable films which had been altered prior to commercial screening at the producers' or distributors' request, and in ways that changed their directors' original intentions. Ridley Scott's version of *Blade Runner* as it was before changes made in response to adverse, pre-release screenings, is arguably a darker, more disturbing film where the audience's insecurity about authentic and simulated personality contaminates the central character. Scott's first version of the film did not have Deckard's voice-over spoken in a hard-boiled Philip-Marlowe style to explain key aspects of the plot and ambience in Los Angeles AD 2019. This voice-over established an empathetic and unproblematic connection between the audience and the gum-shoe blade runner. At key moments he explains for us, and moralizes on the action: Deckard in this way is the figure with whom we identify as we move through the action.

But both the director and actor, Harrison Ford, disliked Deckard's narration, and lacking this voice-over, the 'director's cut' presents the hero much more objectively and enigmatically, and it is even possible to be nostalgic for Ford's comforting tones when we are left much more to our own devices on the mean streets of the first version, vulnerable to the overpowering, cold visuality of decaying LA. In other words Deckard also becomes a problem. When Rachael first follows him back to his flat after he has administered the Voigt-Kampff test, he brutally tells her the truth about her constructed psyche: in the first-released version of the film, we perhaps put this down to a need for Deckard to protect himself from his own emotions in responding to Rachael – he forcibly reminds himself that she is a non-human construction by telling her the truth. In Ridley Scott's preferred version, it may be that Deckard acts like this because he too is a human-Thing, acting inhumanly because he does not know better.

The motivation for this desolating possibility is one brief sequence, only seconds long, where Deckard dreams a vision of a unicorn, as he becomes drunk, trying to follow clues to Leon's whereabouts. The unicorn sequence is utterly enigmatic in its immediate context, but is resolved by a detail in the closing minutes of the film. Garff, a seedy detective, has throughout the action made origami figures from foil – a chicken, a man, and finally a unicorn, and he leaves this where Deckard will find it. This detail reveals him, perhaps, as Deckard's minder, as someone with access to Deckard's synthetic memories, which have been implanted in just the same way as Rachael's. Scott's preferred version of the narrative ends with Deckard apparently realizing the implications of this, just before leaving with Rachael. The softened ending added footage of them escaping to the north, using materials left on the cutting room floor during the editing of Stanley Kubrick's *The Shining.*

Ridley Scott's first cut of *Blade Runner* creates this desperate ambivalence in its closing minutes, and we are forced back through the narrative seeking clues that will resolve the issue one way or the other. There are none, so the narrative is radically indecidable, rather like Henry James' *Turn of the Screw.* Did Peter Quint and Miss Jessell haunt the children, or was the governess a hysterical murderess? Deckard's angry question to Tyrell, after he has discovered that Rachael is cybernetic, becomes our own anguished question about our hero: 'How can it not know what it is?'

References

BLAKE, William ([1793] 1971), *America. A Prophecy,* Plate 11, lines 115–16, in *The Poems of William Blake* edited by W. H. Stevenson, text by David V. Erdman, p. 199, London: Longman. The plate is reproduced (in black and white only) in *The Illuminated Blake* ([1793] 1975) annotated by David V. Erdman, p. 149, London: Oxford University Press.

BRUNO, Giuliana (1987) 'Ramble city: Postmodernism and *Blade Runner*', in *October* 14: 61–74. Reprinted with related material in Annette Kuhn (ed.) *Alien Zone. Cultural Theory and Contemporary Science Fiction,* London and New York: Verso.

DICK, Philip K. (1968) *Do Androids Dream of Electric Sheep?* All quotations from the Grafton Books edition (1972 and many reprints), now prominently subtitled 'filmed as *Blade Runner*'. Grafton publish several dozen other novels by Dick as well as his *Collected Short Stories* in five volumes.

FISCHER, Norman (1989) '*Blade Runner* and *Do Androids Dream of Electric Sheep?*: an ecological critique of human-centred value systems', in the *Canadian Journal of Political and Social Theory/Revue canadienne de théorie politique et sociale* XIII/3: 103–13.

HARAWAY, Donna (1989) 'A manifesto for cyborgs: science, technology, and socialist feminism in the 1980s', 173–204 in *Coming to Terms. Feminism, Theory, Politics*, Elizabeth Weed (ed.), London: Routledge.

HEIDEGGER, Martin ([1927] 1962) *Being and Time*, translated by John Macquarrie and Edward Robinson, Oxford: Basil Blackwell.

JAMESON, Fredric (1984) 'Postmodernism, or the cultural logic of late capitalism', *New Left Review* 146: 53–92.

—— (1991) *Postmodernism, or the Cultural Logic of Late Capitalism*, London and New York: Verso.

KELLNER, Douglas, Flo LIEBOWITZ, and Michael RYAN (1984) '*Blade Runner*: A diagnostic critique', in *Jump Cut* 29: 6–8.

MULVEY, Laura (1989) *Visual and Other Pleasures*, London: Macmillan.

RONELL, Avital (1989) *The Telephone Book. Technology, Schizophrenia, Electric Speech*, Lincoln and London: University of Nebraska Press.

SCHELER, Max ([1913] 1954) *The Nature of Sympathy* [*Wesen und Formen der Sympathie*], translated by Peter Heath, with a general introduction by W. Stark, London and Henley: Routledge & Kegan Paul.

SCOTT, Ridley (1982) *Blade Runner*. A Michael Deeley–Ridley Scott Production, directed by Ridley Scott, screenplay by Hampton Fancher and David Peoples, produced by Michael Deeley. Available as a Warner Home Video (112 mins, colour) for home viewing only. 15 rated.

—— (1991) *Blade Runner. The Director's Cut*. Warner Home Video. 15 rated.

TOMAS, David (1989) 'The technophilic body. On technicity in William Gibson's cyborg culture', in *New Formations* 8: 113–29.

WARRICK, Patricia S. (1980) *The Cybernetic Imagination in Science Fiction*, Chapter 8 discusses Philip K. Dick's contribution. Cambridge, Mass. and London: MIT Press.

WOLLEN, Peter (1993) 'Modern times: cinema/Americanism/the robot', 35–71 in *Raiding the Icebox. Reflections on Twentieth-Century Culture*, London and New York: Verso.

PART II
Essays on Postmodernism

Two: Architecture and Visual Arts

Introduction

We have seen how some of the debates over postmodernism have been physically realized in the architecture represented by Michael Graves' Portland City Public Services Building (above pp. 41–2 and illustration p. 134). In this section, Julian Roberts argues that most of the supposed postmodern architectural style of the last 20 years is in fact no more than a superficial decorative effect. He describes the philosophical basis of early-twentieth-century architectural modernism, expressed through the writings and practice of Le Corbusier, and then the reaction which it provoked during the 1970s and 1980s. He defines this reaction as anti- rather than post-modernist. Roberts' chapter represents a position that has been consistently held in arguments over the development of aesthetics and design since the 1930s. He argues that there is certainly a need to go beyond the working assumptions of classical modernism, but that this can be done by extending one of its latent traditions, that of artistic and philosophical constructivism. In this way there might be a genuinely postmodern architectural practice which is based in more than a frivolous combining of styles and periods, which is the most familiar image of postmodern building. Roberts' definitions of modernism are based in philosophical assumptions, and therefore extend the discussion of the movement in Part I, which was largely confined to modernism as a literary and artistic category.

It is more difficult to relate the changing kinds of representation in the visual arts of the last 30 years quite so directly to the single category of the postmodern because of the extraordinary diversity of materials in the period. In this section the visual arts are illustrated by works which demonstrate some of the central debates: these are the writing and photographic collages of Yve Lomax, the painting and printmaking of Tom Phillips, and his *TV Dante*, a video made in collaboration with the film director Peter Greenaway. The three chapters explore the following arguments:

Was there an architectural postmodernism?

Has postmodernism contributed to art from the women's movement?

How does theory inform contemporary creativity?

What uses are made of the interplay between verbal and visual meaning in contemporary art?

Is there a place for traditional, painterly skills in contemporary art, when the use of technology is becoming so pervasive?

Postmodernism and the visual arts: the end of painting?

Classical modernism during the first three decades of the twentieth century produced a diverse range of working practices in the fine arts. Analytical, abstract styles competed with the long-established traditions of realism and verisimilitude. Conventional, craft-based skills were challenged by disruptive, seemingly naive modes of drawing and painting, or else they were entirely abandoned in favour of eclectic constructions which could use all sorts of found materials. It is pointless to look for a moment when the values of painterly traditions were 'finally' exhausted, but during the 1970s and 1980s painting increasingly became only one option among many which artists might choose to practise, leaving the current position of painting itself uncertain. Consequently the special status granted to painting and drawing, and their attendant skills, has been increasingly eroded as artists have explored all kinds of alternative means of expression which rely on new materials and technologies.

The particular value ascribed to the 'marks' in paint, pastel or charcoal on the picture surface, made by a human calculation and trained perception, is now challenged by image-making practices based in technology. Paintings and drawings have traditionally been valued partly because they are direct expressions from the hand and eye of a known individual. They are uniquely expressive and therefore uniquely valued, and the prestige of a painting is directly allied to the prestige of the particular artist's 'vision'. Paintings have therefore been valued as luxurious commodities because they are produced with skilful craft, and they are unique objects; as such they can be traded and collected. Images that can be reproduced an indefinite number of times, such as prints or photographs, are not humanly marked to the same degree, and uniqueness is not part of the value which is ascribed to them. Therefore this serial nature of the reproduced image has contributed to the displacement of painting as a medium (Benjamin [1936] 1973: 219–54). Mechanical reproduction produces new kinds of image, but other strategies have moved further away from, or have altogether abandoned, the production of an art object which can be admired or exchanged. 'Post-object' artists produce even more intangible kinds of work such as performance pieces, subtle modulations to the landscape as in land art, film and video texts, conceptual accounts of projected works, and installations which are site-specific and cannot be so easily appropriated by private ownership.

These changing assumptions about painterly values in the recent period are starkly demonstrated by comparing three influential critical books. Kenneth Clark's *Civilisation* (1969) was first a major television series which was hugely influential in popularizing a traditional view of the civilized arts in the late 1960s. Clark's narrative covered the development of architecture, painting and sculpture from the classical period onwards, and concentrated on European achievements. Reacting against Clark's high-cultural account of the arts, John Berger's *Ways of Seeing* (1972), also a television-to-book transfer, was still firmly conceived within the perspective of European painting, but contextualized aesthetics and taste by raising questions of patronage, ownership and audience. *Ways of Seeing* was an early, important contribution to the redefining of culture in historical and material terms, as discussed above (pp. 33–9). The third book in this sequence is a posthumous collection of essays by the American critic Craig Owens, *Beyond Recognition. Representation, Power and Culture* (1992). Owens wrote for the journal *October* which has been extremely influential in analysing and theorizing innovative art of the 1980s, and together with the writing of Rosalind Krauss, Owens' contributions were among the most fruitful.

In two essays on 'The Allegorical Impulse' published in 1980, he proposed six strategies which might characterize postmodern art practice. These were: *appropriation, site specificity, impermanence, accumulation, discursivity,* and *hybridization* (Owens 1992: 58), and they certainly establish terms of reference which had not been apparent to either Clark or Berger. Owens argued that, in trying to move beyond the working assumptions implicit in modernism, artists of the last three decades deployed these strategies in the following ways:

Appropriation The use of photo-mechanical reproduction of imagery in single or multiple form in order to challenge the uniqueness of the art image and its specific 'aura'. For example: Andy Warhol's *200 Campbell's Soup Cans* (1962).

identity [handwritten margin note]

Site specificity The construction of complex environments, installations and sites which locate works firmly within a defined context, and against the supposed timeless and universal application of a great painting within a prestigious gallery. For example: Robert Smithson's *Spiral Jetty* (1970) built in the mud and rock of the Great Salt Lake, Utah.

Impermanence Creating works from ephemeral materials, either in their physical construction, or in their content drawn from mass/popular imagery so as to offend the elite status granted to gallery art. For example: Jeff Koons' *Pink Panther* (1988) combining schlock-kitsch figurines.

Andy Warhol's portraits of pop-culture icons [handwritten margin note]

Accumulation Drawing out the creative process using a repetitive logic, through the production of works in series – 'Thirty is Better than One' (Andy Warhol) – or through a dialogue of contrastive elements. For example: Yve Lomax's *Open Rings and Partial Lines* (see below p. 123).

Discursivity Setting up interference patterns between the mute sensuous appeal of visual imagery and the discursive reflection of written commentary in the same piece, making the silent art work articulate and argumentative. For example: Mary Kelly's *Post-Partum Document* (see below p. 121).

Hybridization The combination of materials, genres, period references to produce highly eclectic constructions, both in content and form, again to contravene the purity of the art object. For example: Tom Phillips' *TV Dante* (see below p. 166).

Aspects of all of these strategies are present in the architecture, photography, prints, paintings and video discussed in this section. But however ingeniously the art work attempts to escape the status of privileged commodity, the art market can always recapture it within the economics and politics of the gallery space. This double bind is another problem inherited from the agitational phase of early modernism, as in Wyndham Lewis:

> I might have been at the head of social revolution, instead of merely being the prophet of a new fashion in art. Really all this organized disturbance was Art behaving as if it was Politics.
>
> (Lewis 1937: 35)

[120]

However, the creative activity which most authentically challenged the aesthetic assumptions of arts institutions, and which has consistently argued against settled social conventions, has undoubtedly been produced within the context of the women's movement. This is a body of work which has very good reason to reject the category of postmodernism as a comprehensive description of contemporary cultural activity.

Art of the women's movement: feminist and/or postmodernist?

A number of female artists and writers came to prominence during the 1970s and 1980s who were motivated and inspired partly by the kinds of critique developed by contemporary feminism. Mary Kelly's involvement with the women's movement during this period informed her work as an artist, and she made a leading contribution to a distinctively feminist aesthetics – 'I don't believe there can be feminist art, only art informed by different feminisms' (Mary Kelly 1990: 61). Her *Post-Partum Document* (created 1973–9, published 1983) is a collection of objects, images and texts which map her own experience of motherhood in relation to her son as he progressed through his early development, from the beginnings of self-consciousness and speech, to the age of seven. The *Post-Partum Document* transforms the genre painting of mother-and-child (and above and beyond this pairing, the madonna-and-child) by exploring the experience from the mother's perspective. The text/installation also articulates the experience through the use of psychoanalytic theory based on the work of Freud and its contemporary developments in the writings of, among others, Maud Mannoni, Michele Montrelay, Melanie Klein, Julia Kristeva and Jacques Lacan.

Traditional portraiture in oil painting aims to convey individual psychology through realistic representation of the subject's 'likeness': 'The great test ... is to turn the picture to the wall and see if it seems that someone has suddenly left the room' (Phillips 1989: 13). By its use of psychoanalytic theory, Mary Kelly's *Post-Partum Document* challenges the ambition of naturalistic portrait painting to explore psychological 'depth'. How is identity constructed and experienced, both for the mother and for the child? What are the dynamics of their growing relationship? What part does language play in the formation of personality? How far is our 'self-image' coincident with our social presence? Mary Kelly articulates these and other aspects of identity in relation to Freud's theories of

Oedipal development, and this is a clear example of writerly modernism, combining aesthetic practice with theoretical perspectives. But her work does not simply serve to exemplify the master-text. Artists such as Kelly, Barbara Kruger and Jenny Holzer are careful not to produce work which is scripted by theory, however closely their making has been prompted or informed by theoretical writing (Kruger 1990: 60; Varnedoe and Gopnik 1990: 398–403).

Works such as the *Post-Partum Document* are post-painterly because they stage a systematic criticism of the status and meaning of representation. They also put themselves into a critical relation with the conventional meanings of painting as a craft-produced commodity, invested as it is with all the prestige of (largely male) painterly tradition, and laden with assumptions about the representation of gender. Kelly's images and texts question the kinds of self-image which women are expected to negotiate in contemporary society, and they pose questions about female – and also, necessarily, male – responses to those constructed images. She continued this critique with the 'extended project' *Interim* (1985–90), the Latin title translating as 'meanwhile, in the meantime', but also 'however, nevertheless'. This installation presented some of the exterior forms through which a woman's life may be articulated when she is no longer defined by the status which society grants to her as a young mother. Her practice turns linguistic meaning against visual cliché, while also being alert to what may be coercive within language itself (Mulvey 1989; Apter 1991). The titles of sections for *Interim* are Latin nouns, *Corpus, Pecunia, Historia, Potestas* – body, money, history, power – where the gravity of the names operates in part as an oppressive weight from within which individual experience has to be articulated. The transitional nature of woman's mid-life experience in *Interim* is presented as a paradigm of the ways in which sexual identity is assembled:

> She can neither look forward, as the young girl does, to being a woman, that is having the fantasized body of maturity; nor can she return to the ideal moment of maturity – ideal in that it allows her to occupy the position of the actively desiring subject without transgressing the socially acceptable definition of the woman as mother. She is looking back at something lost, acknowledging perhaps that 'being a woman' was only a brief moment in her life.
>
> (Kelly 1990: 23)

Yve Lomax is another feminist artist who during the 1970s contributed to this development of a politics of representation by focusing on the social construction of gender (Pollock 1988: 155–99). Her work was included in the influential exhibition *Beyond the Purloined Image* which was organized by Mary Kelly in 1983 and included exhibits by Ray Barrie, Karen Knorr, Judith Krowle, Olivier Richon, Mitra Tabrizian, Susan Trangmar and Marie Yates. Kelly described their work like this:

> the artists in *Beyond the Purloined Image* refuse to retreat into the esoteric realms of pre or post modernism. They are passionately, but critically committed to the contemporary world; yet they are not content merely to pilfer its cultural estate. Instead they are exploring its boundaries, deconstructing its centre, proposing the de-colonisation of its visual codes and of language itself.

> (Parker and Pollock 1987: 249)

It is clear in this statement that Kelly viewed theories and practices associated with postmodernism as obscurantist and dilettante. By contrast the artists in *Beyond the Purloined Image* shared a common concern with the inter-relationship between representational codes as deployed in the mass media and in discourses about sexuality. Poststructuralist and psychoanalytic theory were central to this critique, which used photography to create images in order to challenge conventional expectations about appearance, identity and desire. Lomax's *Open Rings and Partial Lines* consisted of large panels of photographs in three separate sections – in traditional art-historical terms, triptychs – where the two outer images were dislocated by the ambiguous presence of the central, dividing image (Lomax 1982: 9). The panels of *Open Rings and Partial Lines* refused the conventions which categorize individuals through the stark opposition of male/female, just as her prose text *The World is a Fabulous Tale* considers how to circumvent patterns of domination in narration, identity and ecology:

> in the work I have attempted to produce an assemblage where a 'middle' or 'third' term neither unifies nor fragments or divides which in turn calls into question the position of the two sides as two sides. It is this play of neither/nor which excites me.

> (Parker and Pollock 1987: 252)

Lomax's work was also included in *Difference: On Representation and Sexuality* in 1985, an exhibition organized by Kate Linker for the New

Museum of Contemporary Art in New York, which displayed work by Ray Barrie, Victor Burgin, Hans Haacke, Mary Kelly, Sylvia Kolbowski, Barbara Kruger, Sherrie Levine, Marie Yates and Jeff Wall. She has continued to explore questions in the politics of representation through her imagery and the use of theoretical concepts, but she now addresses ideas of difference as experienced throughout culture. Her current work reflects the growth of concern over ecological issues, exploring the relations between science and humanity's impact on the physical environment. [Note: With thanks to Hilary Gresty for material in these two paragraphs.]

The World is a Fabulous Tale was first published in *Other Than Itself: Writing Photography*, edited by John X. Berger and Olivier Richon in 1989. The text plays with opposing terms such as 'truth' and 'fiction', 'signs' and 'things', 'natural' and 'artificial' as a way of questioning the nature of photographic objectivity. Yve Lomax collages imagery, in her writing and montages, so as to unsettle the reader's/viewer's assumptions about the relations between the image and the real, metaphor and logic. By using commonplace imagery, for example from nursery rhymes and birthday cards, she provokes questions that are normally reserved for philosophy: 'By bringing the mythic and metaphorical into play I hope to implicate the reader or viewer in the fragrance of the world. I hope to invite the reader or viewer to participate in a philosophical or theoretical activity.' Her work can be related to the kinds of question raised about documentary truth by Trinh T. Minh-ha in her own writing and film making, which has a similar ambition to unsettle large assumptions and unpick oppressive categories through the innovative use of image and metaphor (see below, section Four).

Art produced within the vigorous political and theoretical debates of the women's movement during the last two decades has actively incorporated theory and reflection to its working processes. Text-as-commentary and text-as-object become intrinsic to the construction of works by artists such as Kelly, Barbara Kruger, Lomax and Jenny Holzer. In this summary of developments in the visual arts their work has been used to exemplify aspects of the postmodern agenda in terms of post-painterly media, the incorporation of theoretical discourse, and the playing between verbal and visual discourses. It's important to emphasize here that the kind of work made by Kelly and Lomax should not be taken as representative of all feminist-inspired visual creativity; it is only one kind of strategy followed within the women's movement. Even so, there is a serious objection to be made to this description, which is that the kinds of critique and the varieties of pleasure which these photographs, writings, films and installations offer should not be subsumed under another, supposedly more comprehensive category, such as that of postmodernity. The critique of domination and exploitation made by artists from the perspective of the women's movement is arguably a more comprehensive and necessary project than the kinds of analysis offered by the language of postmodern critique (Pollock 1988: 156). This would then be a clear example of the appropriative nature of the category of postmodernism, where its all-encompassing ambition actually mystifies the operations of specific oppression, and detracts from more focused argument.

Tom Phillips: painterly skill and postmodern technique

Tom Phillips' career in its various phases and working practices can be related to these developments from a different perspective, demon-strating once more the diversity of art which can be misleadingly subsumed within the global category of the postmodern. Phillips trained in the traditional painterly skills of Camberwell Art School during the late 1950s, where life drawing was the central discipline, but he developed his characteristic interests during the 1960s and 1970s when his paintings and printmaking explored a wide range of themes through the interaction of text and image and the use of controlled series of variations. His long-term project to translate and illustrate Dante's *Inferno* has grown from a de luxe artist's book into a televisual video-text which incorporates extensive use of computer graphics, made in collaboration with the film director Peter Greenaway.

Despite the apparent parallels with a number of the new tendencies in art and theory, Tom Phillips' work over two decades has not so far enjoyed the attentions of postmodern commentators. Given the range and interest of his output, this is puzzling; it may simply be an effect of the generations, that his career has been 'out of phase' with critical fashions. He has major national exhibitions and his work circulates internationally in large printed editions, while his *TV Dante* was broad-cast on prime-time television, but theoretical commentary has so far overlooked him. It may be that his output is so various he embarrasses attempts to categorize it: he paints portraits, makes prints, collages, translates, and writes the best commentary on his own work; he has composed operas and has undertaken long-term photographic projects which record the changes to specific sites in south London.

The sheer diversity of these activities might suggest a postmodern eclecticism, moving between different modes and styles, and giving primacy to none. Phillips' work is also close to the materials and interests of Pop Art, a movement which is often associated with the beginnings of postmodern activity through its incorporation of images and styles from mass culture (see above pp. 33). Phillips makes extensive use, for example, of found materials from postcards and flag imagery, both recurrent obsessions in Pop Art. The interplay of visual and verbal meaning is also a principal theme throughout his work, as for the feminist artists described above. There is also a clear contribution from theoretical writing, specifically the influence of Roland Barthes and the structuralism of the 1960s as it was followed in art schools at the time. Barthes' *Mythologies* ([1957] tr 1972) and *Writing Degree Zero* ([1953] tr 1967) encouraged an alert attention to the materials of everyday life in terms of the underlying patterns which expressed social organization (Rylance 1994: 42–54). But the element in Barthes' structuralism which Phillips did not develop in any consistent way is its role in the critique of social hierarchy and ideological conformism. This lack of overt political critique clearly differentiates his work from much of the art made by the subsequent generation of artists beginning their careers in the later 1970s.

Barthes' enthused analysis of the 'meaning' of the spectacle of a wrestling match, or of the design of the Citroen D. S. was always ambiguous: his structuralism delighted in plotting the coded significations of popular culture, but the reading was always finally intended to reveal the ways in which ideology was at work within the routine detail of daily existence. Phillips, too, maintains a keen attention to the smallest details of his south London environment – a fragment of linoleum, the varieties of water stop-cock covers, the street corners photographed at precisely the same location and time each year, but there is no explicit element of ideological critique present in his images. This differentiates his work very clearly from the installations of Mary Kelly and the photographic practice of Yve Lomax where critique is fundamental to the process of their art.

These issues continue to be controversial, and many commentators write about a sense of cynical exhaustion pervading the visual arts in the early 1990s. The New York Whitney Biennial Show in 1993, for example, was heavily criticized because it exhibited only work that was remorselessly and narrowly 'politically correct' in its focus on issues of race/gender/class mis-representation. But the range of art discussed in this section shows that divergent practices may still move and provoke the spectator. The lens-based art derived from writerly modernism practised by Mary Kelly and Yve Lomax is one option; Tom Phillips' video for 'postmodern television' is another. But so are his portrait paintings executed in oils, and these show that painterly skills and painterly pleasures are still to be seen:

> Painting is a slow manual process, it is something you do alone, and it's something you do with your hands. If you put that in the context of the strangely escalated society we're in where communication is a very rapid thing, where we're bombarded with a lot of imagery from advertising and television and video and so on, it makes painting a strangely subversive activity.
>
> (Huxley 1993)

Further reading

Journals *Architectural Design*; *Artforum*; *Artscribe*; *October*; *Oxford Art Journal*; *Third Text. Third World Perspectives on Contemporary Art and Culture*; *Word and Image. A Journal of Verbal/Visual Enquiry*.

Art in Theory 1900–1990. An Anthology of Changing Ideas, edited by Charles Harrison and Paul Wood (1992) is a 1200-page anthology in seven sections covering topics such as 'The Legacy of Symbolism', 'The Idea of the Modern World', 'Rationalization and Transformation', through to 'Ideas of the Postmodern'. It is the most inclusive collection of this kind, and provides primary materials to explore many of the issues raised in Part I of this book. Mike Davis *City of Quartz. Excavating the Future in Los Angeles* (1990) is a wonderful history of LA as poly-ethnic urban galaxy. Brandon Taylor *Modernism, Post-Modernism, Realism. A Critical Perspective for Art* (1987) is a closely argued polemic for a renovation of artistic practices. Caroline Tisdall *Josef Beuys* (1979) is an accessible account of an influential German artist. Barbara Kruger *Remote Control. Power, Culture and the World of Appearances* (1993) is a collection of aphoristic essays on TV, film and spectacle during the 1980s by a prominent communication-artist. Sandy Nairne in collaboration with Geoff Dunlop and John Wyver *State of the Art. Ideas and Images in the 1980s* (1990), and Robert Hewison *Future Tense. A New Art for the Nineties* (1990) are informed surveys. Rozsika Parker and

Griselda Pollock (eds) *Framing Feminism: Art and the Women's Movement 1970–1985* (1987) is an encyclopaedic archive of statements and descriptions.

References

APTER, Emily (1991) 'Fetishism and visual seduction in Mary Kelly's *Interim*', *October* 58, Fall: 97–108.

BARTHES, Roland ([1953] tr 1967) *Writing Degree Zero*, translated by Annette Lavers and Colin Smith, London: Jonathan Cape.

—— ([1957] tr 1972) *Mythologies*, selected and translated from the French by Annette Lavers, London: Jonathan Cape.

BENJAMIN, Walter ([1936] 1973) 'The work of art in the age of mechanical reproduction', 219–54 in *Illuminations*, edited and with an introduction by Hannah Arendt, translated by Harry Zohn, London: Fontana/ Collins.

BERGER, John (1972) *Ways of Seeing*, London: BBC, Harmondsworth: Penguin.

CLARK, Kenneth (1969) *Civilisation*, London: BBC Publications.

HOLZER, Jenny (1989) *Signs*, London: Institute of Contemporary Arts.

HUXLEY, Paul (1993) Tutor, Royal College of Art, interviewed by Peter Blake, *Opinion: Art Education*, BBC Radio Four, 21 October.

KELLY, Mary (1983) *Post-Partum Document*. [Published version of the original installation work.] Foreword by Lucy R. Lippard, London: Routledge & Kegan Paul.

—— (1984) 'Desiring images/imaging desire', in *Desire: ICA Documents*, London: Institute of Contemporary Arts.

—— (1987A) 'Beyond the purloined image', in *Framing Feminism: Art and the Women's Movement 1979–1985*, Rozsika Parker and Griselda Pollock (eds) London: Pandora Press.

—— (1987B) 'Invisible Bodies: On *Interim*', in *New Formations* 2, Summer, 7–19.

Mary Kelly by Hal Foster. New York: The New Museum of Contemporary Art.

KRAUSS, Rosalind (1985) *The Originality of the Avant-Garde and Other Modernist Myths*, Cambridge, Mass. and London: MIT Press.

KRUGER, Barbara (1990) *Love for Sale. The Words and Pictures of Barbara Kruger*, text by Kate Linker, New York: Harry N. Abrams.

LEWIS, Wyndham (1937) *Blasting and Bombardiering*, London: Eyre and Spottiswoode.

LOMAX, Yve (1982) 'The politics of montage', *Camerawork* 9.

—— (1987) 'Broken Lines: More and No More Difference', text and photographs in *Screen* 28 (1).

—— (1989) 'The World is a Fabulous Tale', in *Other than Itself. Writing Photography*, John X. Berger and Olivier Richon (eds), Manchester: Cornerhouse Publications.

MULVEY, Laura (1989) 'Impending time: Mary Kelly's *Corpus*', in *Visual and Other Pleasures*, London: Macmillan.

OWENS, Craig (1992) *Beyond Recognition. Representation, Power, and Culture*, edited by Scott Bryson, Barbara Kruger, Lynne Tillman and Jane Weinstock. Introduction by Simon Watney. Berkeley, Los Angeles, Oxford: University of California Press.

PARKER, Rozsika, and Griselda POLLOCK (eds) (1987) *Framing Feminism: Art and the Women's Movement 1970–1985*, London: Pandora Press.

PHILLIPS, Tom (1989) *The Portrait Works*, with an introduction by Bill Hurrell, London: National Portrait Gallery Publications.

POLLOCK, Griselda (1988) 'Screening the seventies: sexuality and representation in feminist practice – a Brechtian perspective', 155–99 in *Vision and Difference. Femininity, Feminism and the Histories of Art*, London and New York: Routledge.

RYLANCE, Rick (1994) *Roland Barthes*, Hemel Hempstead: Harvester Wheatsheaf.

VARNEDOE, Kirk, and Adam GOPNIK (1990) *High and Low. Modern Art and Popular Culture*, New York: Museum of Modern Art.

3
Melancholy Meanings: Architecture, Postmodernity and Philosophy

JULIAN ROBERTS

The concept 'postmodern' first came into general currency in the realm of architecture; and it is in architecture that it most rapidly lost its value. For architects, 'postmodern' is now part of history, fading into the palette of client-acceptable styles along with 'tudor', 'Queen Anne' and the rest.

That, of course, is an aspect of the way the term came into use. 'Postmodern', at least in architecture, arose from the critics' inability to say anything substantive about the turbulent range of styles emerging in the last two or three decades. The main thing the buildings seemed to have in common was chronological: they happened later than 'modernism' (which, being a self-conscious programme, is much easier to define). Beyond that, they were also more *ostentatiously finished* than modernist buildings, and could afford to 'quote' other styles in the way that the frugal functionality of their predecessors could not (or would not). But that exhausts the significance of the great majority of postmodern buildings. Po-mo, now, is typified by the bolt-on ornamentation of countless speculative office buildings, distinguished from their dreary forebears only by greater outlay on tinted glass, polished stone facings, and inscrutable fragments of 'classicism'.

However, it is futile to pour scorn on work that was never intended to do more than proclaim the affluence of those who commissioned it. And in any event, the worst excesses of this architectural cynicism were confined to England and the empty boom of the Thatcher years. Meanwhile, there is, or was, a certain manner in post-war architecture which, perhaps, will continue to be called 'postmodern'. The name, though, is not important. Our question is: what is this manner of architecture?

To answer this, I shall assume that 'postmodernism' can be characterized by something to which it is opposed, namely modernism; and I shall explore the express or implicit polemic that a certain architecture conducts against modernism. Beyond this, however, I shall argue that modernism is not the monolithic entity its 'postmodern' critics make it out to be. The dynamics of the opposition are more adequately represented by seeing not modernism, but 'post-modernism' as the initial object of critical revolt. The problem is that modernism in its initial aspect performs this revolt inadequately; only in what I shall argue is a stronger form of modernism – constructivism – does its proper critical force emerge.

In other words, we have a taxonomy not of two, but of *three* competing cultural modes: an initial critique of 'post-modernism' in what is conventionally called modernism, a resurgence of 'post-modernism', and a fuller critique in a revitalized modernism. Moreover, it is obvious from this scheme that terms like modernism and post-modernism lose all chronological content. Certainly, much architecture since the mid-1960s falls into the second of our modes; but there is nothing that binds that mode to particular dates or to a particular place in a sequence.

1 Modernism and mimesis

I start by asking what modernism is, or was, such that 'post-modernism' felt impelled to rebel against it.

Modernism (I define) is a set of attitudes culminating in the belief that we can escape history. It supposes that the world has some independent objective structure or other, and that human beings are able to give an account of that structure in knowledge that is fundamentally isomorphic with it. For 'modernism', the critical properties of knowledge are that it should be 1. *distinct* from its content ('the world'), but 2. *isomorphic* with it – i.e., changes in the world are matched by changes in knowledge (see Roberts 1992). For example, my knowledge that two and two make four matches an intrinsic property of the objective world: two apples plus two apples really *do* make four apples. Moreover, however much the universe may change, the views of it captured in knowledge (or, at least, in 'scientific' knowledge) are anchored in absolute objective constancy. Arithmetic is the firmest example of that; but there is no objection to empirical knowledge or knowledge of the past. For example it is, always was, and for ever will be true that the battle of Hastings was fought in 1066 AD. In other words, although in practice knowledge usually concerns the empirical, the transitory, and the historical, it is not itself any of those things. Knowledge stands above history.

This is a view we would term *mimesis*; it rests on the assumption that knowledge reflects and, in reflecting, lifts the things that it reflects into a higher sphere of generality. This attitude is, in part, platonistic; knowledge, properly, consists of 'ideas', which are somehow continuous with the intelligible aspect of the world, though not with its base sensory matter. Indeed, at its foundational levels, scientific investigation takes place precisely in abstraction from matter and change. Its paradigm, moreover, is arithmetic, which represents the purest of the 'ideas'. Arithmetic is, in this account, absolute mimesis: it exhaustively captures the quantifiable aspects of reality, while at the same time remaining completely distinct from it.

Historically, this position can be reconstructed from the work of many thinkers. It is most commonly associated with Plato, for whom the 'truth' of things did not lie in the way they most directly appeared – not in the shadows on the cave wall, for example, but in the figures who cast them (*Republic* 514a ff); not in the disorder of experience, but in the stately regularity of the heavens (the 'music of the spheres' – *Timaeus*). In the modern era, it is most visible in the efforts of Frege to ground arithmetic in logic. Kant had claimed that arithmetic was 'synthetic' – i.e., that it contained elements of the empirical. Frege insisted that it was purely analytic – i.e., that it arose only in the absolutely non-empirical motions of logic itself. For Frege, moreover, numbers were expressly regarded as 'platonic' entities.

Modernism is the assertion of the mimetic principle in art, and pre-eminently, indeed, in architecture. With it, architecture becomes an epiphany of pure spirit. One manifesto for this position is Le Corbusier's *Towards a New Architecture* of 1923. Le Corbusier, like Frege, invoked Plato in his vision of 'platonic grandeur, mathematical order' (111). This principle, which was associated with the wonders of engineering and modern technology, was opposed to the stuffy sentiment of tradition. Tradition, said Le Corbusier, was capable only of producing the 'Boulevard Raspail' (glossed by his translator as Regent Street!). But this represented a 'contemptible enslavement to the past' (103); such architecture was 'stifled by custom' (92). Contemporary architecture, by contrast, should turn to 'mathematical calculation' which would reveal the 'universal law' (1) and the 'principles which govern our universe' (31). Throwing aside concern with 'style', the 'stifling accumulation of age-long detritus' (288), new architects should be 'intelligent, cold and calm' (127). The fruits of their work would then be 'pure creation of the mind' (1, 201, 209), and a 'manifestation of man creating his own universe' (73).

The principal results of this mathematical art are evident in three aspects. First, constructional methods appropriate only to primitive technology would be overthrown. The thick walls necessary for rough sandstone, for example, would be replaced by the thin cavity structures achievable in concrete. Pitched roofs and basements would be replaced by arrangements that were more efficient in their use of space and better at dealing with damp – flat roofs (with gardens) and buildings raised on pilotis (columns).

Second, Le Corbusier insisted on the compositional supremacy of what he called the 'great primary forms' – cubes, cones, spheres, cylinders and pyramids (29). These were the vocabulary of mathematical spirit. In Le Corbusier's application, square sections were supreme; he praised the 'audacity, austerity and nobility' of the square mouldings of the Parthenon (220). And the dignity of the rectilinear expressed itself also in his declaration that 'architecture is nothing but ordered arrangement, noble prisms, seen in light' (162).

Finally, Le Corbusier's belief in the expressibility of an ideal essence shows itself in his doctrine of the priority of the plan. The plan is the seminal form of the whole structure. It is the seed from which the building grows; and in good architecture all the articulations of the work should be traceable back to the plan, and never appear as disconnected surface articulation. 'Mass and surface are determined by the plan. The plan is the generator' (47). Concentration on the plan re-affirms the pure originatory ideal, and makes possible 'the clear and naked emergence of the Essential' (138). Acccordingly, Le Corbusier rejects any mere 'play of decoration' (51); and, similarly, a building's material is strictly subordinate to its ideal geometry (despite traditional architecture's 'many dissertations on the soul of stones', as he comments sarcastically – 18).

2 Anti-modernism

The practical effects of this programme – at least in the naive modernism of Le Corbusier's successors – were, and are, evident enough. They were, moreover, accentuated by the fact that Le Corbusier's platonist enthusiasms were coupled with a somewhat robust attitude towards social planning. On the basis that 'where order reigns, well-being begins' (54), residential building was to be concentrated in mass units, preferably in widely-spaced 'enormous towers' (58), whose 'jutting prows' (63) would map the heroic new order illustrated by his visionary drawing of a 'city of towers' (57). And (an equally fateful component of the ideology), cheapness was to be prized as an end in itself. 'We no longer have the money to erect historical souvenirs,' Le Corbusier declared dismissively (15).

Modernism by this aegis became an arrogant recipe for cheap mass functionality and the ubiquitous concrete cube; and those features, at least, presented easy targets for revisionists. Canonical 'post-modernism' from that perspective is merely an inversion of the programme of *Towards a New Architecture*, as one can see typically in Michael Graves's

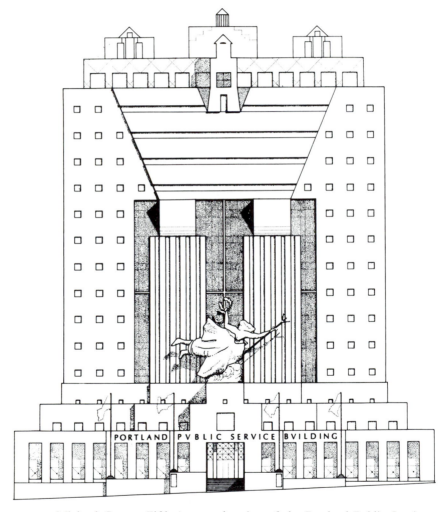

PLATE 1 Michael Graves, Fifth Avenue elevation of the Portland Public Services Building, Portland, Oregon, 1980.

Modernism is a kind of cold death.

Public Services Building in Portland, Oregon, and in his hotels for the Florida Disneyworld. Accordingly, any economies of construction are not to be celebrated, but to be masked by ostentatious embellishment: polished granite comes into its own. The building does not declare its structural rationale (as with Le Corbusier's emphasis on the plan); on the contrary, it plays and dissembles with the odd, the surprising and the redundant. The vocabulary of the building, moreover, ceases to be attached to any 'message', and this semantic disengagement is under-scored by manneristic historical citation. On top of this come certain stylistic gestures such as the rehabilitation of the arch – not structurally, however, but by means of curved lintel beams!

Just as post-modern texts don't necessarily move in a circle – IJ

Whatever substance the express aesthetic of such work may have is, indeed, largely drawn from the positions it attacks. One of the founding texts of postmodernism was Robert Venturi's *Complexity and Contradiction in Architecture*, first published in 1966. In his Introduction, Vincent Scully claimed that it was 'the most important writing on the making of architecture since Le Corbusier's *Vers une architecture*' (Venturi 1977: 9). A more persuasive recent view is that despite the book's 'cathartic' impact it was theoretically modest and relied on a 'bombastic mass of sub-jectively and superficially appropriated historical material' for its effect (Kruft 1991: 511ff). Nonetheless, however reactive its basic structure (Venturi inclines towards gibes such as the conversion of Mies's 'less is more' into 'less is bore') the book does articulate a fundamental motif. This motif is *despair of significance*; and at this point we can start to map out the fundamental structure of anti-modernism generally.

Modernism was mimetic, in that it believed that reasoned language was essentially a reflection of reason in reality. The work of the mathematician, for example, mimetically appropriated *the very same entities* that were evident in the outside world. Equally, all language was ascertainably about things out there. Moreover, the outside was *absolutely* outside human knowledge, in the sense that it was completely independ-ent of it. Our knowledge might be right or wrong; but at least there was always an autonomous world in terms of which it was right or wrong.

Now, anti-modernism in all its guises comes to the conclusion that the first part of this position (reliable mimesis) is no longer tenable. Whatever significance is, it is not the passage of an outside into an inside. The problem lies in the incapacity of knowledge to account for itself. Or, to put it another way, it seems hard to settle on any part of knowledge that is self-evidently distinct from its objects. The basic metaphor of mimesis imagines that the 'ideas' may be imported into mind because they are separable from reality; they have an absolute persistence independent of the reality they inform. The world itself is full of content, ever coming to be and passing away. But the ideas can embrace that content, and they mediate between the world of inconstant change and the realm of intelligibility and constancy.

Now this metaphor only convinces so long as the ideas seem evidently solid. This evidence, as we noted, has usually rested on the drawing of an analogy with what always seemed the most reliable of all the ideas: mathematics. With the exception, perhaps, of colour, knowledge is quantificational in character. All the dimensions of time and space, ranging from the facts of history to the frequencies of electromagnetic waves, are quantifiable. So no part of existence is inaccessible to mathematical description; and mathematics, it was supposed, is self-evidently absolute.

The difficulties of this view have only become apparent during this century – largely in the train of Frege's attempts to ground arithmetic by deriving it from logic and the pure forms of thought. The first problem was Russell's paradox, which demonstrated that the set theory pre-supposed by arithmetic was not self-evident and would only work if assisted by additional and rather counter-intuitive axioms. Such imposition of axioms hardly spoke for the timeless self-evidence one would associate with platonic ideas; rather, it suggested that arithmetic was at some profound level pragmatic and hence itself part of the changing world of content.

The second puzzling result in the philosophy of mathematics was Gödel's theorem. Venturi, indeed, cites it as 'proof of ultimate inconsistency in mathematics' (16). Strictly, this formulation is wrong: the point of Gödel's theorem is not that mathematics is inconsistent, but that the price of regarding it as consistent is that we must accept its *incompleteness* – i.e., that there are certain questions arising purely on its own absolute terrain that cannot be answered, questions comparable with, though more complex than, 'what is two times two?'.

But Venturi is right: the rule of mathematics over the realm of ideas is shaken. Arithmetic seems, contrary to the assumptions of platonism, to be neither self-evident (it involves principles that are pragmatic rather than 'pure') nor self-contained (it is incomplete). With that, the notion of a self-contained realm of ideas loses its central support; and the form supposedly abstractable from reality starts to look as though it too is tainted with the material world.

[136]

With that, Le Corbusier's central metaphor looks in danger of collapsing. The pure geometrical entities that modernist buildings were supposed to incorporate, radiating outwards from the plan, were suddenly rooted not in eternal laws of the universe, but in the activities of particular human beings. And if that was the case, why worry at all about their perspicuity to such ideas? More specifically, why imply any kind of hierarchy, as Le Corbusier does between the plan as 'generator' and the rest of the building as something 'determined' by it? It would be more appropriate to regard 'logic' as merely one rhetoric among many, and, equally, the plan as no more than one expressive resource among others. This, in effect, is the argument implicit in Venturi's polemical advocacy, first, of ambiguity and 'contradiction' (precisely what the logical order of ideas is not able to encompass), and secondly of historical reference (which, for Le Corbusier, was no more than the peddling of 'souvenirs').

3 The aesthetics of melancholy

Venturi's platform is basically Nietzschean. Modernism had imagined that logical and normative consistency could be guaranteed by being anchored to *one* knowing and willing 'subject'; this, popularly, is what Kant's 'transcendental subject' is supposed to have achieved. For example, 'I' (the central 'subject') cannot will or know contradictories; if I desire (or know) p, I cannot also desire or know *not-p*. Nietzsche, however, replaces this sentimental faith in the single subject with a view in which *many* 'knowing' and 'willing' centres occupy the psyche, and where values like truth and consistency are replaced by the anarchic ecstasies of the 'will to power' (Nietzsche's manifesto can be found in section one of *Beyond Good and Evil*).

This has, of course, provided academic architectural criticism with raw materials for an industry whose commodities range from phenomenology to deconstruction. The best opening to the aesthetics of sceptical despair, however, is provided by Walter Benjamin's little-understood theory of *melancholy.* He first developed this in *The Origin of German Tragic Drama* (1928), but it subsequently became the basis of an entire theory of culture (see, especially, 'The Work of Art in the Age of Mechanical Reproduction' ([1936] 1973)), and of his various historical analyses of Paris in the nineteenth century, especially the essays on Baudelaire.

Melancholy, in Benjamin's argument, arises when the connections between this world and the divine world of salvation seem to be lost beyond recovery. Theologically, melancholy is the response to the *deus absconditus*: Christ is dead, a figure in a historical past, but no longer a presence now. Equally, the whole process of reason and signification is cut adrift; in Dürer's celebrated etching (the 'Melancholia I' of 1514), the instruments of higher mathematical learning lie useless along with all the other tools of mere human enterprise. Certainly they no longer provide

PLATE 2 Albrecht Dürer, *Melancholia*, 1514.

us with a bridge to heaven. Thus abandoned, the world and everything in it are no more than a death mask (a *facies hippocratica* – see Roberts 1982: 139ff, 152). However subtle the inquiries of mathematics, it cannot detect spirituality where the spirit has flown. All the researches and compositions of the human mind never go beyond the perverse riddles of anagrams, onomatopoeic conceits and the rebus; signification ceases to be a power of logos, and becomes itself immired in the brutishness of things – denotation *non verbis sed rebus* (146). We are consumed by 'passionate contemplation', in which 'every trivial object, because the natural and creative relation to it has gone, appears as the sign of an inexplicable wisdom, and enters an incomparably rich set of connections' (140).

Using Benjamin's idea as a starting point, we can reconstruct some basic elements of the melancholic world picture. Its starting point is sceptical: the difficulty of grounding mathematics shows that a 'true account' of 'objectivity' is not available even as an ideal. This is not because of the empirical difficulties of 'finding out'; it is because we are unable even to decide what a 'true' account might be. If a container has holes in it, we cannot even consider what the position would be for it to be full up. (This is an interpretation of the views of Hilary Putnam: see Roberts 1992: Ch.1.) For this reason we might as well abandon the whole image of a world 'about which' we could develop true accounts, even on an approximate basis.

Instead, and here the whole Nietzschean paradigm begins to take effect, we resign ourselves to the notion that, yes, we move in a universe of expressive systems (languages, sciences, calculations); but we have no hierarchy in which to fix them, no standard of 'truth' by which to judge them. Mathematics are no truer than any other language; and each language is judged, ultimately, not by how deeply it penetrates into ideal structures, but by the purely internal criterion of expressive vigour.

Hence the favouring of surface over depth that we noticed already in Venturi, and which legitimates the playful eclecticism of styles and provocatively superficial ornamentation of postmodern architecture. The most sustained theoretical exploration of this in the immediately aesthetic realm is to be found in the poet Rainer Maria Rilke's essay on Rodin, which argues that Rodin's sculpture is informed by the principle that 'everything is surface' (see Roberts 1988: 222; and, on a similar theme, Deleuze 1969). The world is a rich weave of correspondences in which the creases, furrows and folds of each object repeat and echo across the cosmos. Rodin's sculptures thematize the emergence of intelligibility as

[139]

local patches within the generality of inarticulate surface; typically, in Rodin, fragments of human form 'surface' in the texture of the rough-hewn rock. But human shapes are no more ideal or absolute than any other natural forms, says Rilke in his commentary; the lines on a leaf repeat themselves in the wrinkles of a face, and so on, eternally. The notion that the world is 'folded', rather than structured according to deep determinations, is explored by Deleuze further in *Le Pli*. (Whether this is directly applicable to Leibniz, as he claims, is another matter.)

This principle has two particular points of application in the production of art and architecture. First, the notion of a universal surface, and the unavailability of depth, destroys the classical understanding of the relationship between soul and body. Bodies, in the classical idiom, are the clothes of the soul. They should, accordingly, be represented as beautiful and calm (to reflect the truth and eternity of the soul, seat of the ideas). The eighteenth-century art historian, Johann Winckelmann, developed a precept of 'noble simplicity and still grandeur' which is seminal for the modern version of this tradition, whether in sculpture or architecture. The classical modernism of, for example, Karl Friedrich Schinkel's 1828 New Museum, in Berlin, is an attempt to present a building's exterior as a calm mirror of its regular and mathematical 'soul'.

In the melancholic impulse, however, the external ceases to be a vehicle for expressing the internal; and the internal in any event disappears as a source of reasoned determination. The internal becomes something threatening and unpredictable, liable to break to the surface and overwhelm it without warning. Recent films are full of this theme: the rational purity of the body is violently disrupted by an interior which reveals itself to be not spirit, but an inhuman nightmare (grotesque

PLATE 3 Karl Friedrich Schinkel, 'Façade der Hauptfronte des neuen Museums', 1819.

parasites in *Alien*; robotic machinery in *Blade Runner*). In architecture, it emerges most strongly in the perverse citations of Ricardo Bofill (see the 'Palace of Abraxas' in Marne-la-Vallée, plate 4), where 'history' intervenes not as the calm discourse of tradition, but as the threatening invasion of uncontrollable dreams. In painting, an analogous effect is achieved most strongly by Francis Bacon, whose work (most obviously in the crucifixion triptyches) thematizes the vicinity of 'body' to 'meat', and the elision of physical integrity with the fleshy mass on the butcher's slab. (This, of course, is a constant theme also of Baroque still life. See Schneider 1989: 334–7.)

A parallel motif, with more direct application in architecture, is the *subversion of structure*. Classical modernism is structurally perspicuous: what holds the building up is presented as such to the observer. For classical thinkers, the power of the Doric rested as much as anything in its structural rationality (which, for example, was obscured by the decadent ornamentation of the Corinthian order; cf. Le Corbusier 1923: 214). For the melancholic, however, structure retains no priority, but, instead, hypostatizes itself into luxuriant autonomy. This is exemplified in Giovanni Battista Piranesi's *Carceri*, with their endless receding perspectives of functionless arches (Plate 5), and, in a different variant, in Charles Meryon's 1850 engraving of the Petit Pont, where Notre Dame and the pre-Haussmann houses along the Seine tower over the indeterminately located viewer. (Meryon, a contemporary of Baudelaire's, was for Benjamin a model of the melancholic's dissolution of structural sense into mysterious and inscrutable correspondences in his etchings of modern Paris: see Roberts 1982: 191.)

Exaggeration and deformation of structure are also evident in what is often mistakenly regarded as 'high-tech' architecture, namely, the Hong Kong Shanghai Bank (Norman Foster), Richard Rogers's buildings for the Pompidou Centre and the Lloyd's insurance market. Here, structural and service elements sprout ostentatiously on the outside, but their supposed functionality owes more to the science-fiction fantasies of Archigram or Lebbeus Woods than to constructional rationale (see, for example, Lebbeus Woods's 'Geometrical Tower' in his 1987 collection *Centricity. The Unified Urban Field*).

4 Constructivism

Melancholy, in the end, invests all in an imagery of *memento mori*. Its most intimate emblem is the ruin, the declaration that proclaims its own

PLATE 4 Ricardo Bofill, *Les espaces d'Abraxas,* interior, 1979–83.

PLATE 5 Giovanni Battista Piranesi, plate 14, second state, *Carceri d'Invenzione*, 1760–1.

transience. However, as Benjamin argued in relation to the Baroque, this stoic apathy serves too readily as a pretext for intellectuals who, for all their professed grief at the ills of the world, are glad to retain the comforts of office (Roberts 1982: 152). So what alternatives are there to mimesis and melancholy?

The better form of modernism, I would suggest, is *constructivist*, where this is understood to include philosophical constructivism as well as the post-revolutionary Russian movement. Constructivism is the view that, yes, melancholy is right to reject mimesis; the notion that there is a world, and there is 'knowledge' which somehow appropriates it into a distinct and self-justifying system, is an incoherent model. However, melancholy resorts too abruptly to scepticism, because after concluding that the mimetic account of knowledge does not work it fails to take the next step of considering whether a better account might not be found.

Constructivism takes that next step. In its view, knowledge is not a state, it is an activity (for more details of this argument, see Roberts 1992: chs 1 and 5). That means, in sum, that knowledge is never recoverable as a state of affairs, or even as a system. If Gödel demonstrated that

[143]

arithmetic is forever incomplete, then that, for the constructivist, need be no problem: for constructivism, systems are only *derived from an activity*, rather than, as in typical platonist or formalist schemes, knowing being the *implementation of a system*. 'Completeness', however important for systems, has no application in the context of activities. For a melancholic such puzzles merely serve to emphasize the irresistible force of scepticism; for constructivists, however, they usefully confirm their root intuition that *knowledge is practice*.

In constructivism, semantic groundrock lies not in an 'outside world', but in the constructive activity of reasoning itself. This, moreover, articulates itself in what might in the widest sense be called political intersubjectivity. In that respect, the 'world' of constructivism is essentially changeable; and history ceases to be a derogation from the timeless realm of ideas, and becomes the medium of science and knowledge of any kind. Moreover, to the extent that history has a 'logic' (one might say: it lies in *reconstructibility* – what has once been 'constructed', can be constructed again), so does 'reality' in general. Melancholy as the *deus absconditus*, in this approach, is replaced by constructive critique of practice: we *can* understand where we are, and what we have to do. In the twentieth century, this project is most readily associated with certain successors of Husserl, notably P. Lorenzen or, in a very different way, J. Habermas (Roberts 1992). Further back, Hegel's project in the *Phenomenology of Spirit* can be interpreted as an attempt at the same thing (Roberts 1988). Much of Benjamin's work revolves around this same release from the dream-filled sleep of the melancholic into an 'awakening under the clear sky of history' (Roberts 1982).

Now, if we look carefully, we can see exactly this same anti-melancholic position in architecture. In the first place, there is a strongly constructivist thread in *Towards a New Architecture*. Le Corbusier's apparent platonism in that work is, in fact, less important than the non-mimetic arguments that constantly break through. His platonism exhibits itself in the recourse to 'laws of nature' (73), 'principles which govern our universe' (31), and so on. But the constructive impetus – that the universe is constructed by us, rather than being platonistically imposed – is equally powerful. It centres around the notion of human 'units of measure', the 'first condition of all' (70). This is what Le Corbusier later appropriated to his doctrine of the *modulor*, which affirms that the human stature provides the basis for architectural proportion. The idea (which strongly resembles contemporary notions in the work of Husserl) is that the world emerges from the

(human) construction of repeatable and comparable measures of quantities, in other words.

Far from being pre-given, moreover, these are created in technology.
Geometry, for example (as Lorenzen argues) emerges from a technology
capable of producing matching plane surfaces; probability from the
construction of chance machines ('dice'). Le Corbusier's advocacy of
mass production and standardization (in *Towards a New Architecture*) is
not a perverse delight in uniformity; it is a celebration of the idea that
the world is created by, and ultimately at the disposal of, human beings.
'Architecture is the first manifestation of man creating his own universe'
(73). And the real sin of the stylistic eclectics is that they fail to engage in
this process of reconstructive creation. The product of such traditional
academic training is 'a lyrical poet let loose with a halter round his neck,
a man who knows things, but *only things that he has neither discovered for
himself nor even checked*' (74; my emphasis).

The constructivist strand in twentieth-century art is quite explicit.
In music it is associated with techniques of atonal composition. In the
cinema, it can be found in Eisenstein and the use of montage. In the visual
arts, it has its forerunner in Suprematism and its fruition in early Soviet
constructivism. In artistic theory, the notion of construction assumes a
central position in Adorno's *Aesthetic Theory* (see Roberts 1988: 276ff). Soviet
constructivism has in recent years been revived in *de*-constructivism (as
modish critics have, quite unnecessarily, dubbed it; see Johnson and
Wigley 1988).

The basic aesthetic motif in all these is constant. The technology of
constructibility is pushed to its limits, with two aims. First, the naturalism
of its opponents (and particularly often, indeed, of melancholy) is
combated. Construction wishes to exhibit itself as itself, as construction;
tonal centres, foundations, narrative integrity, assimilation to or depiction of 'nature' – these are all rejected. The mimetic impulse, in other
words, is eradicated entirely; what is mimetically reproduced is always
an other, not a self – a construction in the past, not an activity in the
present. (In Adorno's account, this distantiation is ironical and in his sense
'melancholy'; but it can equally well be optimistic, as it would be, say, in
Schiller's aesthetics.) Skill delights in itself, not pathetically, as (self-)
expression, but playfully, as the exuberant realization of objectivity. We
are not beholden, platonistically, to eternal ideas or pre-existent essences; we make our own world!

This motif is readily apparent in Soviet constructivism, for example

PLATE 6 Vladimir Tatlin, *The Monument to the Third International*, sketch of the inclined axis, 1919.

in the work of Melnikov, Lissitsky, or Rodchenko. The paradigm example is perhaps the 'Tatlin tower' (Vladimir Tatlin's 'Monument to the Third International'), which, in direct contravention of Le Corbusier's insistence on the primacy of plan, platonic solids and the like, explodes in unrestrained geometric complexity. In its purest form, artistic constructivism surmounts both mimesis and function, and achieves sublimity by the uncompromising pursuit of concepts to their furthest point. The sublime is what exceeds measure, according to Kant (see Roberts 1988: 55–66). In this respect it is associated with the excess of reason over instrumentality, function, and mimesis. It aspires to the totality that can never be captured in the understanding; it is, like the *ideas*, a thinking to the extreme end (*Critique of Pure Reason* B377–89).

Such elements can make contemporary constructivist buildings difficult to realize (e.g., Zahar Hadid's Hong Kong Peak project), except perhaps as small-scale provocations ever in danger of being consumed by their own irony (see work by Frank Gehry, and the 'addenda' to existing buildings by Coop Himmelblau, for example at Falkestraβe 6 in Vienna).

It may be, indeed, that the most successful realization of a conceptual, non-pathetic sublime is to be found at greater historical distance, in works by Balthasar Neumann (who, understandably, was one of the architects prized by Venturi – see *Complexity and Contradiction*, 28, 78). Neumann's church ceilings spring from a plan that reveals little of the complex three-dimensionality above, or of the sophisticated vaulting techniques that make such interpenetrating volumes possible (see, for example, Vierzehnheiligen or Neresheim). For Neumann, structural complexity affirms a world of Promethean self-confidence. His staircases for Schloβ Augustusburg near Cologne, or the Vienna Hofburg, are a direct counter to the nightmarish infinities of Piranesi. Neumann's spaces also recede without apparent end, but the calm fluidity of the transitions from one to the next dispels the melancholic claustrophobia of Piranesi's prison. It may be, as Colin St John Wilson has suggested, that the closest analogy to Neumann in this century is to be found in Finland, in the work of Alvar Aalto and successors such as Kaiko Leiviska.

5 History

These aesthetic modalities issue, eventually, in differing attitudes to history. For the mimetic view, truth is timeless and history is an illusion:

we merely need to recover what is universal, eternal and 'natural'. Human practice, in that respect, is derivative and never constitutive of anything.

For the melancholic, history is an indication of decay and transience, and underlines the futility of human striving. Significance only arises in the longing for transcendence – i.e., for a mortification of this world in the hope of something better in a 'beyond'.

For the constructivist, history is the arena of truth and humanity; 'here is the rose, here jump', as Hegel puts it in the preface to the *Philosophy of Right*. Whatever transcendence is, it starts here, with the instruments we have at our disposal in this world.

Nonetheless – and this, crucially, is what distinguishes constructivism from blind technological optimism – what we have here is indeed no more than our own construction, and that construction is bounded by the terminality of physical existence. The melancholic *memento mori* is, in this respect, carried over into the world picture of constructivism. The world's baseless fabric fades and dissolves; but it is precisely by incorporating such considerations that the grandeur of co-operative human striving manifests itself. Transcendence lies not in escape, but in the affirmation of hope despite suffering. Beauty reaches full expression only in its passing, as Benjamin argued at the end of *Goethe's 'Elective Affinities'* (Roberts 1982: 132). It is in the fragility of construction that this motif is expressed – not as trauma, but as the dance that will come about, despite everything. Constructivism is neither heroic, as mimesis can be, nor embittered, like the melancholics; it is tragic. But tragedy is where the sublime finally emerges.

References

BENJAMIN, Walter ([1936] 1973) 'The work of art in the age of mechanical reproduction', 219–54 in *Illuminations*, edited with an introduction by Hannah Arendt, translated by Harry Zohn, Glasgow: Fontana/Collins.

DELEUZE, Gilles (1969) *Logique du sens*, Paris: Les Éditions de Minuit.

—— (1988) *Le Pli. Leibniz et le baroque*, Paris: Les Éditions de Minuit.

JOHNSON, P. and WIGLEY, M. (eds) (1988) *Deconstructivist Architecture*, New York: Museum of Modern Art.

KRUFT, Hanno-Walter (1991) *Geschichte der Architektur-Theorie*, Munich: C. H. Beck.

LE CORBUSIER ([1923] 1987) *Towards a New Architecture (Vers une architecture)* translated by F. Etchells, London: The Architectural Press.

RILKE, Rainer Maria ([1903] 1946) *Rodin*, translated by Jessie Lemont and Hans Trausil with an Introduction by Padraic Colum, London: The Grey Walls Press.

ROBERTS, Julian (1982) *Walter Benjamin*, Basingstoke: Macmillan.

—— (1988) *German Philosophy. An Introduction*, Cambridge: Polity.

—— (1992) *The Logic of Reflection*, New Haven and London: Yale University Press.

SCHNEIDER, Norbert (1989) *Stilleben. Realität und Symbolik der Dinge*, Köln: Benedikt Taschen.

VENTURI, Robert (1977) *Complexity and Contradiction in Architecture*, New York: Museum of Modern Art.

WOODS, Lebbeus (1987) *Centricity. The Unified Urban Field*, Berlin: Aedes.

4

'The World Is Indeed a Fabulous Tale': Yve Lomax – a Practice around Photography

HILARY GRESTY in dialogue with YVE LOMAX

A is for abstraction. And why you may well ask, should abstraction be placed in that privileged position which the Greek alphabet reserves for the letter A? Why should abstraction star as the first? A voice pipes up from the back of the room: 'But it's mental [sic] to put abstraction first. Abstraction doesn't concern real things. *Real life, that's what comes first. With abstraction there is a withdrawal from worldly things. To say that A is for abstraction is really to upset the apple cart.'*

Yes, I had thought it elementary, that A is for apple. I had learnt that A, in designating apple, referred to the primary existence of the real thing in the world. The real thing, or referent as some might say. To say that the real thing comes before the sign, the abstraction which is A for apple, had seemed perfectly true to me. And now it seems that I have to eat my words and say this is not so. Has someone, I ask, been telling tales?

F is for fiction (and also fable). As a child I was rebuked for telling tales. No matter who had done what, where and when, parents would sternly warn against telling tales. Playmates, moreover, would thrust their faces forward, glare and emit the following ditty: 'Tell tale tit, your mother can't knit and your father can't walk with a walking stick.'

Once upon a time, Plato, the most Grand Father of Western Philosophy, also warned against telling tales. For Plato, true philosophy did not tell tales, but poetry on the other hand, could be accused of spinning stories foreign to truth. Plato's line, so I've heard tell, is that true philosophy rises above the charms and double dealings of rhetoric; it neither tells tales nor practises the art of persuasion. The task of philosophy is to safeguard the truth from tall stories and the fabrications of fiction, which are the source of error, lies and illusion. The gates of Plato's ideal city are shut to those who spin yarns and tell tales: the poet is banished and fiction is relegated to the other side, opposite the truth.

Truth/fiction: a line is drawn and fiction is excluded from entering truth's domain.

Truth/fiction. 'Oh no' moans the child, 'do I have to hear about binary oppositions again?'

[150]

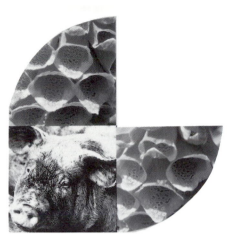

PLATE 7 Yve Lomax, 'Listen, listen' (photocollage), 1993–4.

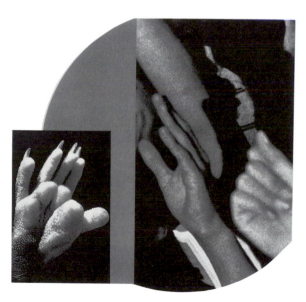

PLATE 8 Yve Lomax, 'Day-break' (photocollage), 1993–4.

The animals went into the ark two-by-two and I may well say that B is for the binary tale where difference is told in terms of two. Yet within this tale of two only one is ever primary. The binary tale proceeds two-by-two, yet for all the twos one is (Hurrah! Hurrah!) whilst the other is not. Truth is not fiction, the same is not difference and man is not woman. And so the history goes on.[1]

HG: I have chosen *The World is a Fabulous Tale* as the starting point from which to open a conversation about your work because it raises a number of issues pertinent to any discussion of a postmodern practice. It questions assumptions such as binary opposition which, philosophy aside, still inform and limit much daily understanding, in particular where oppression is deployed. The text plays on the differing levels and applications of myth and metaphor which make up discourse, a richness of allusion and history denied by traditional empiricism, and the self-perfecting modernity of the industrial age. Language is seen to be made up of interacting particles rather than as a closed and unified system. It is in this diversity that the text exemplifies an important shift from the pioneering work of many feminist artists in the the 1970s when theory provided a rigorous template for development of a visual practice which would challenge totalizing modes of thought and place art within the complex web of social and cultural relations. Rather, theory is now seen, to quote Russell Ferguson, as 'a narrative like any other – as a kind of story, or myth from which to draw'.[2]

Any challenge to the predominant Western cultural heritage of rationalist thought is an immense task and one closely allied to a discussion of the nature of photography in its ascribed role as the purveyor of empirical evidence upon which, amongst other things, scientific classification has been based. It is in this role that photography can be seen as the harbinger of the modern age's mastery through representation. In past conversations we have talked about the camera as 'one of the great revealing devices', so loved by the nineteenth century, and how this is closely bound to Western culture's privileging of vision over the other senses, compared with, for example, the Judaic tradition, a listening culture, where significantly the curtain in the tabernacle is pulled back to *reveal* nothing. A starting point might be to look at how electronic media and the computer override any remaining vestige of credibility that the photograph as evidence of this type might still have had – the irony being that such credibility was ill-founded in the first place.

YL: There is no denying that with the advent of the computer, image manipulation *par excellence* has been born. Here is a technology where images can be combined, recombined and altered endlessly and seamlessly – a montage machine of infinite possibilities. For fields as diverse as meteorology, medicine and the advertising industry a host of possibilities has been opened up. In terms of such endless possibilities we are hearing today endless tales, a whole cacophony of stories about the effects that these may have. One such story is that the computer-generated image threatens the photograph as evidence. The story goes that computers can simulate the 'real' of a piece of photographic evidence whilst simultaneously dissimulating that this 'real', this evidence, is only a simulation. In short, the photograph's objectivity is threatened. However, the notion of an objectivity, the very idea that an observer can observe without affecting, or being affected by, the observed has been repeatedly thrown up in the air not only by quantum physics but also by photographic theory (and practice). We may think that computers threaten photographic objectivity but isn't this objectivity a myth? Yet as Michel Serres reminds us: 'There is no myth more innocent than that of a knowledge innocent of myth.'

I is for image (in all senses of the word). As a child I was greatly excited at the prospect of my birthday. The night before was invariably sleepless; I would lie awake imagining what the birthday would bring. What was it I was looking forward to the most? Was it the present I so desperately wanted but wasn't sure that I would receive? Was it the favourite food that I could eat and eat and eat? Was it the cake that was to be baked and decorated with candles and my name? . . . Or was it the birthday cards that I would receive through the post? (Oh, the thrill of those envelopes which bore the mark of having made a journey.)

On the 18th December it is my birthday, the anniversary of the day on which I was born. Each year on the same date the anniversary returns. 'Many Happy Returns.' As the cards are posted and kisses given again, is it assumed that the recipient is one that has also returned the same? Upon the birthday there is, so I am told, a returning to the 'day of one's birth'. Once upon a time, one day there was a birth. And is this day returned to as the birth of a one? You may well say that such a one provides the birthday with an origin and point of return. In which case I ask the following question: is the image you have of the birthday one behind which there remains a primary and essential one? If you take such a one to be behind the birthday images or signs, all the cakes and candles, kisses and cards. If you assume that it is towards this one that you turn back, then it seems to me that images are taken as coming after, as posterior.

[153]

HG: *The World is a Fabulous Tale*, like much of your writing, uses fragments, (or as you would say, in order to avoid connotation of a whole, 'assemblages') of autobiography and forms borrowed from ditties and popular story telling. One of the images which sticks in my mind from an earlier piece is that borrowed from the nursery rhyme 'The Pied Piper' in your discussion of 'the crisis of representation'.[3] This raises a number of interrelated issues. 'The Pied Piper' is laden with suggestion, not least that of blind belief in an absent, an unknown, which just because it is unknown demands a charismatically inspired and deluded following; on the other hand in using the reference you are actually asserting a very recognisable, or 'real' image. This use of heavily endowed and accessible images is a characteristic shift away from what you have termed the 'quasi-scientific, bleached out' use of language in an attempt to 're-inscribe authority' beyond the vagaries of individual self-expression, which was practised not only by yourself, but many artists during the 1970s.[4] This shift is further reflected in the use of found images, codes and forms borrowed from documentary, cinematic and popular photography in your visual work. I am always surprised afresh by the way that I find the images you make familiar, even when it is one that you have constructed. Is this a recognition that science, theory and their underpinning philosophies are, together with folklore and other popular forms, just examples of many stories that can be told and that no one story is necessarily exclusive to the representation of a single reality? It seems that the imaginary spaces beyond the image are on a parity with those within it. This begs many questions regarding the so-called crisis of representation, which has been used as a basis for much postmodernist image making. Your position is one within which the 'crisis' necessarily 'warps'.

YL: In terms of the logic of representation, a representation, whatever this may be, must refer to something beyond itself. Classically, representation has been conceived of as 'surface appearances' beyond or behind which there is a depth. This depth is the realm of the essential, the realm of the 'founding presence' upon which representation is based. Now the crisis of representation revolves around the idea that we have irrevocably lost this presence. (As we have lost it we assume that it must have been there in the first place.) All that we are left with is surface, images that only refer to other images, signs that only refer to other signs. However, my question has been, if representation ceases to refer to anything beyond representation then how can the terms of representation still

[154]

apply? Doesn't the logic of representation warp? For me the twist is that if there is no 'depth' then how can we speak of the 'surface'? Doesn't the very notion of the surface become meaningless? This provided for me the twist in the debate about the postmodern image as mere surface. If the very idea of image-as-surface-appearances becomes meaningless then surely it is a matter of asking: what and how does an image *affect*? It is no longer a matter of seeing images as substitutes which replace the real world but rather understanding the effectivity of images *in* the world.

One of the stories we hear, one of the theories perhaps we fear, is that the real world is a fiction.

    L is for the line in the middle and also for long, long ago. 'Fadófadó or a long time ago, if I were then I wouldn't be here now; if I were there now and at that time I would have a new story or an old story, or I might have no story at all'. And so repeats the Irish story teller before the telling of the tale.

    Nothing solid or substantial stands behind the surface of the image ... the real world is a fiction. And what may you make of these lines? What might be your interpretation, your story? Perhaps you have a new story or an old story ...

HG: One of the implications of a fixed reality behind the image has been a relegation of metaphor to secondary status as an unscientific or unverifiable discourse.

YL: There is a tradition, which for convenience's sake I will call the *critique*, and which maintains that in order to theorize or philosophize properly one must banish metaphor. In the *critique* tradition philosophy is not a story, not a pictorial description, not a work of literature. Making a firm distinction between the literal and the figurative, the *critique* declares its status by breaking with the 'domain of images'. Univocality is what the *critique* loves – one word, one meaning. Yet this univocality, this image-free language, this literalness is somewhat spurious. As Michèle le Doeuff reminds us so wonderfully in *The Philosophical Imaginary*, philosophy is stuffed full of images: Plato poured out fables. Kant was fascinated by the image of an island.[5] In the *critique* tradition it is believed that if one does bring an image or a metaphor into play this is only to decorate the discourse. A metaphor can only speak indirectly, it can only imply. To be properly theoretical one has to *explicate*, one has to *open out* the folds. What the *critique* tradition so conveniently forgets is that metaphor, pictorial description, and style can *implicate* the profoundest of philosophical or scientific ideas: a poem by Lucretius can be a valid

[155]

PLATE 9 Yve Lomax, 'The observer affects the observed' (photocollage), 1993–4.

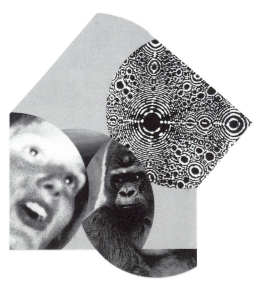

PLATE 10 Yve Lomax, 'More than meets the eye', (photocollage) 1993–4.

treatise in physics, a novel by Virginia Woolf can tell us about wave mechanics. So-called 'scientific' semiology (as widely practised in the 1970s) partook of the tradition of the *critique* – one could expose or explain the codes through which language worked by employing a (meta)language which was miraculously free from those very codes – a language which could be bleached of all its 'ideological' content. Yet as Barthes realized, one can only play one code against another and Derrida said very much the same thing when he said that in any attempt to define or explain metaphor there will always be one metaphor in excess.

language itself is metaphorical

The implication of metaphor brings a much richer knowledge of the world. To speak by way of implication is not about standing back and attaining the correct distance in order to see things clearly; implication is about being plunged into things, finding oneself in the middle of things.

HG: There is an apposite quote from the novel *Waterland*, by Graham Swift, in which he is questioning the methodology of conventional history: 'But man [sic] – let me offer you a definition – is the story telling animal.'[6] Such story telling, folk lore and 'old wives tales', are inherently metaphorical.

YL: Yes, likewise the *critique* tradition assumed that such so-called popular culture is a denigration of true knowledge. In the *Wind Spirit* Michel Tournier says that a myth is a story that everybody already knows.[7] In my work, both written and visual, I bring into play a variety of images which have already been heard or seen. By bringing the mythic and metaphorical into play I hope to implicate the reader or viewer in the fragrance of the world. I hope to invite the reader or viewer to participate in a philosophical or theoretical activity, which maintains that we can generate philosophy quite properly with fairy tales and nursery rhymes and pictures of pussy cats from greetings cards.

HG: One alternative to acknowledging and celebrating this richness of metaphor is to use appropriation either as a bland statement of nihilism (that is, to beg the irony of the photographic medium in its indexical relationship to the objects it represents), or to plunder style without questioning the political status of the appropriated material (that is: to 'image-scavenge' with complicity). Your visual work, like your writing, uses found images and conventions from different types of image making – these are materials of appropriation, but your use is firmly embedded in the contemporary world and the adoption of an ethical stance within that world. I recall you saying that you want people to address, for example, an image of a monkey 'in all its fullness', to consider human-kind's relationship to animals, to make a choice and to take up a position. Would you like to elaborate on what you have called the 'specificity' and the 'power to affect' that all images have?[8]

YL: It was Deleuze who first introduced me to Spinoza's questions, 'what is a body capable of?'; 'What affects is it capable of?'[9] A body can be anything: an idea, an animal, a visual image, a body of sound, a photographic body, a mountain, a child or a wind. A body is never separable from its relation with the world. It is these interrelations which make the child, the wind or the photographic image; they are not defined or distinguished by internal essences which condition or structure the mode of their being. A body is constituted by and composed of relations, of *affects*. The power to affect concerns the relations into which a body is capable of entering and which come to define it. What does this image affect? What affects this image? Bodies affect each other. As Deleuze reminds us, affectivity is a two-way process, indeed a process which goes in more ways than one. It is a complex of interactions. Both specificity and heterogeneity are retained and as we enter into this specificity we find not a discrete element or thing in itself, but rather a set of relations. Specificity is continually opening onto multiplicity and vice versa.

L is for the line in the middle ... It had appeared that the line in the middle came in between, enabling one to distinguish itself and an opposition to be settled. The line in the middle appeared to form a sort of medium, the means whereby to establish the difference between the one and the other. Yet with this medium we find something else also happens: the one comes to be mediated by the other; both become mixed up in the middle. In coming between, the line in the middle ineluctably involves the one with the other. It dances across the two terms and unsettles them both. Just as difference has become settled we find that it becomes unsettled ...

'Ding dong merrily on high' the child impishly sings, 'it remains undecided as to whether I shall be one or the other. Ding or dong, dong or ding? Perhaps I shall be both but then maybe I shall be neither.'

In mid flow the binary tale turns into a tale of oscillation ...

HG: There are two things that seem particularly relevant in your assumption of photography as part of an ecology (rather than as a mere tool or consequence of representation). Firstly issues around difference – whether of, for example, gender, race or culture. Secondly the formal conventions and devices that you employ visually – montage and collage, irregular and abutting frames which confuse inside and so confound the very means of representation itself, abstract and given signs which break up sequences, colour and pattern which reject the possibility of illusionistic depth, and more recently the circular frame, with its monadic properties. Together these all lead to, or implicate, a multiplicity of readings and a deliberate blurring of the distinction between fact and fiction. The writing echoes this image-making process – juxtaposition, repetition, displaced narrative and the use of a multiplicity of conventions. The position you adopt is very much an *ethical* one – something influenced by your work in the *Format* picture library, and the way that images are actually employed on a day-to-day and often commercial basis.

YL: Yes. One thing always involves others: one thing and another and another. In fact we don't have definite things so much but more states of affairs, sets of circumstances. A set of circumstances may be a photographic montage which combines a picture of a rain forest with a picture of a crowd of people which is hung upon a gallery wall and viewed by a child at 2 o'clock in the afternoon. In terms of these circumstances we have a photographic image and a rain forest and a child and 2 o'clock in the afternoon. All these elements compound together and a multiplicity is formed which adds up to something quite specific. An individuality is formed, yet as Deleuze would say this individuation is quite different from that which pertains to a unified subject. In *Mille Plateaux*, Deleuze and Guattari reserve the name 'haeccity' for this idea: 'The child ceases to be subject, to become an event, in an assemblage that is inseparable from an hour, a season, an atmosphere, an air, a life.'[10] With such assemblages or sets of circumstance we find all sorts of unnatural participation, which is one way of saying that with a set of circumstances nature always implicates culture and vice versa: as such no firm distinction can be made between the natural and the artificial.

M is for middle and many things. M is for many stories and meanings that may be told. That we are neither one thing nor the other, that we are neither inside nor outside but somewhere between, may soon be a tale of numbing neutralisation ... There is yet another story which I have heard told, a tale which is somewhat more lengthy. In unsettling the one and the other, such that we become unsure which is either and which is or, the line in the middle begins to gather momentum. The story here is that the line in the middle picks up speed and whilst doing so turns into a stream. In this tale a stream flows and gnaws away at its two banks; it picks up speed in the middle and carries away the one and the other ... suddenly we find ourselves moving in the very middle – midstream – of things, no longer attempting to grasp the banks of binary difference.

YL: Given that with any one thing others are always involved, will this particular action augment or diminish another's capacity to interact? For Spinoza this is an ethical question. Once we consider the affects we have on others, be they animals, images or human beings, then doesn't the question of ethics and prudence come into play? For Spinoza the ethics in question concerns a body's ability to affect and act, and this power to affect refers to the *potential* a body has for combining with others. Sometimes affects may weaken another such that its potential for further interaction is diminished ... Here we feel wretched. We feel less. A broken spirit. These are sad times. For Spinoza, however, there are more joyful times when one affects another such that the potential to interact is augmented.

The World is a Fabulous Tale ends by posing this question of ethics and multiplicity; in turn this question becomes the starting point for subsequent writings. Where this question will lead me I never know in advance. I am continually surprised ... How can we think difference differently? In *The World is a Fabulous Tale* I wanted to make the logic of binary oppositions surprise itself. In the very middle of its logic I wanted binary opposition to find itself breaching itself and there become exposed to multiplicity. If deconstruction has taught me anything it is that one can't simply or antagonistically oppose the logic of binary opposition. To oppose it will not surprise this logic one bit. The surprise happens when binary logic is made to *fold in* upon itself, such that *something else becomes involved.*[11] In short, one has to practise what Michel Serres refers to as the 'baker's logic'.[12] Now this idea of the baker's logic holds a particular charm for me as my father was a baker. As a small child I would watch him kneading dough, a process of continually folding in, of implication. In terms of perfecting the baker's logic we have to knead binary opposition: to make the two terms fold in such that it is shown that both sides implicate each other and that as such they become, as Derrida would say, 'both and neither/nor'. Neither positive nor negative, neither one thing nor the other. What we have here is a state of affairs where *something else is involved*, where something else is implied, where we continually find ourselves *between things*. And being between things do we not, once again, find ourselves in the very middle of multiplicity?

[160]

HG: In *The World is a Fabulous Tale* you are careful to avoid the notion of 'multiplicity' collapsing into 'anything goes' by suggesting a fluid ethic, an ecology, but doesn't this still beg the questions as to whose ethics, whose ecology?

YL: Yes it is precisely this question which Michel Serres bids us to plunge into as he bids us to plunge into the question of chaos. For Serres multiplicity opens onto the question of chaos: how can we involve ourselves with chaos without subjecting this to the tyranny of the 'one'? As Serres reminds us, the 'one' tyrannizes when it unifies at the cost of crushing, capturing and diminishing the potential of multiplicity. The 'one' suppresses chaos by explaining it as impure, irrational mixtures of dis-order; by fixing it into a binary system chaos becomes the negation of order.

Understanding that something else is always involved means that an ethics of multiplicity continually involves itself with surprises and unpredictability; it invites us to participate in a reality – a life – which is multiple and circumstantial without the feeling that order has been lost or negated. As such this ethics remains open and continually moving. Yes, a fluid ethics. Such fluidity brings with it a life of experimentation but also lasting prudence. How do you know beforehand what affects or implications you are capable of? This is another way of saying the affects or implications that one thing has on another can only be judged in terms of the circumstances of each situation, or as Serres would say 'la logique des circonstances'. There aren't definite things which gain territories, position or presences by employing the binary logic of inside and outside, of inclusion and exclusion. Here the inside and outside are continually turning inside out. One has to consider the map and the circum. One has to circumnavigate with a map (an ethics) which changes depending where and when you enter or begin. Stances aren't denied. One can always stop and take up a position. One can always think with your feet firmly on the ground. Yes, one can always think in terms of all that which this image implies, that is, assume a singular and unitary position. However what is special here is that one's *stance* is one part of the *circumstances*, only one locality in the multifaceted richness of the world(s) we live in and of which images, metaphors and ourselves are part.

So the child remarks with zest, 'maybe I shan't be speaking of a loss of an independent and real world or telling tales of the death of the referent. Perhaps I shall say that the existence of an independent real world is one story amongst others. As for apples and images — well I might just tell the tale that with both "things" and "signs" (both nature and culture) we always start in the middle and in so doing the question of the referent, its absence or presence, becomes more a question of connections, of effects and affects. As the philosopher may indeed say, more a question of ethics than of epistemology or ontology.'

Notes

1 All quotes within the body of the text from Yve Lomax, 'The World is a Fabulous Tale', in *Other Than Itself: Writing Photography,* John X. Berger and Olivier Richon (eds), Manchester: Cornerhouse Publications, 1989.

2 Russell Ferguson, 'A Box of Tools: Theory and Practice', in *Discourses: Conversations in Postmodernism, Art and Culture,* New York: New Museum of Contemporary Art; Cambridge (Mass.), MIT Press, 1990, pp. 5–7. In the same volume Lynne Thornton writes, 'In some cases the deployment of Theory, as a prescriptive or legitimizing device, becomes just another mode of commodification', from 'If upon leaving what we have to say we speak: a conversation piece', p. 50.

3 'The pied piper of the signifier played an enchanting tune. The children who followed its "line", were never to return and affirm the authority of the parental signified. The signified, the representative, has ceased to spring forth from a known descent; it has no lineage, no family tree. We fear that the signifier is a "ringer" of an empty centre. We fear that we no longer know who "we" are ....' from *Future Politics/The Line in the Middle,* Yve Lomax, self-published, 1986.

4 In conversation with the artist, January 1992.

5 Michèle Le Doeuff, *The Philosophical Imaginary,* trans. Colin Gordon, London: The Athlone Press, 1989.

6 Graham Swift, *Waterland,* London: Heinemann, 1983.

7 Michel Tournier, *The Wind Spirit,* London: Collins, 1989, p. 157.

8 In conversation with the artist, January 1992.

9 Gilles Deleuze and Claire Parnet, *Dialogues,* New York: Columbia University Press, 1987, p. 60.

10 Gilles Deleuze and Félix Guattari, *A Thousand Plateaus: Capitalism and Schizophrenia,* London: Athlone Press, 1987, pp. 261–2.

11 Barbara Johnson, *A World of Difference,* Baltimore: Johns Hopkins University Press, 1987.

12 Michel Serres, *Rome, Le Livre des Fondations,* Paris: Grasset, 1983.

5
Televising Hell: Tom Phillips and Peter Greenaway's TV Dante

NIGEL WHEALE

Tom Phillips' painting and printmaking, together with the *TV Dante* which he made in collaboration with the film-maker Peter Greenaway, are discussed here from three perspectives, each of which have been important in debates over postmodern culture. These are:

Inter-relations of visual imagery and verbal text in works that actively combine the two kinds of meaning.

Exploitation of the technology and conventions of television and video to construct complex, non-naturalistic narratives.

Contrasts between pre-modern styles of reading based in allegory, compared with nineteenth- and twentieth-century theories of the symbol and image.

Painting language

Tom Phillips was born in London in 1937, and growing up near the huge railway junction at Clapham during the war was a formative experience for him. In the mid-1950s he went on to read English Literature – 'mainly Anglo-Saxon' – at Oxford. Subsequently, while teaching in a Brixton secondary school Phillips continued his childhood passion for drawing by attending life classes in the evenings at Camberwell School of Art. His teacher there was the painter Frank Auerbach, and at this point Phillips realized that he had to give his full attention to painting: 'Camberwell was the last surviving "fundamentalist" art school, where one's studies consisted almost completely in drawing from the life, which I did every day and all day for three years with rare excursions into other fields' (Phillips 1975: 16).

This intensely figurative training was subsequently overlaid by more experimental interests. Phillips elaborated many of his concerns and projects during the 1960s and has maintained them with great consistency over several decades. He experimented with painting and defacing verbal text, repetition-and-cancellation exercises, collage, the use of musical motifs (he has also written an opera), and making paintings from the colours left on the palette at the end of the week. He welcomed the play of chance and indeterminacy into the processes of composition, 'aleatoric' techniques that were exploited at the time by a number of artists, for example John Cage, for whom Phillips wrote a moving obituary (Phillips 1992B). All of this was done with the intention of sustaining 'the greatest possible diversity within a single thing' (Phillips 1975: 62). He included all kinds of information within his pictures, from art-historical reference to popular-cultural forms such as the postcard. Phillips refers several times to the influence of ideas from structuralism which were in the air during the 1960s. The kinds of reading which Roland Barthes made of French culture in the mid-1950s (published as *Mythologies* in England in 1972) seem to inform aspects of Phillips' working practice in, for example, the desire to derive general social meaning from fragmentary texts. In a brief essay on the postcard as a genre Phillips formulated sixteen axioms, the seventh of which is:

> The postcard creates the future of the site shown in it. After two or three postcards had appeared, Carnaby Street started to become *a postcard reproduction of itself.*
>
> (Phillips 1975: 232)

the barn!

This sense of the insidious power of mass-produced imagery to de-realize its subject is very well treated in Don DeLillo's novel *White Noise* (1985), a cautionary satire on postmodern times.

A vigorous eclecticism was current among a number of London-based artists at the time, but each practitioner was inevitably exploiting the technique for different purposes. Phillips shared the aims of artists such as R. B. Kitaj, Richard Hamilton and Joe Tilson which included incorporating scholarly-intellectual materials within the processes of their work. This immediately established a tension between purely graphic, image-based perceptions, and textually-derived meanings which are produced by verbal (as opposed to visual) language. Kitaj for example made use of a very diverse range of visual reference in his oil paintings and screen prints, but he drew on much more explicitly political materials than Phillips. Kitaj could include reference to fascist imagery from the Spanish Civil War in a painting such as 'Primo de Ribera' (1969), or address the threatening domination of American power in his prints like 'Truman in the Whitehouse' (1965) (Aulich 1987).

[164]

Phillips tended to work within the formal themes of art-historical traditions, or else, in a strict sense, on more banal subjects such as benches in public parks – where banal means 'open to the use of all the community' (*OED*). Phillips' treatment of national totems such as flags character-istically focused on the de-formation of the colours and design, rather than on explicitly ideological dimensions. When he did paint overtly 'political' subjects, as in 'Berlin Wall with German Grass and Skies' (1973) the affront which the wall represented was ironized and played against an 'a-political' collage comprising blue/green elements of grass and sky.

Playfulness, being receptive to serendipity – the chance collocation of meanings in objects – and good jokes animate much of Phillips' creativity, including, for example, a group portrait of the Monty Python team. One of his most sustained projects has been his systematic defacing of a dull late-nineteenth-century novel, W. H. Mallock's *A Human Document*, an activity he began in 1966. In the best traditions of surrealist serendipity Phillips wanted a suitable text to work over in the style of Tristan Tzara, the founder of Dadaism, who used a cut-up technique in order to exploit the combinations produced by hazard, where this included the operations of chance as well as danger:

> ... the first (coherent) book that I could find for threepence (i.e. 1 ¼p) would serve.
>
> Austin's the furniture repository stands on Peckham Rye, where Blake saw his first angels and along which Van Gogh had probably walked on his way to Lewisham. At this propitious place, on a routine Saturday morning shopping expedition, I found, for exactly threepence, a copy of *A Human Document* by W. H. Mallock, published in 1892 as a popular reprint of a successful three-decker.
>
> (Phillips 1980: Notes [1])

Phillips kept his defacement of Mallock's novel as a spare-time game, a recreational art that was not intended to detract from the day's serious work. Each page was painted or drawn over, leaving selected words and phrases from the Mallock Ur-text untouched, in this way generating a loosely related series of new narratives out of the gaseous original. When the spacing between type on the page of any text becomes too wide and irregular it can form intrusive patterns in the reader's scanning of the words, creating what printers call 'rivers' of white which appear to fracture the type area. Phillips followed these interstitial tracks, linking selections of words from Mallock's text, or blocking particular statements in isolation. This technique combined impersonal, formalist method with individual creative expression:

> In a sense, art is in a neo-classical phase at the moment; formalism, system and procedure abound as well as the cult of the cool and detached. My own work is dominated by various processes.
>
> (Phillips 1975: 211)

This method was formalistic because the working process established a grid on which to operate where meanings were generated within the given parameters of the novel text. In Craig Owens' terms it was the strategy of accumulation (see above p. 120). But it was also individually expressive because the *Humument* followed the Surrealist ambition to elicit meaning from discontinuities and collisions of disparate materials, so that unconscious interpretations and the multiple significations of texts might be revealed. The sense-texture of each page of *A Humument* is a virtuoso demonstration of meanings snatched from a set of possibilities, and individual statement is seen to have been wrested from a matrix of impersonal terms.

This combination of formalism and literacy is found throughout Phillips' painting and printmaking, as in the painting 'Benches' (1971), now in the Tate Gallery. Here the iconography of people sitting or strolling in public parks is framed by chronological colour catalogues of the hues used in the painting itself. In making the triptych, Phillips used no 'photographic or other transfer procedures' (1975: 153). Therefore artisan, draughtsman skills – his three years in the Life Class – mimic the conventions of mass reproduction; people at ease in the park are set about with vivid displays, which are a spectrograph of the colours which compose them, and beneath the visual image runs the forbidding text 'FOR ALL FLESH IS GRASS ... MCMLXXI'. The connection between fine-art and literary values is again made with this biblical legend, which might be found in one of the renaissance emblem books which Tom Phillips studies and collects.

Televising Hell

In 1983 Phillips published a de luxe 'Livre d'Artiste' edition of his own translation of Dante's *Inferno* with the Talfourd Press, a venture he created specifically to manufacture the volume. This monumental book was constructed over seven years, using sources accumulated during the

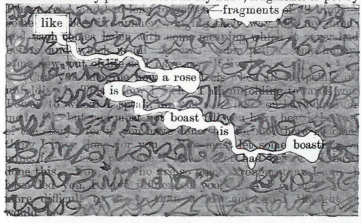

PLATE II Tom Phillips, 'I drew so many words', from *A Humument. A Treated Victorian Novel*, 1980.

previous twenty. In the tradition of fine-art publication it consists of etchings, lithographs and screenprints which illustrate a superbly printed hand-set text, and it utilizes the finest materials and methods of production – 'The paper, made in Somerset at a site where the rents were once collected by the father of Dante's Beatrice, costs £1 per sheet' (Thomas 1983). The book appeared in a subscription edition of 180 copies; 60 were sold in advance for £1000 each, and a proportion of the remainder were priced at £10,000 each. Phillips himself estimated that the edition had cost £150,000 to make, plus £100,000 in lost income, and he considered that he would be lucky to break even. The heroic scale of the 'hazard' of this project is demonstrated in the fourth plate illustrating Canto XXIX, where Phillips incorporates an account statement from the 'Maddnill Bank' indicating a personal debit scenario of £49930.80.

The Talfourd edition was followed by a 'people's edition' in 1985, published by Thames and Hudson at a more popular price, and using laser-scan offset-lithography to reproduce as faithfully as possible the artisan qualities of the original printshop work. And even though the second edition reduces the scale of the initial format, it is still a generous 29 by 21 cms, comprising 138 plates, four to each of the 34 Cantos of the poem, plus a frontispiece of Dante in his study, and an initial half-title emblem. The text of the poem is Phillips' own translation of Dante's terza rima into blank verse, and it has won the approval of academic scholars of Dante, and of Sir John Gielgud, when he recited the text for the *TV Dante*. In addition Phillips added 27 pages of commentary glossing the imagery of his illustrations to the poem, material not present in the Talfourd text.

Dante Alighieri (1265–1321) probably wrote his *Commedia* during the last 14 years of his life, but he set the action of the poem in his thirty-fifth year, which in the medieval Christian view is the mid-point of anyone's existence. Dante is a viator, a traveller on a spiritual journey, who having lost 'the right way' finds himself in a dark wood. He is guided out of this threatening crisis by the spirit of the Roman epic poet Virgil, but the only route to resolve the crisis lies by way of a road through Hell and Purgatory, in order to reach Paradise. This journey is also fiercely contemporary because it includes the shades of numerous politicians, priests and malefactors from Dante's Italy, and the outcome cannot be a foregone conclusion, because it will depend on the worthiness of the traveller as he is tested by the experience which he undergoes. The one hundred cantos and three books of what came to be called *La Divina Commedia* were quickly acknowledged as one of the great poetic epics, a worthy successor to the *Aeneid* of Virgil, who is Dante's mentor only during the first two books. At the end of Canto XXVII of the *Purgatorio*, Virgil entrusts Dante to be conducted to the celestial Paradise by Beatrice, Dante's ideal beloved.

As with other European epics such as the *Odyssey, Iliad, Aeneid* and *Paradise Lost*, the graphic brilliance of the *Commedia* has consistently attracted artist-illustrators. Phillips is well aware of other artists' responses, such as those of Botticelli, Michelangelo, da Vinci, Blake, Doré and Rauschenberg. But in the prospectus to his first edition of the *Inferno* he distinguished between his own project and that of all previous illustrations to the poem. Rather than simply picturing the action of the epic, he intended to provide a visual commentary for Dante's text which would form 'its notes or apparatus [in order to] make a bridge in time and reference'. Within most of the illustrative plates Phillips also encrypted a further commentary. This is a collaged series of statements cut out from the text of W. H. Mallock's *A Human Document*, the novel he previously mined for his *Humument*.

It is the ingenuity and richness of medieval allegory which allows so much creative freedom to Phillips' illustration of the *Inferno*. The wood in which the fictional traveller is lost is an obvious, traditional allegorical emblem for the confusions and entrapments of the world; to be lost in the wood is to have lost the right way of virtue. So far so good. The traveller then begins to climb a hill on which early morning sunlight is playing: allegorically this is more obscure, but might mean that he attempts to leave error in some hope, though with difficulty (Sayers 1949: 75). But no sooner has he set out than he is confronted by three ferocious beasts in succession: a leopard, a lion, and finally a she-wolf. As with so much of medieval and renaissance imagery, these symbols derive from a biblical text. The *Book of Jeremiah* describes the judgement of God on the people of Jerusalem in these terms:

> Wherefore a lion out of the forest shall slay them, and a wolf of the evenings shall spoil them, a leopard shall watch over their cities: every one that goeth out thence shall be torn in pieces: because their transgressions are many.
>
> (Jeremiah 6.6)

Allegorical convention interprets the leopard as the lighter, more inconsequential sins of the world such as lust, because its pelt is spotted – 'che di pel maculato era coverta' (*Inferno* I. 33). The lion represents the more threatening, obdurate sins of pride and ambition, and the she-wolf is the gnawing, penetrating sins of envy and covetousness. The bestial trio are the first of many trinities in the poem, which remind the reader of the place of the Holy Trinity as the means to salvation. Allegorical ingenuity allows the threefold structure of the beasts to be read in a variety of other contexts, which can be moral, theological or political. Therefore they may also be seen as characterizing the sins typical of particular stages of life, those of youth, middle age, and old age, or else they stand for the major categories of sin active at any time of life, such as self-indulgence, violence, and malice (Sapegno 1968: 7–8). The political reading, drawing on the complex historical context of the poem, associates the leopard with Florence, the lion with the Royal House of France, and the she-wolf with the Papal State (Wicksteed 1900: 11).

Tom Phillips' *Inferno* presents the three beasts as the first plate opposite the opening text of Canto I, in the form of three chevrons or V-figures, at the top of which is a trace of commentary from Mallock's *Human Document*, 'the restless advance to the devil'. The leopard is signified by its pelt, a maculated pattern, which seems to be made of microbes. The lion and the wolf are signified by successively closer views of the beasts' two faces. The working processes of the printshop are incorporated into the allegory since the lion is drawn on 'stubborn stone', as a lithograph, and the wolf is 'deeply etched by acid on copper since it is here we find the ingrained sins of envy' (Phillips 1985: [11] and 285).

The allegorical meanings so far have been explicable by reference to biblical precedent, conventional beliefs, theological-moral systematics and historical context. They are allegories which may be 'derived' via reference to external sources. But there is one more beast which is cited at the end of the Canto and which is allegorically enigmatic. After retreating in fear from the animal trinity, the traveller meets the shade of Virgil, 'lo mio maestro, e il mio autore' (*Inferno* I 85). Virgil offers to guide Dante through Hell and Purgatory as the only way to escape from the she-wolf, the covetous malice of later life (or the secular corruption of the Papacy). Only the Veltro, the Hound, will eventually overcome the Lupa:

> He shall not feed on land and property,
> but wisdom rather, love and moral strength.
> Between twin Feltros shall he rise and reign,
> saviour of that downtrodden Italy . . .
>
> (Phillips 1985: 12/14)

The middle ages produced a vast literature of prophecy linked to apocalypse and political renovation, and the question whether the Veltro is a specific individual or an idealized projection is unresolvable. Many historical figures have been cited but the favourite candidate is Can Grande della Scala, whose name actually translates as 'great dog'. Can Grande ruled in the appropriate region of northern Italy, and was also, conveniently, one of Dante's patrons. Opposed to this elite saviour figure there is an attractive, populist reading of the Veltro emblem which seizes on a pun with 'feltro', interpreting this not as a geographical region but as 'felt', the coarse cloth of the people. This is taken to imply that salvation might emerge from among the weak and the impoverished (Sayers 1949: 77).

Phillips illustrates the figure of the Veltro in a very striking way by using the Hound as a graphic demonstration of the workings of allegorical interpretation (see illustration p. 172). In a letter sometimes ascribed to Dante, and addressed to Can Grande della Scala, there is an explanation of the structure of the *Divine Comedy*. The letter explains that

> the meaning of this work is not of one kind only; rather the work may be described as 'polysemous', that is, having several meanings; for the first meaning is that which is conveyed by the letter, and the next is that which is conveyed by what the letter signifies; the former of which is called literal, while the latter is called allegorical, or mystical.
>
> (Anderson 1982: 333–4)

And following a common medieval definition of allegorical method, the Can Grande letter distinguishes no less than four separate kinds of allegory within the poem. Plate 1/4 of Phillips' *Inferno* transcribes the passage quoted above (in the original Latin) as a frame to the illustration, and then images the ascending layers of meaning: first, the Literal, being the Hound as referent, a dog racing across grass – in fact, grasstrack, since the image came from *Greyhound Times*; second, Direct Allegory, with the Veltro as political saviour, collaging images of selected candidates – Can Grande, Gramsci, Mussolini, Dante – against the Italian tricolour; third, Moral Allegory, as a sword representing spiritual and temporal powers; fourth, highest and deepest meaning, the Anagogical Allegory, or meaning addressed to the fate of the individual soul, where it is signified as DVX – leader, conductor, guide – or 'the moral force implicit in leadership itself' (Phillips 1985: 285). The cross-referencing between illustrations is also extensive, so the DVX image recalls a significant detail

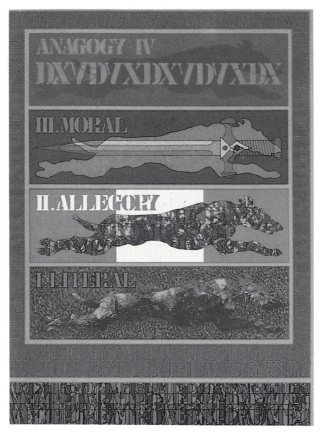

PLATE 12 Tom Phillips, 'The Greyhound', from *Dante's Inferno*, 1985.

of the frontispiece to the whole volume, where Dante in his study pores over a book opened at the same word.

Phillips' *Dante's Inferno* is therefore an extraordinarily involved and involving dialogue between the poem and the illustrations which are in fact graphic interventions and commentaries, rather than mute picturings of the text. The volume is an extremely elaborate sequence of laminations created by the superimposition of visual response to verbal text. It is possible to distinguish at least seven archaeological layers – a usefully mystical total – within Phillips' Dante project:

1 *Inferno*: Dante's text, the first of the three sections of the *Commedia* and itself a monstrous collage;

[172]

2 The tradition of illustration and gloss from 1200 to the present;

3 Phillips' own translation;

4 The facing visual commentary;

5 The facing encrypted Mallock commentary;

6 The iconographical notes and commentary.

The final, seventh circle of response is the transposition of the *Inferno* to the medium of television. Tom Phillips and Peter Greenaway were brought together by Michael Kustow in his role as Arts Commissioning Editor for Independent Television's Channel 4. Kustow was responding to the visual complexity of Phillips' illustrations to the *Inferno*, and he also admired the individuality of Peter Greenaway's film-making. He saw analogies in their methods of working, and part of his brief as Commissioning Editor was to encourage artistic experiment with television as a broad-cast medium. The affinities which he perceived between Phillips and Greenaway's work included 'their quest to make rich artefacts of multi-levelled meaning, their serious use of games, systems and catalogues, and their fascination with old modes of thought yoked to the most modern forms of expression' (Phillips 1990B: [1]). Kustow describes the resulting eight episodes of *A TV Dante* as 'a rich example of television art rooted in a classic text of the human condition' which are 'virtually designed for' repeated viewing. Phillips himself speculates on the day that 'art history may be tempted to categorise this television version as the authentic voice of Post-Modernism' (Phillips 1990B: 8):

> It was only recently that I discovered the most exciting of all forms of referential collage, where reference itself becomes liquefied in a stream of pictorial metamorphoses ... In the editing process [of *A TV Dante*] ... a seamless parade of juxtapositions in motion can be achieved.
>
> (Phillips 1992A: 192)

The television text of *A TV Dante* screens the complexity of the first eight Cantos of the *Inferno* together with its accumulated traditions of commentary through use of multiple layerings and window-insets of information. The screen surface is no longer efficiently transitive, neutrally delivering a view on to a single naturalistic space, but has become rather more like a computer terminal, zoned for information, with each Canto programmed into stylized informatic areas. The borders surrounding inset information windows are colour-coded specifically for each Canto. Different overlays

PLATE 13 'A multitude following a blank flag', from *A TV Dante*, 1990.

are patched around the windows, with upper and lower zones to indicate divisions between the world and hell. Within the information window itself the background can also be utilized for another array of materials. All of these combinations provide a richly encoded screen, as in Canto VII where at one point there are no less than 16 kinds of image displayed simultaneously (Phillips 1990A: 12). The sound-track is also multi-layered, and raises in a different form the issue of verbal-visual relations which is so persistent in Phillips' painting. The sound-track uses very little music, but 'treats' and distorts – or 'disidentifies', to use Phillips' term – words taken from the commentary and poem, occasionally incorporating Italian words which emphasize the translated quality of the TV version.

The protagonists of the poem provide human continuity throughout the image manipulations; Dante is played by Bob Peck, Virgil by Sir John Gielgud, and Beatrice by Joanne Whalley-Kilmer. They are presented in close-up, reciting the poem to camera, so that action as such is relegated to the imagery displayed on the various elements of the screen.

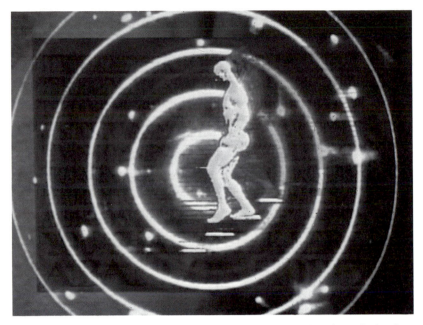

PLATE 14 'A mighty figure is approaching from above, passing through the Gate of Hell', from *A TV Dante*, 1990.

The formality of the construction of the Cantos quickly becomes apparent, as a number of elements recur. Phillips lists the major visual devices, which include the triangle, used as an emblem of the Trinity, and which can be parodically inverted as in the image of the three beasts of Canto I; concentric circles, imaging the structure of the celestial spheres or the circles of Hell; the use of Eadweard Muybridge's photographic sequences of people and animals in movement; and writing, as an extension of the graphic presentation of language which is so much a feature of Phillips' work. 'Indeed, there is one way of looking at the Cantos which suggests they are *entirely* made up of such thematic devices' (Phillips 1990B: 14).

In exploring just some of the allegorical aspects of the four beasts mentioned in Canto I, it will have been obvious how much contextual information and accumulated reference can be brought to the *Commedia*. The *TV Dante* installs the dimension of commentary as a central device of the programme. A variety of experts speak as talking-heads on different

[175]

aspects of the poem, their speech being roughly edited with jump-cuts left in place. This establishes a different level of convention from the performance of the poem text itself which is more fluently edited.

The experts who gloss the detailed meanings of the *Commedia* text in *A TV Dante* are not simply medieval explicators of allegory. They bring late-twentieth-century information to the action and imagery of the poem, so there are experts in natural history, the stock exchange, meteorology, and psychology, as well as professional medievalists, Dante scholars and theologians. A vivid use of contemporary knowledge and visuals occurs at the beginning of Canto V, where entering the Second Circle of Hell Dante and Virgil are engulfed by a storm,

> La bufera infernal, che mai non resta,
> mena li spirti con la sua rapina:
> voltando e percotendo li molesta.
> (*Inferno* V 31–3. Sapegno 1968: 55)

> The hellish hurricane unresting sweeps
> the swirling souls in its rapacious wake
> and thrashes and torments them as they whirl.
> (Phillips 1985: 42)

These are the carnal sinners, tormented for their tempestuous and disorderly living, and the poem likens them to large crowds of starlings in cold weather, or cranes chanting mournfully as they fly 'indian-file' in lines:

> E come i gru van lor lai,
> faccendo in aere di sé lunga riga,
> (*Inferno* V 46–7. Sapegno 1968: 56)

> And just as cranes strung out in stretching lines
> chant dirges as they travel through the air,
> (Phillips 1985: 42)

This kind of simile from the natural world is always effective in the *Commedia*, the poetry of commonplace observation which animates action through similitude. (In literary conventional terms, it is also the kind of simile expected of epic, as in the *Aeneid* XII 472ff.) Phillips writes that the picture library available as the archive on which *A TV Dante* draws was not very extensive, but despite this the range of visual reference has great variety and ingenuity. The *TV Dante* brings extraordinary footage of hurricanes and tornados to visualize the simile of the 'bufera', and has ornithologists explain the behaviour of starlings and cranes, so the meaning is naturalized even as the allegorical sense still works at the level of the poem's action. It is as if pull-down information windows had been added to the poem as a means of laying bare the narrative devices which are at work.

Is this postmodern television, as Tom Phillips conjectures? In so far as *A TV Dante* is not *Pee-Wee's Big Adventure* or *Twin Peaks*, then the answer has to be No. *A TV Dante* was not commissioned by a major channel in order to capture huge audiences for advertisers. It is not addressed to the prime-time mass audience, and does not make relentlessly knowing use of the vocabulary of popular television. Above all, it is not ironic and self-parodic. *A TV Dante* is a brilliant example of television arts patronage intended for a minority audience (which is still of course measured in millions), fulfilling the Channel 4 brief to commission innovative and culturally rewarding programmes. But some aspects of *A TV Dante* do map on to areas of the debates about postmodern culture. These include: the transposing of classic works into popular format; the intensive, eclectic manipulation of imagery within narrative; and a preference for allegorical rather than symbolic meanings. The following final section discusses these changing attitudes to allegory, and some aspects of the debate over the relations between images and words.

Theorizing text and image

The two previous sections of this chapter have explored the very consistent way in which Tom Phillips has included the inter-relation of visual and verbal meanings in his various forms of art. The visual signature which was most firmly associated with his style from the early 1970s onwards was probably the use of uniform capital letters as both text and subject in his paintings and prints. His most widely known work, the *Humument*, now circulating in over three million copies, displays a seemingly limitless ingenuity in combining graphic images and frag-mented text. Commenting on his series of panel paintings 'Curriculum Vitae', he writes:

> Once more I emphasise the fact that I regard texts as images in their own right: treated as they are here with words ghosted behind words to form a (literal) subtext they are all the more image for being doubly text.
>
> (Phillips 1992A: 29)

The *TV Dante*, directed in co-operation with the film-maker Peter Greenaway, takes his exploration of the collusions between literary and visual meaning into quite new areas.

An adverse response to this ambitious combining of different practices may object that for a fine artist to rely so extensively on words and literature is a sign of visual insecurity: if the graphic imagery cannot establish meanings on its own terms, then it must be weak imagery. Another objection to Phillips' mixed modes might claim that they are the product of a kind of English art-academicism, that is, of a visual art produced within a national culture which does not have a vigorous and confident community of painters, and where painterly values have to take refuge in literary culture. But I am arguing that Phillips' scripto-visual art celebrates the pleasures of combination, and for this dialogue to be successful, the categories of text and image must be maintained as reciprocally dependent: it is not the case that the picture 'illustrates' the word, or the text 'explains' the image. This kind of hierarchy of meaning is unsettled by the processes of his paintings, texts and video.

Understanding and explaining the nature of the relationship between visual and verbal meanings has been a persistent problem for a number of related disciplines, which include art history, aesthetics, linguistics, philosophy and psychology. It is self-evident that the mute, sensuous appeal of visual values is different in kind from the connected, discursive semantics of words, and to attempt directly to equate what we see with what we speak or read would seem to be futile. The waywardness of the relation between images and words has traditionally been resolved by subjugating the visual realm. For medieval Christianity, the visual arts were subordinated to belief, and employed to illustrate every aspect of theology, mediating the written word to a largely illiterate congregation. But iconoclasm – a mistrust of visual aids, as it were – was always present, and for Islam remains a continuing debate.

With the growing secularization of imagery from the period of the renaissance, the relationship between the written and the seen necessarily changed. Reading artistic theory from the fifteenth through to the eighteenth centuries, it can seem that what we value in painting now was simply not apparent to early-modern viewers of pictures, or more accurately, that the aesthetic discourses of the time found no place for the appreciation of visual values which we now try to articulate (Bätschmann 1988). European theories of painting from the renaissance to the eighteenth century elevated the genre of 'history painting' to the

[178]

highest rank in the visual arts. This theory only valued canvases which contained literary narratives relating grand religious or political themes. The more inarticulate, purely visual genres such as landscapes, still lives and portraits were demoted exactly because they were more painterly. Qualities in painting which are literally unspeakable because they are expressed visually – tone, hue, form – were denigrated as being only the means by which a discursive semantic sense was conveyed. When the French genre painter Greuze paused before a still life by Chardin and could only sigh, he was acknowledging the inarticulate virtues of Chardin's painting which he felt should be inferior, but to which he felt himself responding against his better judgement (Iversen 1990: 212–13).

Allegorical signification was therefore one of the main conventions whereby visual forms were translated into discursive, literary meaning, and within writing it was also the convention by which figurative meanings in language were translated into non-representational codes. The four beasts encountered by the traveller in Canto I of the *Commedia* have a literal, figurative meaning as animals in the text, and as recognizable animals in Phillips' visual representations of them. But by virtue of the four-fold translating mechanism described in the letter to Can Grande della Scala, the simple animal existences of the leopard, lion, she-wolf and hound are granted all kinds of increasingly abstracted meaning. Allegory therefore transmutes immediate, visual sense into elaborated, discursive value.

Various kinds of ambitious claim are made for the continuities which can be traced from the establishment of 'modernity' during the eighteenth-century European Enlightenment, to the supposedly postmodern condition of the late twentieth century. One of the arguments advanced for a new postmodern sensibility proposes that the structure of taste and the kinds of aesthetic emotion established during the period of European romanticism, that is from approximately 1780 to 1820, are now dissolving, in favour of new orders of pleasure which have more in common with earlier, pre-romantic sensibilities from the period of the Enlightenment, and earlier (Jameson 1991: 11–16). This argument can be tested in relation to the different kinds of meaning which may be derived from allegorical (medieval and renaissance) schemes, and symbolist (romantic and early-twentieth-century) traditions of interpretation.

Allegory is defined as 'speaking otherwise than one seems to speak', or as the 'Description of a subject under the guise of some other subject or aptly suggestive resemblance' (*OED* 1). On this basic definition, allegorical meaning is comparable to the operations of irony as a figurative use of language, since irony is defined as 'A figure of speech in which the intended meaning is the opposite of that expressed by the words used; usually taking the form of sarcasm or ridicule' (*OED* 1) (for example: 'Postmodernism really explains everything so clearly'). Because allegory can insist on the interpretive distance between the literal presence of a visual figure and the attributed, abstract sense – this she-wolf connotes 'corrosive envy' – it is valued by traditions of representation which emphasize the conventional, rather than the natural, derivations of meaning. Postmodernism can certainly be said to be such a tradition, and therefore allegory has enjoyed a revival of interest within theorizing and practices which are called postmodern (Owens 1992: 52–87). Any convention which exploits irony and self-consciousness will also enjoy the potentially ironic gap between figure and sense which is intrinsic to allegorical practice.

the allegory is the signifier and the meaning is the signified

For Christian theology and exegesis the literal and the figurative meanings of the Bible were inseparable components of reading: historical, literal narrative simultaneously figured forth typological truths. It was not a case of 'adding' additional layers of sense to the divine text, but rather of adequately discerning the prophecies which were divinely but obscurely inscribed within the figures of the narrative. This kind of interpretive tactic is common to many religious traditions, but was acutely necessary for Christian interpretation because the meaning of the Old Testament, a Jewish text, had to be radically revised in order to bring it into accord with the schismatic revelation of the New Testament. This fundamental dichotomy within the foundation of Christian textual authority may be one of the contributory factors in the very different kind of interpretive tradition which subsequently developed in Christianity when compared with Islamic attitudes, which derived from the supposed unity of the Qur'an (Prickett 1986, 1990). The violent dispute over Salman Rushdie's novel *The Satanic Verses*, as we shall see in section Three below, can be given a context within these conflicting styles of reading (Ahmed 1992; Gellner 1992).

For medieval and renaissance allegory, interpretive ingenuity could therefore seek out extremely obscure or indirect meanings from the Bible, or from the created world, which was also regarded as a divinely ordained text full of enigmatic senses: because the pelican plucks her breast to provide nesting materials, therefore she is a sign of Christ's love, appearing to feed her young by wounding herself. Rival schools of

interpretation developed, some arguing for as many as 12 different layers
of sense within any text, though one of the most influential schemes
proposed a relatively modest four levels of meaning, the system ex-
pounded in the letter to Can Grande. Allegorical schemes and interpretations were therefore one of the most widely established hermeneutic procedures – that is to say, one of the most powerful interpretive
attitudes – throughout the European middle ages and renaissance. The
consonance or 'fit' between the text which was carrying the imputed
allegorical sense, and the meaning which was constructed upon it, could
vary. The sense might be reasonably self-evident because it drew upon
conventionally agreed meanings, for example that wearing red clothes
signified an amorous character, or more usually the allegorical meaning
was 'darker', and had to be drawn out via special knowledge and
interpretive skill. Allegory in these more obscure readings required
author-ity, the power granted by textual knowledge, for its explication
and validation. Allegorical interpretation might in this sense be described as a mode of reading which was policed by the clerisy who
belonged to the dominant institutions of church and state, and who were
keen to retain the modes of understanding as endorsed by particular
allegories. Alternatively, as Chaucer's Wife of Bath well knew, disagreement and schism could also be articulated via dissident allegorical
interpretation. The history of Christianity is the history of its heresies,
which were often argued through new readings perceived as illegitimate
by authority (Leff 1967).

Allegory however lost this supreme position within writing and
interpretation during the post-renaissance period in Europe. In the
course of the seventeenth and eighteenth centuries there was a retreat
from this kind of sustained allegorical construction as new assumptions
about the nature and taxonomies of knowledge developed. What we now
regard as systematic, empirically verifiable knowledge – particularly in
the natural sciences – displaced the earlier kinds of understanding
derived from traditional theological assumptions. By the late eighteenth
century, for example, readers of poetry expected to be able to understand
poems more intuitively and sympathetically, and to be able to associate
personal experience more directly with the poem. This therefore
allowed empathy to play a part in the construction of their 'own'
meaning. To accuse a text of being merely allegorical in our own time
is to imply that its metaphorical quality is unconvincing, and allegory
in aesthetic debates since the romantic period has therefore been

disparaged, and the symbol has been valued as the superior mode of metaphorical meaning:

> A symbol is indeed the only possible expression of some invisible essence, a transparent lamp about a spiritual flame; while allegory is one of many possible representations of an embodied thing, or familiar principle, and belongs to fancy and not to imagination: the one is a revelation, the other an amusement.
>
> (Yeats [1897] 1938: 116)

allegorical meaning is ambiguous multiple interpretations

symbolic meaning is supposed to be self-evident, like empirical knowledge

Allegory declined in the pre-romantic period as a technique because it came to seem too artificial. Within an allegorically constructed text, there is an explicit tension between the worldly, phenomenal interest which we take in the literal level of the writing or image, and the abstracted hierarchies of meaning which allegory then draws from that figure. In Canto V of the *Commedia* we are charmed by the imagery of the starling flocks, or the cry of the cranes, and then appalled as the simile is mapped on to the scheme of the souls in torment. These intrinsic confusions can contribute some of the most interesting kinds of complexity to allegorical writing, where our empathetic response to detail as part of the physical texture of life interacts with conceptual levels of understanding in the poem which are 'only' allegorically authorized: 'it is in the nature of allegory that it devastates its own subjects' (Harrison 1991: 166). In terms of postmodern debate, allegorical meaning divides between our phenomenological response to 'figure' and our textually prompted response to 'discourse': this is another aspect of the exploration of interference patterns that are created by text-and-image relations, and which are so much a part of current creative work (Barthes 1977: 15–78; Iversen 1990). Postmodern theory has therefore rediscovered the joys of allegory because it lays bare the merely conventional nature of the derivation of meaning, and also because it can act as a kind of distancing process, prompting reflection within the inevitable gap between visual and verbal codes. Allegory allows the insertion of a chilly blade between figure and discourse.

The prints, paintings and films of Tom Phillips and Peter Greenaway persistently draw attention to the ways in which meanings can be constructed out of their content. Or else, the distinction between 'content' and 'interpretation' is elided to the point where the process of interpretation takes on the status of meaning itself. Allegory is therefore a premodern tradition of writing and reading that lends itself very well to postmodern concerns. By returning to positively ancient forms of signification such as allegory, artists like Tom Phillips and Peter Greenaway

[182]

are not so much post-modern as pre-romantic, as they delight in the varieties of ways in which the ascriptions of meaning to signs can be deployed. In Peter Greenaway's film *Prospero's Books* (1991), for example, an adaptation of Shakespeare's *Tempest* made with the encouragement of Sir John Gielgud, Greenaway took the central theme of Prospero's learning as a visual motif. A complete library of renaissance knowledges was invented and displayed through computer animation, overlaying and intercutting with the performance of the play text. The books demonstrated textuality-as-magic through the commentary and animations which elaborated their contents, much as the talking-heads glossed the senses of the *TV Dante*. We again meet continuities in creative practices, from postmodern to the oldest kinds of writing, since allegory and irony are present in the earliest literary traditions: there is no cleverness in contemporary writing that cannot be found in earlier texts.

Allegorical exegesis displays meaning, and cools our immediate, feeling-with responses through its commentary. Affective response is of course still there – *A TV Dante* and *Prospero's Books* are passionate works, and it is only a dull parochialism that could say otherwise. Reflection is incorporated to the processes of pleasure, rather as, one imagines, was the case for renaissance readers of Donne's poetry or of Spenser's *Faerie Queene*, and even perhaps as for the first audiences of *The Tempest* in 1611. The pre-modern culture of the medieval and renaissance periods is fascinating for all kinds of reasons, but within the context of debates about postmodernity, it might be said that the sixteenth and seventeenth centuries are compelling, partly because society was not yet subjected to commodity and surplus materiality to the same degree as ourselves, and that subjectivity was therefore organized and expressed in significantly different forms from today. The point is not to be nostalgic about these lost forms of subjectivity, but to appreciate the critical distance between our own commodity-oriented mentality, and the strangely different processes of ego formation in early modern society. Postmodernism is dead. Long live the Renaissance.

References

Selected Works by Tom Phillips

1975 *Tom Phillips: Works/Texts to 1974*, Stuttgart: edition hansjörg mayer.
1980 *A Humument. A Treated Victorian Novel*, London: Thames and Hudson

by arrangement with edition hansjörg mayer, Stuttgart. [Revised reprint of Tetrad Press edition.]

1983 *Dante's Inferno. The First Part of the Divine Comedy of Dante Alighieri translated and illustrated by Tom Phillips*, London: Talfourd Press. [Version including etchings, screenprints, lithographs and hand-set text.]

1985 *Dante's Inferno. The First Part of the Divine Comedy of Dante Alighieri translated and illustrated by Tom Phillips*, London: Thames and Hudson. [Laser-scanned offset-lithograph version.]

1987 *A Humument. A Treated Victorian Novel*, London: Thames and Hudson by arrangement with edition hansjörg mayer, Stuttgart. First Revised Edition. [This substitutes 55 new pages within the 367 pages of the 1980 edition.]

1989 *The Portrait Works*, with an introduction by Bill Hurrell, London: National Portrait Gallery Publications. Published in association with the exhibition at the National Portrait Gallery, London: 6 October 1989–21 January 1990. [Includes a provisional checklist of miscellaneous published writings.]

1990A *A TV Dante*, Tom Phillips with Peter Greenaway. A KGP Ltd Dante BV Co-production for Channel 4, first broadcast July 1990. Translator, Tom Phillips.

1990B *A TV Dante. Notes and Commentaries*, London: Channel 4 Television in association with the Talfourd Press.

1992A *Works and Texts*, with an introduction by Huston Paschal, London and New York: Thames and Hudson.

1992B John Cage, the *Independent*, Friday 14 August: 17.

Editions of The Divine Comedy

SAPEGNO, Natalino (1968) *Dante Alighieri. La Divina Commedia*, three volumes, Florence: La Nuova Italia Editrice.

SAYERS, Dorothy L. (1949) *The Comedy of Dante Alighieri the Florentine*, three volumes, Harmondsworth: Penguin.

WICKSTEED, Philip H. (1900) *The Inferno, Purgatorio and Paradiso of Dante Alighieri*, three volumes, parallel text with commentaries. [The edition read by T. S. Eliot while writing *The Waste Land*] London: J. M. Dent and Sons.

Secondary Studies

AHMED, Akbar S. (1992) *Postmodernism and Islam. Predicament and Promise*, London and New York: Routledge.

ANDERSON, William (1982) *Dante the Maker*, New York: Crossroad.

AULICH, Jim (1987) 'The difficulty of living in an age of cultural decline and spiritual corruption: R. B. Kitaj 1965–1970', *The Oxford Art Journal* 10/2: 43–57.

BARTHES, Roland (1977) *Image-Music-Text*, Essays Selected and Translated by Stephen Heath, Glasgow: Fontana/Collins.

BÄTSCHMANN, Oskar (1988) 'Text and image: some general problems', in *Word and Image* 4/1: 11–20.

GELLNER, Ernest (1992) *Postmodernism, Reason and Religion*, London and New York: Routledge.

HARRISON, Charles (1991) '"Seeing" and "describing": the Artists' studio' in *Essays on Art & Language*, 150–74, Oxford and Cambridge, Mass.: Basil Blackwell.

IVERSEN, Margaret (1990) 'Vicissitudes of the visual sign', in *Word and Image* 6/3: 212–16.

JAMESON, Fredric (1991) *Postmodernism, or the Cultural Logic of Late Capitalism*, London: Verso.

LEFF, Gordon (1967) *Heresy in the Later Middle Ages; the Relation of Heterodoxy to Dissent, c. 1250 – c. 1450*, two volumes, Manchester: Manchester University Press.

OWENS, Craig (1992) 'The allegorical impulse: toward a theory of postmodernism', and Part 2, pp. 52–87 in *Beyond Recognition. Representation, Power and Culture*, edited by Scott Bryson, Barbara Kruger, Lynne Tillman and Jane Weinstock. Introduction by Simon Watney. Berkeley, Los Angeles, Oxford: University of California Press.

PRICKETT, Stephen (1986) *Words and the Word: Language, Poetics, and Biblical Interpretation*, Cambridge: Cambridge University Press.

—— (1990) 'Literature and the Bible', 951–63 in Martin Coyle, Peter Garside, Malcolm Kelsall and John Peck (eds) *Encyclopedia of Literature and Criticism*, London: Routledge.

SCHWENGER, Peter (1994) '*Prospero's Books*' and the visionary page, *Textual Practice* 8/2: 268–78.

THOMAS, David (1983) 'The Phillips Inferno', *The Sunday Times*, 30 October.

YEATS, W. B. ([1897] 1938) 'William Blake and his illustrations to the Divine Comedy', in *Essays and Introductions*, London: Macmillan.

PART II
Essays on Postmodernism

Three: Literature

Introduction

If you are a reasonably energetic and indiscriminate reader it's not difficult to be sceptical about the claims made for a specifically post-modern literature. Postmodernity as a period-specific effect might be confidently located in late-twentieth-century popular culture, for which there seem to be no precedents. And postmodernism might be used to describe productions in film, television and video, which are modernity's technological contribution to the arts. But authors, surely, have always known the score, and writing has always been ahead of the game?

Some of the textual strategies which are claimed to be intrinsic to postmodern poetry and fiction are discussed in this section with reference to writing which in different ways has created scandal. John Ashbery's reputation as a major poet can provoke strong disagreement in Great Britain, and to a lesser extent in the United States, where unsympathetic readers find his writing incomprehensible. Altogether more serious disagreement was provoked in 1988 by the publication of Salman Rushdie's novel *The Satanic Verses*, when Muslim opinion in many countries felt that the book was a blasphemous attack on Islamic belief. The polarizations of opinion which these writers have provoked raise the following issues:

What kind of subjectivity is expressed by an innovative poet such as John Ashbery?

Does his poetry make an absolute break with previous literary traditions?

Can the apparently all-pervasive ironies of this poetry be resolved into particular meanings?

And for *The Satanic Verses*:

What is 'magic realism'? Can it be specifically identified with post-modern fiction?

[189]

What is at issue in the violent dispute over the meaning of this novel?

What does deconstruction as a critical method contribute to a reading of *The Satanic Verses?*

John Ashbery: postmodernity's laureate?

Evidence for assessing the place of poetry in readers' affections today is contradictory. Surveys of teaching in England would seem to suggest that only a narrow range of poems are studied, rather reluctantly, in many schools. Students beginning degree courses in English and other literatures do not often seem to have read very widely or have much of a commitment to reading poems. But there are also other contrary indications. We may be mistaken in looking for the reading and writing of poetry primarily within academic institutions, and it would be heartening to think that there is an extensive appetite for poetry among the general community. One clear indicator might be the relative success enjoyed by presses such as Carcanet and Bloodaxe in Great Britain during the 1980s. These ventures have promoted large and eclectic lists of international contemporary poetry, significantly replacing distribution by established publishers (Wheale 1992). Activities such as writers-in-the-community and competitions, often linked to local arts festivals, also demonstrate keen participation in the reading and writing of poetry. In America creative writing programmes are a routine provision in colleges, and provide a training ground as well as a constituency for poets. This looks like a confident and vigorous context for poetic work, when taken together with the funding of publications by the National Endowment for the Arts and other State Arts Councils – or that is certainly how it can appear to British poets when they visit America.

The position of John Ashbery's writing and reputation within this general picture is singular. In 1994 he published *And the Stars Were Shining,* his sixteenth collection of poems (exclusive of small-press and selected editions), and previous writings also include *Three Plays* (1978), *Reported Sightings. Art Chronicles 1957–1987* (1989) and a comic novel of suburban manners, *A Nest of Ninnies* (1969) which he co-authored with James Schuyler. The dust wrapper to the British edition of his thirteenth collection, *April Galleons* (Carcanet 1987), quoted a review from *The Times:* 'On both sides of the Atlantic a substantial and increasingly coherent body of opinion accepts that he is quite simply the finest poet in English of his generation', together with another notice from *The Sunday Times*, 'Ashbery *is* a really good poet, a legitimate though rebellious heir of Eliot, Pound, Stevens and Auden.'

The blithe assertion that your man is 'quite simply the finest' betrays an imperious confidence. Nothing is ever straightforward where literary reputation is concerned, and particularly the status of poets, where the stakes are often fought over with an appalling intensity. This kind of league-table claim is essentially meaningless, because it is clear that the ways in which different poets and poetries are valued must depend crucially on the constituency which is making the argument. So for example a number of British and American readers would propose Seamus Heaney as 'finest poet in English of his generation', and be prepared to make elaborate arguments for him, and against the claims made on behalf of a poet like Ashbery. Another readership with different preoccupations might propose the work and career of Adrienne Rich. Even so, this kind of ambitious estimate of John Ashbery's achievement is not uncommon, and the arguments are often made with reference to particular qualities of modernity in his work.

Academic appreciation of Ashbery's poetry has grown since the mid-1970s, and a more widespread interest is usually credited as beginning with his eighth collection, *Self-Portrait in a Convex Mirror* (1975). The ways in which major poetic reputations come to be established is a study in itself (Rainey 1989), but John Ashbery's achievement today is often analysed as a particular contribution to postmodern style. The *Times*'s notice from *April Galleons* already gives an indication of the sort of genealogy which can be proposed for him: Eliot, Pound, Stevens, Auden. This is a difficult family grouping: heterogeneous, all-male, and belonging distinctly to the heroic phase of twentieth-century modernism. On this view Ashbery's poetry is valued because theoretical, academic commentary of the past 15 years has been able to make claims for his writing which reinforce its own intellectual agenda. In this way Ashbery's reputation has come to be complicit with the kind of commentary which it provokes, and is therefore closely tied to academic valuation and, inevitably, circulation. I will argue here that the poetry is not in fact absolutely coterminous with postmodern theory, but only looks that way. In cutting the apparent ligature between poem and secondary commentary, I hope to relieve the impression that John Ashbery is therefore only of academic interest. He was once asked: 'Do you think of yourself as a philosophical poet and do you read much in philosophy?' To which his uncharacteristically curt answer was 'No' (Labrie 1984: 31).

Arguments for Ashbery-as-postmodernist can be summarized as follows. His poems display:

1 *Critique of the subject*   Here 'subject' means the formation of individual identity, where any sense of the continuity of personality is replaced by analysis of the determining structures by and through which identity is articulated. On this view, language itself is the most formidable determining institution, followed by gender, class and culture, which are themselves mediated exclusively through language. What anyone takes to be their 'personality' is only the delusive sense of identity which individuals experience by courtesy of these external structures. From this point of view Ashbery's poetry can be related to the postmodern preoccupations described in 'Subjectivity and subjection, history and nature' (above pp. 52–6), and also to the various analyses of identity in the art works of Mary Kelly, and in the critique of postcolonial experience and representation by Gayatri Spivak and Trinh T. Minh-ha.

2 *Critique of representation*   If language is the most powerful determinant of subjectivity, then postmodern writing needs to demonstrate the ways in which this is the case. Ashbery's poems put disparate repertoires of language into playful relationship, slipping between elaborately literary tones, extreme colloquialism and prose rumination without giving due notice, and at such a speed that the reader has to be aware of this gaming if s/he is to have any means of making sense of the vertiginous changes of register. Positions offered by particular genres and idioms of language are briefly occupied within the poems, and then clashed or elided with other contrasting idioms, so that the partiality of each position can be appreciated within the dynamic of the reading. On this description, postmodern interpretation is groundless, deprived of constitutive truths whether from time, place, person, or morality. Postmodern reading is 'interstitial' or 'diacritical' because it is said to generate meaning differentially, making reference only *between* sets of imagery, and not to the status of any 'real' object/person/period which the image deictically indicates.

These two critical-reflective strategies combine to generate the entire spectrum of undecidability which is the pleasure of the postmodern reader: eclecticism displays traces of meaning which we enjoyably

[192]

identify, and then put into conflict with a subsequent citation. For this argument no explicit politics can be enjoined in Ashbery's writing, and the past is not offered as evidence or inspiration, but only as another language form. The nature of conclusions drawn from such reading – how we totalize our sense of what has been written – is therefore definitively elusive. The adequacy of this postmodern reading is tested here in Chapter 6, 'A new subjectivity? John Ashbery's *Three Poems*'.

'It was and it was not so': the politics of fiction

John Ashbery's poetry is evidence of a genuine continuity of writing strategies from the period of early-twentieth-century experimental art, and as such can still meet with incomprehension. Salman Rushdie's fiction is also allied with some aspects of European modernism, and has provoked a violent reaction for exactly this reason. In his controversial novel *The Satanic Verses* (1988) Rushdie asked 'how does newness come into the world?' and this was in part related to the making of new art forms. For Rushdie, this newness was both the stark, challenging novelty of Muhammad's vision of Islam, and simultaneously the newnesses created by late-twentieth-century migration and cultural change. Perhaps it was also the newness of a novel which tries to put new questions in novel (new) forms. The dynamic which then developed between these different areas of his writing provoked the violent intransigence of the *fatwa* against him. Rushdie's critique of Muhammad's newness inflamed communities which were already being urged to oppose 'Western Modernism' because it was perceived to be a corrupting product of Great Satan – that is, of America.

Everywhere in the late twentieth century there are complex processes at work by which different regional and national cultures converge and interact with each other. 'Integration' is far too bland a word to describe these convergences, because the cultural and political reactions taking place all around are often so convulsive. These conflicts created by the interaction of formerly distinct cultures are certainly a major topic in all of the discussions of postmodernity, and postmodern fiction is often characterized by its playful combination of radically diverse kinds of narrative which break the decorum which readers might expect to encounter. In *The Satanic Verses* Salman Rushdie explored the cultural mixing and confusion undergone by two migrants who travel 'from Indianness to Englishness, an immeasurable distance. Or, not very far at all, because they rose from one great city, fell to another' (Rushdie 1988: 41; hereafter *SV*). Rushdie did this by counterposing one comic-realist strand of narrative set in the contemporary world with another much older story, set in a distant historical period. '"It was and it was not so", as the old stories used to say' (*SV* 35). It is exactly the promiscuous, fictional mixing of these two tales which has provoked argument and violence.

The Satanic Verses begins with Mr Gibreel Farishta and Mr Saladin Chamcha being blown out of the air at 29,002 feet when their Bombay–London jumbo flight 'Bostan' is destroyed by a Sikh terrorist bomb. They fall to earth in 'a rain of limbs and babies' (*SV* 6), and as they fall they sing, are metamorphosed, and miraculously begin to fly. Both of the heroes have made and remade themselves many times in the course of their lives, and a central theme of the novel is the constructed, seren-dipitous nature of identity, and of Indian identity in particular. Zeenat Vakil, for example, is a doctor working with the Bombay homeless and the victims of the 'Amrika cloud' at Bhopal. In addition to this admirable engagement with daily intransigence in India, Zeeny is also an art critic who has written a critical-theoretical polemic. Her text is in fact a postmodern argument against national 'purity' and 'cultural heritage', it is a theorization of the characters and plotting of *The Satanic Verses* itself. She argues against 'the confining myth of authenticity, that folkloristic straitjacket which she sought to replace by an ethic of historically validated eclecticism, for was not the entire national culture based on the principle of borrowing whatever clothes seemed to fit, Aryan, Mughal, British, take-the-best-and-leave-the-rest?' (*SV* 52).

The term often used to describe this combining of apparently incon-gruous narratives is 'magic realism', and it is associated with novelists such as Milan Kundera, Gabriel Garcia Marquez, Thomas Pynchon and Angela Carter, all of whose fiction conspicuously mixes generic effects, laying an apparently sound basis in reality and verisimilitude and then warping the reader's expectations by moving into fantastic events. The survival of Gibreel and Saladin having fallen 29,002 feet from their hijacked jumbo is one miracle; that Gibreel then turns into a parodic angel, while Saladin grows horns and hoofs is also magical. But they have fallen into the grinding realism of London's racism and poverty: the fantastic details heighten their experience of grim reality: magic conflicts with realism. It is then not difficult to associate this kind of fictional genre-bending with analogous effects in other very self-consciously postmodern items such as the films of David Lynch. Magic realism in film or fiction can give offence through its apparently gratuitous fantasy which may be perceived as a puerile category mistake because it is promiscuously combined with a naturalistic style and materials.

Again it is not difficult to dissolve this category as a specifically postmodern effect by finding earlier traditions which appear to do exactly the same thing. The Russian novelist Mikhail Bulgakov (1891–1940), for example, completed *The Master and Margarita* in 1938, and as an extremely unnerving combination of narrative kinds, it is admired by Salman Rushdie. The novel opens with the events of Christ's trial and crucifixion, told with a compelling detail and conviction, but this sacred narrative is intercut with the story of the Devil's visit to Moscow of the 1930s and his various punishments visited on the literary establishment. Bulgakov's absurdism may be explained as an allegorical attack on Stalin's reign of terror, but here the magic realism is in fact part of the aesopian tradition of writing, where an apparently innocuous and fantastic narrative doubles as a coded fable. However *The Master and Margarita* unnerves the reader because it cannot be accounted for quite so precisely, it escapes the neat reduction of a consistent allegorical reading, as the characters at the close escape any determining ending.

Violent misreading

In Rushdie's narrative, Saladin Chamcha, only son of India's richest manufacturer of fertilizers, has throughout his life dreamed of quitting the bitch-city of Bombay for his dream-city of London. Saladin wishes to change himself into a 'goodandproper' Englishman as part of his complete rejection of Bombay and his father (*SV* 36). This cultural transfusion is a painful thing, 'England was a peculiar-tasting smoked fish full of spikes and bones, and nobody would ever tell him how to eat it' (*SV* 44). In the process of transforming himself goodandproper Saladin suffers alienation from his family and natal country. Chamcha's style of metamorphosis is very particular: he is a perfect mimic and has made a famous (anonymous) career being the voice of commodities such as garlic-flavoured crisps, carpets, and ketchup, so that he became a dark star of the voice-over business (*SV* 60–1). ('Ketchup' is a precise example of the flavoursome mixings which the novel develops: 'Catchup' came into English in 1690, meaning 'High East India sauce', of Chinese-Malay-Dutch derivation.) Change and mutation are everywhere in *The Satanic*

Verses. Change through trauma, migration, love, and age – a man's corpulent body shrivels over the years until 'he seemed to be roaming about inside his clothes like a man in search of something he had not quite managed to identify' (*SV* 67).

Gibreel, son of a humble Bombay tiffin carrier (lunch-runner), had been for 15 years the biggest star in the world's largest movie industry, chief actor-god of the Bombay Theologicals. He had played the supreme deities of both the Hindu and Buddhist religions, Vishnu, Krishna and Gautama (*SV* 16). India's other major religion is Islam, which forbids the profane representation of God or of its founder, the prophet Muhammad. But in a series of disturbing dreams, Gibreel finds himself acting out central roles in a parodic version of the founding of Islam. It is this thread of narrative which has caused the controversy and provoked the death sentence against Salman Rushdie.

Gibreel dreams that he is an angel watching Mahound, a 'business-man-turned-prophet' who is struggling to establish his vision of a monotheistic religion in Jahilia, a city built entirely of sand. 'Water is the enemy in Jahilia . . . it must never be spilled . . . for where it drops the city erodes alarmingly' (*SV* 94). Mahound's vision and certainty represent a 'terrifying singularity' (*SV* 102), and they constitute a powerful conviction that cuts through the dispersed beliefs and mild compromises of Jahilia, like water through parched sand. This fierce singularity is a value which stands intransigently opposed to the shiftings and mutations of the contemporary narrative in the novel. What is its relation to the modern action? It is perhaps a dream which is functioning as Gibreel's wish fulfilment for certainty, but simul-taneously also as a punitive threat to Gibreel the dreamer for his own lack of conviction. Or else it is 'an imaginative way of charting the migrant's path from faith to scepticism, his shifting perspective of women, his attempted exorcism – consciously or otherwise – of child-hood archetypes' (Appignanesi and Maitland 1989: 22).

Mahound climbs the mountain to seek further revelation, and Gibreel's dream changes alarmingly as he finds that he becomes the prophet as well as simultaneously the angel. This collapsing of identities and categories, which is so much part of the novel's content, takes the most extreme manifestation when the prophet thinks that he has been duped by Shaitan – Satan – in place of the archangel. The Devil has dictated false verses which pollute 'the true recitation, al-qur'an', and these are the verses of the novel's title. Rushdie has said that this was the central motivating episode: 'the image out of which the book grew was of the prophet going to the mountain and not being able to tell the difference between the angel and the devil. The book is about the wrestling match which takes place between the two' (Appignanesi and Maitland 1989: 40). Many aspects of the Jahilia narrative gave offence, and were even taken to be blasphemous by some significant sections of Muslim opinion. These included the parody of the divine inspiration which established the Qur'an's text; the renaming of Muhammad as Mahound, a medieval insult associated with false prophecy; the defaming of the holy city of Mecca with the name Jahilia, meaning 'ignorance'; and the mimicking of the wives of the prophet by whores in a brothel named 'the Curtain', which was taken to be a reference to the 'hejab' or veil worn by Muslim women.

The novel was published in the United Kingdom by Viking/Penguin on 26 September 1988. Controversy began in India when Syed Shahabuddin, a Muslim MP, called for the banning of the book because of its 'indecent vilification of the Holy Prophet'. Like many other participants on both sides of the controversy, Mr Shahabuddin had not read the novel, and had no intention of doing so. Rajiv Gandhi, the Indian Prime Minister, quickly responded by banning sale of the book in India: the decision was certainly made with the country's Muslim electorate in mind. Ten other countries with substantial Muslim populations rapidly followed suit, including Pakistan, Saudi Arabia and Indonesia. Political expediency may have played a large part in having the novel banned in India, but Syed Shahabuddin also invoked Article 295A of the Indian Penal Code which legislates against the 'deliberate and malicious intention of outraging the religious feelings of any class of citizens . . . or . . . [which] otherwise, insults or attempts to insult the religion or the religious beliefs of that class' (Appignanesi and Maitland 1989: 48).

Attempts by the Union of Muslim Organisations in Britain to have Rushdie and his publishers prosecuted under the Public Order Act (1986) and the Race Relations Act (1976) were turned down by the then Prime Minister, Margaret Thatcher, who replied to their request, 'It is an essential part of our democratic system that people who act within the law should be able to express their opinions freely' (Appignanesi and Maitland 1989: 57). It also emerged that the author could not be prosecuted on a charge of blasphemy in Great Britain, since this was applicable only when offence was given against the Christian religion. By late November one of Islam's most authoritative theological institutions, the Al-Azhar institute in Cairo, endorsed attempts by British Muslims to have *The Satanic Verses* withdrawn from sale and the edition destroyed.

On 12 February 1989 a crowd of several thousand attacked the U.S. Information Centre in the Pakistani capital Islamabad, protesting against *The Satanic Verses*, and five people were killed and dozens injured when police fired on the demonstrators. Similar riots in Kashmir the following day killed one and injured over 100 more people. On 14 February Ayatollah Khomeini, the spiritual and political leader of Iran, proclaimed a *fatwa* or decree informing 'all the intrepid Muslims in the world that the author of the book entitled *The Satanic Verses*, which has been compiled, printed and published in opposition to Islam, the Prophet and the Qur'an, as well as those publishers who were aware of its contents, have been sentenced to death' (Appignanesi and Maitland 1989: 84). Khomeini and his Iranian theocrats proclaimed Rushdie's novel to be a product of 'world-devouring' America's conspiracy against Islam: one sermon denounced *The Verses* as 'no doubt one of the verses of the Great Satan or one of his surrogates, where one of the member of the British royal literary society [sic!] was forced to write a book ...' (Appignanesi and Maitland 1989: 87–8).

The Satanic Verses became one of the great-unread books of the decade, along with Stephen Hawking's *A Brief History of Time*. The *fatwa* initially made the novel difficult to obtain as booksellers withdrew it from display or ceased stocking it in fear of violent attacks on staff and property. Although this might be expected to have increased curiosity about Rushdie's book, it seems on anecdotal evidence that even among habitual readers of contemporary fiction, there was still a reluctance actually to engage with the novel, which a widespread whispering campaign labelled as 'unreadable'. In the British popular press, and in certain sections of the political establishment, Rushdie was openly vilified as a trouble-maker and opportunist, an immigrant who attacked the British police in his writing but who was then happy to accept the protection of the security forces at taxpayers' expense (Tebbit 1990). Religious intolerances rapidly promoted racist insult and mutual suspicions, in Great Britain as elsewhere. During the intervening period more deaths and injuries have followed, sometimes in riots, and in several cases as the result of assassinations. Fundamentalist intolerance continues to find new literary targets: the Bangladeshi feminist Taslima Nasreen was forced into hiding in June 1994 when Muslim fundamentalists accused her of calling for the Qur'an to be thoroughly revised in her book *Shame*. In fact Nasreen was arguing for a relaxation of some of the stricter Islamic laws as they affected women, and her book was consequently banned in Bangladesh.

Gayatri Spivak: deconstruction and postcolonial fiction

Can theory be articulate about this tangled and murderous dispute? The confrontation might be described as a clash of reading styles: Islam venerates the extraordinary beauty of the Qur'an as a pure revelation, the direct word of God, and no sustained critical tradition within Islam has ever developed which could examine the Qur'an as an historically mediated text. In Christianity, by contrast, textual criticism has for centuries analysed the Bible as a religious document which is compromised and made fallible by secular transmission, and where the revealed meanings have to be interpreted with that understanding. The Qur'an for Islam is absolutely infallible. Therefore, as Rushdie himself says, 'the battle over *The Satanic Verses* is a clash of faiths, in a way. Or, more precisely, it's a clash of languages' (Appignanesi and Maitland 1989: 75). Or more precisely still, it is a clash of hermeneutic assumptions. In satirizing the process by which the text of the Qur'an was dictated to the Prophet Muhammad Rushdie is perceived to be attacking the foundation of Islamic belief.

There is no place for postmodern moral relativism over the central issue in this debate: the threatening and violent responses made against Rushdie are wrong and utterly deplorable. The *fatwa* is a cynical incitement to murder that was undoubtedly made for calculated political motives in the wake of Iran's defeat after eight futile years of war against Iraq. As of March 1995 Salman Rushdie still has to remain in hiding, and has every reason to consider himself, as he puts it, 'the last of the (British) hostages' to fundamentalist political terrorism. *The Satanic Verses* is at the very least a complex, witty, and informative novel: non-Muslim readers can be educated about Islam by reading it. There are many passages which convey the kinds of attraction which an austere and often lyrically beautiful religion might exert on its believers. The novel's telling satire directed, for example, against intolerance and misogyny within Islam raises a legitimate challenge to aspects of Muslim culture and belief (and see Sabbah 1984).

But the argument becomes more intransigent when we consider the responses to the novel from the generally poor communities of Muslims in western countries such as Britain and France. Here the textual play of

The Satanic Verses is easily misrepresented as a malicious attack on the most cherished values which those communities hold, often maintained in defensive reaction to the difficulties of living among an indifferent or actively hostile society. Daniel Easterman, a scholar of Islamic culture, argues that Islamic societies have in common a very developed sense of personal privacy and the 'inviolability of domestic space', seen for example in the organization of traditional domestic architecture where the house is turned inward. This valuing of privacy is part of a network of attitudes deriving from the Arabic root **hrm*, or 'forbiddenness'. That which is 'sacred' or 'prohibited' is *haram*; the *harem* can be the area of the palace set aside for women, or it can be a sacred area. As a category of belief and behaviour *haram* is therefore applied to holiness, impurity and sexuality (Easterman 1993: 217). In Islam, biography developed as a genre which extolled the holiness of its scholars and saints, and so it was a form which particularly observed the pieties of what is *haram*. Personal idiosyncracy and the intimate details of confessional diaries are completely absent from Islamic biographical form, which has been dominated by the conventions of hagiography, that is, of the lives of saints. Therefore Rushdie's novelization of the most intimate aspects of the prophet's life was offensive at several levels: it was perceived as a defamation of Muhammad, but it also constituted a violation of the codes of personal and familial privacy which should be respected for all Muslims:

> By drawing freely on the prophetic biography while subjecting it to the transformations of the novelistic form, Rushdie brought to light the deepest fears of Muslim culture: the fear that one's own inner self may be brought to view, that hagiography may become biography and biography a vehicle for doubt.
>
> (Easterman 1993: 219)

Because *The Satanic Verses* could easily be portrayed as an offence against these proprieties, Khomeini was able very effectively to misinform 'the poor and illiterate masses, the so-called "mustad-hafin" or "the feeble ones", among whom he recruits his most devoted "volunteers for martyrdom"' (Appignanesi and Maitland 1989: 95). If Rushdie can be said to have made an error of judgement in writing the novel as he did, it must be here, in the likelihood of extreme offence being given to large numbers of vulnerable and impoverished people. In theoretical terms, to press this aspect of the argument, *The Satanic Verses* contravenes the values of a

sensitive and very specific 'interpretive community' to an unacceptable
degree. It may be that given the immense scope for mutual incomprehension and misunderstanding between the 'reading communities' concerned, the textual politics of the novel should have intervened in the
debate with a more strategically considered fiction. Salman Rushdie's
reply to this kind of prudent argument was given early in the development of the controversy: 'I cannot censor. I write whatever there is to
write... There are no subjects which are off limits and that includes God,
includes prophets. I refuse to think that I should shut my mind off to
subjects which are not just of interest to me but which have been my
concern all my life' (Appignanesi and Maitland 1989: 40–1).

But is the appeal to the writer's supreme privilege of imaginative
autonomy an adequate defence? The situation may be analogous to that
described by Gayatri Chakravorty Spivak in considering the relation
between 'First World' feminist argument and 'Third World' populations:

> How, then, can one learn from and speak to the millions of illiterate rural
> and urban Indian women who live 'in the pores of' capitalism, inaccessible
> to the capitalist dynamics that allow us our shared channels of com-
> munication, the definition of common enemies? The pioneering books that
> bring First World feminists news from the Third World are written by
> privileged informants and can only be deciphered by a trained readership.
> The distance between 'the informant's world', her 'own sense of the world
> she writes about,' and that of the non-specialist feminist is so great that,
> paradoxically, *pace* the subtleties of reader-response theories, here the
> distinctions might be easily missed.
>
> (Spivak 1986: 38)

Gayatri Spivak's article 'Reading *The Satanic Verses*' is included in this
anthology because of its individual critical perspective and style. Her
own biography gives her particular insight into the experiences described
by post-colonial migrant literature:

> The 'choice' of English Honors by an upper-class young woman in the
> Calcutta of the fifties was itself highly overdetermined. Becoming a
> professor of English in the U.S. fitted in with the 'brain drain.' In due
> course, a commitment to feminism was the best of a collection of accessible
> scenarios. The morphology of a feminist theoretical practice became clear
> through Jacques Derrida's critique of phallocentrism and Luce Irigaray's
> reading of Freud.
>
> (Spivak 1986: 37)

Gayatri Spivak's critical practice can be related to significant areas of the debates over postmodernism because she consistently works with ideas and strategies adapted from the writings of Jacques Derrida. Spivak's 'peculiar theme is always *persistent* critique' (*Third Text* II: *55*), that is, a persistent examination of the terms and relations in which particular discourses are transacted: 'and, I must emphasize, an *asymmetrical* persistent critique, focussing on different elements in the incessant process of recoding'. A discourse is a specific vocabulary which articulates a particular regime of meanings which can be, for example, literary, philosophical, or political. In 'Reading *The Satanic Verses*' Spivak makes connections between each of these three kinds of discourse in a complex fashion because she argues that a simple reading of Rushdie's novel is now impossible due to the way in which the text has become implicated in the tangled and (literally) violent disagreements sketched above. This kind of deconstructive criticism therefore focuses on what it takes to be the hidden assumptions within the terms of any argument, and is concerned to reveal the unacknowledged, even unconscious implications of a particular position. For Spivak, Derrida is a philosopher who is 'not an overthrower of myths but rather who is interested in seeing how a myth works both as a medicine and poison'.

There are three main emphases in Spivak's ambitious reading of *The Satanic Verses*:

1 She defines the central theme of the novel as a portrayal of the instabilities created within an identity which is split between a migrant and a specifically national allegiance. Yet, she argues, the literary construction of the novel itself is not neutral between these two areas of experience, because it derives in so many ways from the traditions of European modernist writing, and therefore in its actual construction is committed to forms of representation which are already specific to western understandings. That is, the literary form in crucial respects compromises the content, and its author's declared intentions. Salman Rushdie as author is unavoidably present to readers of his novel: in response to the *fatwa* he has written eloquently in defence of his position, and therefore the status of the novel text is implicated in these various statements of principle (Rushdie 1990). But Rushdie as author-effect is also written into the narrative of the novel, that is, the novel stages questions of authorial control within its fiction. Spivak is critical of this tactic, which could be termed pseudo-modernist rather than postmodern.

2 Female characters and their roles within the plot development are also significantly foreshortened, according to Spivak. The definition of blasphemy is the central problem for the novel, and 'As so often, woman becomes the touchstone of blasphemy.' Spivak notes that magic realism is used in a particular way for the episodes dealing with rural experience in contemporary India, around the figure of the orphan saint Ayesha. As an example of actual, intransigent difficulties faced by Muslim women in India, she cites the example of a notorious divorce settlement that provoked widespread debate, the 'Shahbano' case from 1985. Rushdie's version of magic realism as a postmodern tactic is not equal to complexities such as these. Because the novel never genuinely questions the coding of gender, Spivak argues that *The Satanic Verses* is in effect limited to being 'a realist reading of magical realism'.

3 Spivak's final argument in the third section of her article is the most general and most abstract. She sketches the development of the idea of secular reason in Europe from the period of the Enlightenment, and by historicizing the concept of rationality in this form, she seeks to identify it as '*necessarily* Eurocentric'. At this point, the deconstructionist tendency in postmodern critique continues eighteenth-century debates over the status of abstract universals such as the true, the real and the good:

> Human rights are supposedly universal and human rights claims presuppose universal moral truths. In fact, morality can exist only as part of the fabric of particular social forms of life. Rights, therefore, if they exist at all, are social and relative to particular cultures.
>
> (Freeman 1990: 167)

NOTE: Owing to constraints of space, the last five pages from Section II of Gayatri Spivak's article as it appeared in *Third Text* 11 are omitted in this reprinting. Professor Spivak goes on to discuss the 'production' of Ayatollah Khomeini, and cites interpretations from Black British, Iranian, Turkish, and Palestinian activists/scholars.

Further reading

Journals *Boundary 2. An International Journal of Literature and Culture*; *Critical Inquiry*; *Critical Quarterly*; *New Literary History*; *PN Review*; *Representations*; *Textual Practice*; *Third Text. Third World Perspectives on Contemporary Art and Culture.*

Poetry

PN Review 99, September–October 1994 contains an extensive set of appreciations, 'Ashbery in Britain', pp. 32–81. The poetry of John Ashbery's friend, Frank O'Hara, is a lyrical and sociable body of work, represented in *The Selected Poems of Frank O'Hara* edited by Donald Allen (1991). Geoff Ward's *Statutes of Liberty. The New York School of Poets* (1993) provides contexts for Ashbery and O'Hara, and his pamphlet *Language Poetry and the American Avant-Garde* (BAAS Pamphlets in American Studies 25, British Association for AmericanStudies, 1993) is a helpful overview of poets such as Charles Bernstein, Bob Perelman, Ron Silliman, Stephen Rodefer, Lyn Hejinian, and Susan Howe, set against the competing tendencies in American poetry since the 1950s. *In the American Tree* (1986) edited by Ron Silliman, is a generous selection of this poetry. British poets with a distinctive form and content are represented in *A Various Art* (1987) edited by Andrew Crozier and Tim Longville. *Poets on Writing. Britain 1970–1991* (1992) edited by Denise Riley is a helpful anthology of essays and statements.

Fiction

The *Ulysses* of post-war fiction is still probably Thomas Pynchon, *Gravity's Rainbow* (1973), which takes, among many other things, the development of missile telemetry as a way of linking the end of the Second World War with the emergence of the Cold War stalemate. Don DeLillo has written some of the most ambitious novels about America during the 1970s and 1980s: *White Noise* (1985) was his 'breakthrough' novel, a comic tale of family life and ecological disaster. *New Essays on 'White Noise'* (1991), edited by Frank Lentricchia, is a good introduction. *Libra* (1988) is a densely researched fiction about Lee Harvey Oswald and the Kennedy assassination; see Frank Lentricchia *Introducing Don DeLillo* (1991). DeLillo's television essay for BBC's Omnibus, *The Word, the Image and the Gun* (1991) is a brilliant audio-visual compilation of his central themes, but alas lost to the airwaves. William Gibson's *Necromancer* (1984) is the cyberpunk classic which mapped the culture and politics of cyberspace. Gibson's *Virtual Light* (1993) is more firmly grounded in a near-future Californian dystopia, where the Golden Gate bridge has become a postmodern version of the Ponte Vecchio. Andrew Ross's 'Cyberpunk in Boystown', Chapter 4 of *Strange Weather. Culture, Science and Technology in the Age of Limits* (1991) is a useful overview of cyberpunk in relation to paranoid conceptions of the technological future. The fiction and essays of Angela Carter are a wonderfully satirical body of writing, alert to all of the issues of form and ethics posed by the debates over postmodernism and fiction: *Nights at the Circus* (1984) is one of her most imaginatively textured books. Linda Hutcheon's *A Poetics of Post-modernism: History, Theory and Fiction* (1987) and *The Politics of Postmodernism* (1990) contain very full bibliographies of the secondary literatures on many aspects of postmodern works.

References

APPIGNANESI, Lisa, and Sara MAITLAND (eds) (1989) *The Rushdie File*, London: Fourth Estate.

ARBERRY, Arthur J. (1955) *The Koran Interpreted*. [A respected translation of the Qur'an in poetic forms.] London: Allen and Unwin.

ASAD, Muhammad [translator] (1980) *The Message of the Qur'an*, Gibraltar: Dar al-Andalus.

EASTERMAN, Daniel (1993) 'Still lives', 210–22 in *New Jerusalems. Reflections on Islam, Fundamentalism and the Rushdie Affair*, London: Grafton.

FREEMAN, Michael (1990) 'Human rights and the corruption of governments 1789–1989', in Peter Hulme and Ludmilla Jordanova (eds) *The Enlightenment and Its Shadows*, p. 167: citing M. Sandel (ed.) (1984) *Liberalism and Its Critics*, Oxford.

LABRIE, Ross (1984) 'John Ashbery: an interview', *The American Poetry Review*, May/June: 29–33.

NEWELL, Stephanie (1992) 'The other God: Salman Rushdie's "new" aesthetic', *Literature and History*, third series 1/2: 67–87.

RAINEY, Lawrence (1989) 'The price of modernism: reconsidering the publication of *The Waste Land*', *Critical Quarterly* 31/4, Winter.

RUSHDIE, Salman (1988) *The Satanic Verses*, London and New York: Viking/Penguin. [The novel was reissued in 1991 by an anonymous grouping of publishers, The Consortium, Inc.]

—— (1990) 'In good faith', the *Independent*, 4 February, and 'Readers' Reactions' to the essay, 11 February.

RUTHVEN, Malise (1990) *A Satanic Affair: Salman Rushdie and the Rage of Islam*, London: Chatto and Windus.

SABBAH, Fitna A. (1984) *Woman in the Muslim Unconscious*, translated by Mary Jo Lakeland, New York: Pergamon.

SPIVAK, Gayatri (1986) 'French Feminism in an International Frame', excerpted pp. 36–9 in *Feminist Literary Theory. A Reader*, Mary Eagleton (ed.), Oxford: Basil Blackwell, from *Yale French Studies* 62 (1981).

TEBBIT, Norman (1990) 'Salman Rushdie by Norman Tebbit', in the 'Heroes & Villains' opinion page, the *Independent Magazine*, 8 September. And see the replies in the following issue, 15 September.

Third Text. Third World Perspectives on Contemporary Art and Culture: *Beyond the Rushdie Affair* (1990) Summer, no. 11, Rasheed Araeem (ed.), London: Kala Press.

WHEALE, Nigel (1992) 'Uttering poetry: small-press publication', in Denise Riley (ed.) *Poets on Writing. Britain 1970–1991*, London: Macmillan.

6

A New Subjectivity? John Ashbery's Three Poems

NIGEL WHEALE

Three Poems is a wry title because the medium of the work is in fact prose, an essay of over one hundred pages which is divided into three sections. These are 'The New Spirit', 'The System' and 'The Recital'. In a 1984 interview Ashbery volunteered that this was one of his two favourite works from his own writing, together with *Houseboat Days* (1977) (Labrie 1984: 31), and *Three Poems* deserves more attention than it has so far received. It is very hard to find anything comparable to *Three Poems* in contemporary British poetry, though there are a number of possible models in American and European writing, and also in pre-modern English writing. This is one index of John Ashbery's singularity, and an indication of the distance between his writing practice and what is generally understood to be poetry in Great Britain (Ward 1993A: 'The English Ashbery', 83–94). A useful text for gaining a sense of Ashbery's interests and fellow poets at a formative stage of his career is the excellent small-press journal *Locus Solus*, published in five issues from 1960 to 1962; Ashbery edited the double issue III–IV (see the bibliography below for details).

The three 'poems' are prose meditations which occasionally break into lyric flights (organized on the page as 'poems'). By adopting the para-doxical genre of the prose-poem the text immediately puts itself into a cryptic relation with our expectations; what kind of reading response is appropriate here? Prose-poems in English are usually quite brief – T. S. Eliot's 'Hysteria', for example – so Ashbery's *Three Poems* must be one of the most sustained prose-poem performances in this language. Stephen Fredman's is the most focused study of *Three Poems* so far, and he usefully contextualizes the work in relation to other prose-poem texts such as William Carlos Willliams's *Kora in Hell: Improvisations* (1920) and Robert Creeley's *Presences: A Text for Marisol* (1976) (Fredman 1990). The work begins as an enquiry into how we register our experience, and how simultaneously we might represent it to our selves and to others as writing: the reader is addressed from the beginning as absolutely complicit in this process and in the questions which it raises for writer and reader together. The urgent complicity of the reading-relation may partly derive from the fact that the ideal-other who is addressed is said to have been inspired by the poet's analyst (Ross 1986: 181). These strategies so far would seem to conform in general terms to the academic agenda for Ashbery as postmodern writer.

But this reflexion on writing is also a journal of the spirit which registers a progress through the stages of a life in such a way that any reader can enter into the (auto-)biography simultaneously with the writing persona. It is here that *Three Poems* can be described as a very pre-modern work, because this form of life-writing in fact has a huge number of antecedents. These are the various forms of confessional biography which were commonplace in the seventeenth century, and before, in which a life was examined in very general terms, using categories from the established traditions of Christian confession and self-examination (Fredman 1990: 118). This pre-modern version of identity was much less particularized than we are accustomed to, and was content to describe its self, and undergo its experiences, in categories of collectively recognized event. In this chapter I shall observe the early-modern convention of writing the pronoun forms 'our self', 'my self', and so on, as separated elements, since this conveys the kind of distanced, im-personal identity which is implied in this kind of self-consideration.

Three Poems on this description is like any number of early-modern spiritual guides and autobiographies: John Bunyan's *Grace Abounding* (1666) or *The Pilgrim's Progress* (1678), Thomas Traherne's so-called *Centuries of Meditations* (written in the 1660s), or Jeremy Taylor's *Holy Living* (1650). *Three Poems* of course is not simply a spiritual treatise set in Christian theological traditions. In fact each time that 'the transcendent' or 'the holy' is approached within the narrative, the text turns it down as a final option, and religious belief is folded back into the arrays of our experience as simply one more possible option. Religion in this way is humanized as another of the tropes to which people are prone, and no more than that. Nevertheless *Three Poems* does often read like the work of an uncensorious New England divine, writing on how to live a good and reflective life. Andrew Ross locates theological influence in Ashbery's poetry like this: 'the discussion of time in Ashbery's later work increasingly comes to refer, directly or not, to the "case" of Eliot', and Ross describes the spirit-manual aspect of *Three Poems* very acutely as an 'aped confessional banality' which 'allows Ashbery access to areas of religious

discourse where the reader knows he has no serious business to conduct'
(Ross 1982: 190–1). This is well said, but on my description it does not
give enough scope to the function of the soul-journal convention in the
organization of the whole work. Ashbery himself describes the variety of
tones in *Three Poems* like this: 'at times it sounds like journalism or letter
writing or philosophy, both Cracker-barrel and Platonic, and so on. I
guess I was trying to "democratize" language' (Labrie 1984: 31). This
notion of 'democratizing language', including apparently superannuated
forms of spiritual confession, is a useful description of the process through
which the text opens so many language registers to the reader's habita-
tion, which is the work of this prose, as much as of Ashbery's regular
poetry:

> What need for purists when the demotic is built
>   to last,
> To outlast us, and no dialect hears us?
>   ('Purists Will Object', Ashbery 1984: 17)

Three Poems is therefore partly an emptied autobiography, one of those
pre-modern forms where the general tendencies of any existence are
sketched so that they can be coloured in with the particularities of each
life that speculates about its self. In this way the prose deploys impersonality as a freeing of the irrelevant or embarrassing particularities of the
writer's life in order to offer instead the fiction of a larger, generalized
format where other lives – those of its readers, for example – may be
inspected through an active occupation of the opened form. *Three Poems*
provides a generous, non-specific biographical mode which is mercifully
free of confessional display or heroisms on the part of the poet. These
are qualities of medieval and early-modern conventions of biographical
description, not the expressive-individualism of high modernism, but
they also share some significant aspects of early twentieth-century
experimental styles. European modernism also cultivated impersonality
as a formal tactic in writing and painting, partly as a means to articulate
new kinds of perception. Ashbery's criticism and reviews of the visual
arts demonstrate a wide knowledge of, and consistent interest in
Surrealism, and a prose récit such as Giorgio de Chirico's *Hebdomeros*
(1929) is another analogy for the wilder aspects of the narrative conduct
of *Three Poems* (Ashbery 1989: 10–11, 401–4).

The radical selflessness of *Three Poems* for example recalls Virginia
Woolf's novel *The Waves* (1931), which she described not as prose-poem

but as a 'playpoem'. Here six characters speak successive monologues so that the entire business of the novel is transacted through their words. Their speeches are given at various stages of life, again like the subject in *Three Poems*, and the stages are disposed into nine sections. Each section is prefaced with the brief italicized description of a beach at successive times of the day. This gives the sense that the characters' progress through their lives is synchronized with this progress through one over-arching diurnal period. Other than this temporal frame there is no descriptive writing and the only parts of the novel free of the characters' perspectives are the introit phrases 'Susan said', 'Bernard said', 'Jinny said', 'Louis said', 'Neville said', 'Rhoda said'. Woolf intended her writing to be 'pliant and rich enough to provide a wall for the book from oneself' (Bell 1972: 73) and this was inspired by her desire to recast novel form so as to escape kinds of narrative conduct which she felt were restrictive, and predominantly male-oriented. But her organization of narrative in the novels after *Jacob's Room* (1922) also produced a series of extraordinary arrangements of time in relation to the subjectivity of her characters. Ashbery's writing of a transparent subject-position in *Three Poems*, and the ways in which temporality is central to the text, again ally his work with classic modernism rather than creating an entirely novel category of the postmodern.

Therefore I would argue that this 'new' subjectivity, which theorists have offered as a distinctive formation of identity 'under postmodernism' can actually be referred to well-established forms of representing historical subjectivity from other periods:

> The wind is now fresh and full, with leaves and other things flying. And to release it from its condition of hardness you will have to take apart the notion of you so as to reconstruct it from an intimate knowledge of its inner workings.
> (Ashbery 1972: 19–20. Referenced by page number subsequently.)

The characteristic attention of *Three Poems* is a phenomenology of the spirit, a writing which attends to the shifting reception of the world by our selves as subject. It explores the ways in which we might catch a view of our selves as we involuntarily change, or alternatively as we behave with complete predictability. What knowledge do we need, and how might it be seized? I will give quite lengthy quotations from *Three Poems* to convey a sense of the writing and argument because there is a fundamental problem in excerpting from texts like this: it is very easy to misrepresent their quality through isolated statements which in fact depend crucially on being modified by their context within the sequence of writing. So it would be possible to make an anthology of pious remarks from *Three Poems*, rather as authors like George Eliot or Rudyard Kipling were turned into mottoes for calendars and commonplace books. This is obviously the case with any kind of quotation, but in Ashbery's poetics, the textual tactic which silently qualifies or cancels one register with another produces a continuous interference pattern, a shifting moiré of intertextuality, so that a remark which might appear to be substantive and free-standing is glossed or elided by what follows in the narrative. This is another aspect of the writing's 'undecidability', and of the postponement of conclusive meaning within the text.

> In this scheme of things what is merely pleasant has to die to be born again as pleasure, and although it seems unfair this includes your outside view, openness, your penetrability and force to penetrate through outside agents that are merely the logical extensions of your inner decision to act and and to bring this action to bear on the constellation of everyday phenomena. And so a new you takes shape. You can stand it at first. If the beloved were an angel, then this you would be the nameless spirit that watches from afar, halfway between heaven's celestial light and dull Acheron. (21)

The second person pronoun is a fundamental resource in Ashbery's address to the reader, as it was for Auden in the 1930s (Ward 1993A: 106; Fredman 1990: 116). 'You' accesses the poem immediately to 'us', and its use is a strategy that seems to allow us to take on the fictions and propositions of the poetry in a very direct manner. As a vacant language-position, or 'shifter', the pronouns also function conjunctively to link together the disparate statements made by the poetry and prose. The meaning-crisis of the writing in this way bears acutely on the personal name which we are offered. But as reader we can also resist the ascription of 'you' and 'we', and refuse to be included within these pronominal categories. By means of this reader-scepticism we can inspect the too-tidy forms of identity which the pronoun appears to offer. Employing this tactic of feigned intimacy, Ashbery's writings are never concerned with a particular, identifiable third-person subject, they do not have an obvious social realism that evokes other persons by description and analysis. They would have received the Thumbs Down from Andrey Zhdanov and comrades at the Soviet Writers' Congress in 1934. Their

address is always via the much more gently coercive ligature of 'you' –
Who, me, tovarich?

> But it is hard, this not knowing which direction to take, only knowing that
> you are moving in one, not because no rest was decreed for you but
> because the force that shot you here remains through inertia ... (29–30)

Three Poems formulates in its prose and metrics the nearly impercept-
ible changes in tone of lived experience, the lining of any one's life. The
narrative is quietly unglamorous but persistently acute as it enacts the
ways in which experience modulates under the weight of habit. There
are few dramatic interventions:

> the other, unrelated happenings that form a kind of sequence of fantastic
> reflections as they succeed each other at a pace and according to an inner
> necessity of their own – these, I say, have hardly ever been looked at from
> a vantage point other than the historian's and an arcane historian's at that.
> The living aspect of these obscure phenomena has never to my knowledge
> been examined from a point of view like the painter's: in the round, bathed
> in a sufficient flow of overhead light, with 'all its imperfections on its head'
> and yet without prejudice of the exaggerations either of the anathematist
> or the eulogist: quietly, in short, and I hope succinctly. Judged from this
> angle the whole affair will, I think, partake of and benefit from the
> enthusiasm not of the religious fanatic but of the average, open-minded,
> intelligent person who has never interested himself before in these matters
> either from not having had the leisure to do so or from ignorance of their
> existence. (56)

But the prose also describes the dynamics of nameless crises, un-
locatable anxiety, as a general perspective on the modalities of our
experience, and always with a compelling sense of time at work in the
heart of being:

> the everyday glamor of a 'personal life,' keeping a diary and so
> forth, is the outward sign of this progression that is built into us like the
> chain of breathing. So there is no need to wait to be transformed: you are
> already. (23)

The fluctuation of affect is explored, as the changes in our emotions can
drain value and attachment from the world before us. The place of objects
throughout Ashbery's writing is telling, they can be articulate and full of
interest for the perceiver, or bleached of meaning. These changes in the

kind of value which we give to things act as a fluctuating measure of the psyche's projection, of how perky we feel at any given moment. Delicate changes of registration like these are described as they are undergone through the process of maturing, growing older:

> When one is in one's late thirties, ordinary things – like a pebble or a glass of water – take on an expressive sheen. One wants to know more about them, and one is in turn lived by them. Young people might not envy this kind of situation, perhaps rightly so, yet there is now interleaving the pages of suffering and indifference to suffering a prismatic space that cannot be seen, merely felt as the result of an angularity that must have existed from earliest times and is only now succeeding in making its presence felt through the mists of helpless acceptance of everything else projected on our miserable, dank span of days. One is aware of it as an open field of narrative possibilities. (41)

How true, feels the reader in his late-thirties; younger travellers will glide over this section with only a politely feigned interest. This might therefore be a passage which some readers could receive unironically and, as it were, authentically, in the manner of a soul-journal. But since the description is no more than 'an open field of narrative possibilities', it can be reconstructed and re-ironized at any moment, which is what occurs next. Mock-astrological determinisms are deployed in the high-medieval manner which used the star-sign system as a way of amplifying human emotions and rites of passage. The use of this antique mode here in *Three Poems* seems to establish the merely rhetorical nature of authenticity itself: 'All this happened in April as the sun was entering the house of Aries, the Ram ...' (43).

An unnamed erotic crisis is building at this point, presented with humour, and it offers a rare opportunity to observe Ashbery making a revision. In the first printed version of 'The New Spirit', which appeared in *Paris Review* 50 (Fall 1970), page 148 includes 11 sentences which are cut from page 45 of *Three Poems* as it appears in book form:

> Defenestration had become quite common. A lot of people stood around in public chuckling to themselves at not having doped it out before ... Yet it bothered her obscurely. Why so much fuss if things were just following their natural course? Where was the glamor? Who was left to see it? But she decided to shut up about it for the time being.
>
> (Ashbery 1970: 148)

The revision takes out some buffoonery and lightness, as well as removing a rare female figure who is the subject of the meditation's free indirect narration at this point.

The central section of *Three Poems*, 'The System', begins ominously:

> The system was breaking down … At this time of life whatever being there is is doing a lot of listening, as though to the feeling of the wind before it starts, and it slides down this anticipation of itself, already full-fledged, a lightning existence that has come into our own. (53)

The competencies and limitations of maturity are addressed, of fortunate and adequately resourced lives undisturbed by social dislocation or personal tragedy on any scale. And there is also consideration of an unfashionable topic, the quality of happiness, described as exultation, but also as diffused good feeling or bonheur, as it is caught up with low-level background anxieties about the kinds of progress we are making:

> the bases for true reflective thinking had been annihilated by the scourge, and at the same time there was the undeniable fact of exaltation on many fronts, of a sense of holiness growing up through the many kinds of passion like a tree with branches bearing candelabra higher and higher up until they almost vanish from sight and are confused with the stars whose earthly avatars they are … (57)

The lack of consideration given to the intransigence of the world, political idiocy, social catastrophe, has been set aside from this agenda. The entire narrative focuses inwardly, like a renaissance pastoral which might be mistaken for landscape but which is actually psychical space: 'Yet this space wasn't made just for the uses of peace, but also for action, for planned assaults on the iniquity and terror outside' (82). This terrain is the kind of militant 'paradise within happier far' (*Paradise Lost* XII 587) that can work through the world because of the benign assurance that it brings to the possessor:

> we carry both inside and outside around with us as we move purposefully toward an operation that is going to change us on every level, and is also going to alter the balance of power of happiness in the world in our favor and that of all the human beings in the world. (82)

How do we gain a sense of totality, in what frame of mind do we persist, persevere? 'The Recital' is the final short third section of *Three Poems*, a brief coda that becomes more desperate in face of the repetition of life's insoluble problems. What is the relation of unreflective to reflective living? The desire for summation is consistently present in this prose-poem, the hope that we might obtain a grasp on this all-enveloping process, and hope for a degree of objectivity which might be cast back over self and actions. Therefore the text rehearses some of the forms of appeal which are conventionally made in order to define any one's progress through their life. The cramping, functional, mercenary view of existence-as-career is examined – 'And this way of speaking has trapped each one of us' (70), or more anthropologically, 'life-as-ritual':

> Here again, if backward looks were possible, not nostalgia but a series of carefully selected views, hieratic as icons, the difficulty would be eased and self could merge with selflessness, in a true appreciation of the tremendous volumes of eternity. But this is impossible because the ritual is by definition something impersonal, and can only move further in that direction. (71)

Frank O'Hara, Ashbery's friend and contemporary, famously described Ashbery's poetry as forever 'marrying the world', and this may be all that needs to be said about his writing. Ashbery's meditations through democratized language in *Three Poems* put language as our human field inescapably before our attention, and continually embrace the largest categories of time and space in such a way as to show that the world is only comprehended in its naming:

> that gorgeous, motley organism would tumble or die out unless each particle of its well-being were conserved as preciously as the idea of the whole. For universal love is as special an aspect as carnal love or any of the other kinds: all forms of mental and spiritual activity must be practiced and encouraged equally if the whole affair is to prosper. (58)

This kind of totalizing gesture is like the action of 'Ithaca', the penultimate chapter in Joyce's *Ulysses*, where Leopold Bloom and Stephen Dedalus are presented in conversation, but through a speech rewritten as a mock-scholastic dialogue which persistently expands to fill all known limits. The language of 'Ithaca' outruns its characters, naming the limits, and metamorphosing everything it describes into nothing but language. But this is not to say that therefore Ashbery's modern text abdicates from moral argument in a weak postmodern fashion.

L=A=N=G=U=A=G=E: Ashbery's postmodern successors

During the later 1970s, just as Ashbery was beginning to find wider recognition with *Self-Portrait in a Convex Mirror*, a number of American poets had begun writing who were more firmly and explicitly identified with postmodern theory. These were the so-called Language poets, who include, among others, Charles Bernstein, Ron Silliman, Bob Perelman, Stephen Rodefer, Susan and Fanny Howe, and Lyn Hejinian (Silliman 1986; Ward 1993B). Where Ashbery's poetry can be derived from a particular version of European high modernism, and is then often approached via description constructed from academic theory, the poets of the Language tendency were more directly inspired by the reception of European critical theory in the United States during the 1970s, in some cases writing programmatically from consciously adopted theoretical positions (Fredman 1990: 150–61). Again in contrast to Ashbery, poets such as Charles Bernstein and Bruce Andrews write with an explicitly political intention, having a commitment to what they see as the subversive possibilities of poetry as an alternative form of language:

> It is our sense that the project of poetry does not involve turning language into a commodity for consumption; instead, it involves repossessing the sign through close attention to, and active participation in, its production.
> (Andrews and Bernstein 1984: x)

Charles Bernstein's poetry therefore becomes at one level more explicit than Ashbery's, because it is intended as a critique of the values of consumer capitalism, but in another way it is more obscure than Ashbery, as it simultaneously attempts to reflect on the materiality of language itself as a social fact. For Bernstein, poetry should adopt stylistic practices that undermine the false clarities of the 'authoritative plain style' of discourse, 'a voice that was patriarchal, monologic, authoritative, impersonal' (Bernstein 1981: 587). Bernstein's theoretical description of how this might be done actually conforms quite closely to the kind of description which I am making here about the effect of reading Ashbery's *Three Poems*. Bernstein describes a text which

> calls upon the reader to be actively involved in the process of constituting its meaning, the reader becoming neither a neutral observer to a described exteriority or to an enacted interiority. The text formally involves the process of response/interpretation and in so doing makes the reader aware of herself or himself as producer as well as consumer of meaning.
> (Bernstein 1981: 595)

This could be exactly the process of reception which I envisage for a reader of *Three Poems*. Bernstein's own poetry, however, is narrower than this description suggests, exactly because it is more politically directed and linguistically disrupted than Ashbery's characteristic manner. It might be the case that a poetry which offers a more generalized subject-position for the reader to engage with actually provides more scope for reflection than texts written as self-conscious agit-propaganda.

In conclusion: a pre-modern, homeric truth

Hearing the poet read her/his own work, in the same room, a person speaking to persons, without benefit of printed relays or other facsimile modes, the listener can find it difficult not to inhabit every metaphoric site which the declamation of the poet offers (Oliver 1989: 159–72). The voice inflects its particular meaning, and the figure of the poet's presence commands a kind of attention which is utterly specific and poignant. The vibrating column of voiced air is grammar's address to the hearer. 'You' is notoriously a shifting value, which in the shared room of the reading can be possessed with a complete conviction as it is hearingly received. In the silent and solitary reading of poems however the strategy is much more risk-laden. Sometimes the affective connection can be made to the invitation of the open pronoun, at other times the textual address is blank. Perhaps this is why even individual reading in the renaissance was reading-aloud, so that the text should be heard as well as seen. There is a humanism in Ashbery's poems, which we discover when for whatever subliminal reasons we are inhabited by a line or sequence within the poem. This is a theoretically indefensible position which says something like 'Go and hear the poet, and you will understand – at least, on a good night, when all the intangibles are at work, and the omens favourable.' The performed dimension is actual, even if it perpetually escapes analysis, and is in danger of becoming no more than a mystical value.

Therefore I am arguing that John Ashbery's writing should not be simply conflated with a postmodern trickiness, nor understood only through the stratagems of a 'deconstructive' reading (Connor 1991; Rand 1991). The apparent subjectlessness of *Three Poems* renders the writing habitable in very direct ways by any reader, and within the traditional categories which I have indicated. This seems to be the kind of reading which Robert Creeley made of *Three Poems* when he described the book as being 'as near a communal self as I've witnessed' (Fredman 1990: 117). When as reader/auditor we occupy the address of the poem, questions of value are immediately and necessarily implicated by this process. If

relativism or nihilism is just democracy with a bad name

the narrative of *Three Poems* is only tricksy, and works simply by ironic juxtaposition, by the undercutting of one tonal discourse by another which is more 'knowing', then it is a hollow and cute exercise. It would be no more than the anomic circulation of the possibilities of discourse, one 'slipping' under another, suffering occlusion, a victim of the modish indecidability theories of meaning and subjectivity. My preferred reading is one that finds a hierarchy of meaning in the text, that takes certain moments as immune from corrosive irony and relativism, and effectively reads the discourse as an ethical address. But just where those moments may be is an issue that is minutely particular to each reading subject:

> And yet it results in a downward motion, or rather a floating one
> In which the blue surroundings drift slowly up and past you
> To realize themselves some day, while, you, in this nether world that
>   could not be better
> Waken each morning to the exact value of what you did and said,
>   which remains.

('Definition of Blue', Ashbery 1970: 53–4)

Inhabiting the open subject-position offered by the text the reader is then involved with the inescapable question of 'exact value' through these points of application. These are moments of 'nisus' – of pressure, exertion, striving, effort – which oblige the interpreter to take an option, attitude, or bearing. 'Nisus' is a fine old word, used in classical and patristic Latin, as in Augustine's *City of God*, and appearing in English late in the seventeenth century as a description of physiological movement. This is to say that at some level the best texts are always also a form of moral philosophy, though the ethical options are transacted through the colours, tones, textures of the aesthetic elements deployed (Ward 1993A: 'Postmodernism and the end of representation', 146–56). They have the possibilities which prompt diverse reader-responses in the direction of the true and the good, which because it is defined in a context-free manner, can be applicable to different moral constituencies.

Three Poems was composed during the late 1960s and early 1970s, at the time of the national traumas of defeat and withdrawal from Vietnam, and the nadir of Richard Nixon's presidency. Events in the public world are never overtly mentioned in this writing because *Three Poems* is the kind of inward narration which does not include the world in any manifest way. Therefore the text allows any reading awareness to import con-temporaneous politics into its apparent quietism, and register the consequences: 'the poet's polygamous inheritance is not poethood itself, nor its privileges, but the whole symbolic, or social order, which comes with a given language' (Ross 1986: 177).

References

ANDREWS, Bruce, and Charles BERNSTEIN (1984) *The L=A=N=G=U=A=G=E Book*, Carbondale and Edwardsville: Southern Illinois University Press.

ASHBERY, John (1970A) 'The New Spirit', *The Paris Review*, Fall, 50: 115–53.

—— (1970B) *The Double Dream of Spring*, New York: E. P. Dutton & Co., Inc.

—— (1972) *Three Poems*, New York: The Viking Press.

—— (1984) *A Wave*, Manchester: Carcanet.

—— (1987) 'The System', *Selected Poems*, 127–64, London: Paladin, Grafton Books.

—— (1989) edited with an introduction by David Bergman, *Reported Sightings. Art Chronicles, 1957–1987*, Manchester: Carcanet.

BELL, Quentin (1972) *Virginia Woolf: A Biography. Volume Two, Mrs Woolf 1912–1941*, London: The Hogarth Press.

BERNSTEIN, Charles (1981) 'Writing and Method', 583–98 in Silliman (1986).

CONNOR, Steve (1991) 'Points of departure: deconstruction and John Ashbery's "Sortes Vergilianae"' in Antony Easthope and John O. Thompson (eds) *Contemporary Poetry Meets Modern Theory*, Hemel Hempstead: Harvester/Wheatsheaf.

DE CHIRICO, Giorgio ([1929] 1964) *Hebdomeros, A Novel*, translated from the French with an introduction by Margaret Crosland, London: Peter Owen.

FREDMAN, Stephen (1990) *Poet's Prose: The Crisis in American Verse*, 2nd edn, Cambridge: Cambridge University Press.

LABRIE, Ross (1984) 'John Ashbery: an interview', *The American Poetry Review* May/June: 29–33.

LEHMAN, David (ed.) (1980) *Beyond Amazement. New Essays on John Ashbery*, Ithaca and London: Cornell University Press.

Locus Solus (1960–2) A small-press journal in five issues edited by James Schuyler (I and V), Kenneth Koch (II), John Ashbery (III–IV, double issue), and Harry Mathews, Lans-en-Vercors, Isère, France. Ashbery's

294-page 'Double Issue of New Poetry' included work by LeRoi Jones, Larry Rivers, Robin Blaser, Diane di Prima, Frank O'Hara, Barbara Guest and a section of 'Three French Poets', Denis Roche, Marcelin Pleynet, and Pierre Martory, parallel texts with translations by Ashbery. *Locus Solus* took its name from the title of a novel by Raymond Roussel (1877–1933) published in 1914. On Roussel, see *Reported Sightings* pp. 170–1.

MOHANTY, S. P., and Jonathan MONROE (1987) 'John Ashbery and the articulation of the social', *Diacritics* 17/2 Summer.

OLIVER, Douglas (1989) 'Emotion in literary response', in *Poetry and Narrative in Performance*, London: Macmillan.

RAND, Richard (1991) 'Sortes Vergilianae', in Antony Easthope and John O. Thompson (eds) *Contemporary Poetry Meets Modern Theory*, Hemel Hempstead: Harvester/Wheatsheaf.

ROSS, Andrew (1986) *The Failure of Modernism. Symptoms of American Poetry*, New York: Columbia University Press.

SILLIMAN, Ron (1986) *In the American Tree*, University of Maine: The National Poetry Foundation.

WARD, Geoff (1993A) *Statutes of Liberty. The New York School of Poets*, London: Macmillan.

—— (1993B) *Language Poetry and the American Avant-Garde*, British Association for American Studies Pamphlet 25, Keele: BAAS.

7
Reading The Satanic Verses

GAYATRI CHAKRAVORTY SPIVAK

In post-coloniality, every metropolitan definition is dislodged. The general mode for the post-colonial is citation, re-inscription, re-routing the historical. *The Satanic Verses*¹ cannot be placed within the European avant-garde, but the successes and failures of the European avant-garde are available to it.

Peter Bürger pointed out to Jürgen Habermas some time ago that all deliberate attempts at integrating the aesthetic sphere with the *Lebenswelt* must take into account their profound and continued separation.² But, in post-coloniality, all metropolitan accounts are set askew. The case of *The Satanic Verses* is a case of the global *Lebenswelt* – the praxis and politics of life – intercepting an aesthetic object so that a mere reading of it has become impossible.

The case of Mr Fukuyama, fully 'assimilated' Asian-American, who, put off as a graduate student by the nihilism of Derrida and Barthes, has written an article on Hegel's End of History as USA Today, bored but in charge, indolently defending freedom of expression against terrorism, is not outside of this contemporary fact of life. The United States is not outside the post-colonial globe.³

Here is a metropolitan aphorism. 'The birth of the reader must be at the cost of the death of the Author.'⁴ Faced with the case of Salman Rushdie, how are we to read this sentence? I have often said that the (tragic) theatre of the (sometimes farcically self-indulgent) script of post-structuralism is 'the other side'.⁵ The aphorism above is a case in point. Let us read slowly, word for word.

Barthes is writing here not of the death of the writer (although he *is* writing, quite copiously, of writing) or of the subject, or yet of the agent, but of the *Author*. The author, who is not only taken to be the authority for the meaning of a text, but also, when possessed of authority, possessed *by that fact* of 'moral or legal supremacy, the power to influence the conduct or action of others'; and, when authorizing, 'giving legal force to, making legally valid' (*OED*). Thus, even on the most 'literal' level of the dictionary, 'the birth of the reader must be at the cost of the death of the Author' takes on a different resonance.

Barthes is speaking of the birth not of the critic, who, apart from the academically certified authority of the meaning of a text is, also, in the strictest sense, a judge. It is not of such a being that Barthes announces the birth. He announces the birth of the reader who 'is simply that *someone* who holds together in a single field all the traces by which the written text is constituted'.[6] It is the birth of this someone that is conditional upon the death of the Author. The writer is, in this robust sense, a reader at the performance of writing. Or, as Barthes writes, '*writing* can no longer designate an operation of recording..., rather, it designates exactly what linguists, referring to Oxford philosophy, call a performative... in which the enunciation has no other content... than the act by which it is uttered'.[7] When Barthes writes, further, that 'the reader is without history, biography, psychology', I believe he means there is no specific set of history, biography, psychology, belonging to the writer-as-privileged-reader or the ideal reader implied in the text, that gives us the Reader as such. When the writer and reader are born again and again together, the Author(ity)-function is dead, the critic is not mentioned. There is the pleasure of the text.

In the next decade and a half, Roland Barthes will tone down the binaries that seem entailed by these pronouncements. But the words 'the Death of the author' have become a slogan, both proving and disproving the Authority of the Author. And Foucault's question 'What is an Author?' has been construed by most readers as a rhetorical question to be answered in the negative.[8] I reckon with these signs of the times by turning, as usual, toward Derrida.

Derrida usually comes at these things from the other end. He is not an overthrower of myths but rather is interested in seeing how a myth works both as medicine and poison. For him the Author is present in excess. I have not yet read *The Critical Difference*, but I believe I will agree with Barbara Johnson's distinction between Barthes the anti-constructionist and Derrida's *de*-construction.[9]

Moving with Derrida, I can say, that when Barthes and Foucault are monumentalized as marks for the death and nothingness of the Author, everything happens as if the sign 'Author' has no history, no linguistic or cultural limits. I turn back to the dictionary, where I began, and I see that, in the Rushdie affair, it is the late Ayatollah who can be seen as filling the Author-function, and Salman Rushdie, himself, caught in a different cultural logic, is no more than the writer-as-performer. Let me now turn to another aspect of the excessive presence of the author in Derrida's reading habits: what he calls 'the politics of the proper name'.[10]

In order to read the politics of the proper name, Derrida pays close attention to the staging of the author *as* author by the author. 'We would,' he writes, 'be mistaken if we understood it as a simple presentation of identity. (Me, such and such, male or female, individual or collective subject.)'[11] I believe the author of *The Satanic Verses* is 'staged' rather than 'simply presented' in the vestigial rememoration of a face and a proper name in the poem published in *Granta* last autumn.[12] Because the author-function dies hard, that poem is not only outside of technological reproducibility, *hors de reproduction*, but also, and strictly speaking, an artwork, an *hors d'oeuvre*, an exergue or a flysheet, whose topos, like (its) temporality, strangely dislocates what we, without tranquil assurance, would like to understand as the time of life and the time of life's *récit*, or the writing of life by the living.[13]

As I will go on to propose, *in* the novel, Rushdie's staging of the author is more recognizably 'modernist' (not what Barthes, or indeed French critics as a rule would call 'modern'), not de-centered but fragmented by dramatic irony, the question of authorship repeatedly and visibly suspended by foregrounding. But the violence of the *fatwa* continuing the signature after *its* author's death, has jolted modernist playfulness into a Nietzschean *Ecce Homo* in Rushdie's irreproducible poem.

In the first part of my paper, I will attempt the impossible; a reading of *The Satanic Verses* as if nothing has happened since late 1988. The second part will try to distinguish the cultural politics of what has happened, by assembling a dossier of responses from various subject-positions in contemporary political geography. In the third part, I will try to make parts I and II come together in the element of an intellectual history. And perhaps this will allow me a conclusion.

I

First, then, the reading:

The Satanic Verses, in spite of all its plurality, has rather an aggressive central theme: the post-colonial divided between two identities: migrant and national.

As migrant, the post-colonial may attempt to become the metropolitan: this is Saladin Chamcha in his first British phase: 'I am a man to whom certain things are of importance: rigour, self-discipline, reason, the pursuit of what is noble without recourse to that old crutch, God. The ideal of beauty, the possibility of exaltation, the mind' (SV 135–6). This self-definition of the migrant *as* metropolitan is obviously not the book's preferred definition.

The post-colonial may, also, keep himself completely separated *from* the metropolis *in* the metropolis as the fanatic exile. This is represented in the least conclusive section of the book, the place of dark foreboding, the subcontinental Imam ('desh' is a north Indian word which signifies his country), who must destroy the woman touched by the West. This is also not preferred: 'Exile is a soulless country' (SV 208).

What we see in process in the greater part of *The Satanic Verses* is the many fragmented national representations coming together in serious and comic – serious *when* comic and vice versa – figures of resistance. In the hospital, a highly paid male model based in Bombay,

> now changed into a 'manticore' ... [with] an entirely human body, but [the] head of a ferocious tiger, with three rows of teeth ... whisper[s] solemnly ... [while] break[ing] wind continually ... 'They describe us ... They have the power of description, and we succumb to the pictures they construct'.
>
> (SV 167–8)

These monsters organize a 'great escape', and 'take ... the low roads to London town ... going their separate ways, without hope, but also without shame' (SV 170–1).

On another register, and two-hundred odd pages later, 'a minute woman in her middle seventies gives us a related but more upbeat message:

> We are here to change things ... African, Caribbean, Indian, Pakistani, Bangladeshi, Cypriot, Chinese, we are other than what we would have been if we had not crossed the oceans ... We have been made again: but I say we shall also be the ones to remake this society, to shape it from the bottom to the top.
>
> (SV 413–14)

There is framing and dramatic irony everywhere, but never all the way. For example, it is at this meeting that Saladin encounters

> a young woman [who gives] his [conservative British] attire an amused once-over ... She was wearing a lenticular badge ... At some angles it read,

Uhuru for the Simba; at others, *Freedom for the Lion.* 'It's on account of the meaning of his chosen name,' she explained redundantly. 'In African.' Which language? . . . she shrugged . . . It was African: born, by the sound of her in Lewisham, or Deptford, or New Cross, that was all she needed to know . . . As if all causes were the same, all histories interchangeable.

(SV 413, 415)

Most strongly in the hospital section of the book, aptly called 'Ellowen Deeowen', the effect of fragmentation, citation, fast-shifting perspectives is sustained through echoes from British literature. This embedding in the history of the literature of England and Ireland – the echoes from *A Portrait of the Artist As a Young Man* are a text for interpretation in themselves – may prove the most seductive for metropolitan readers.

But the book will not let us forget that the metropolitan reader is among 'the describers'. The post-colonial is not only a migrant but also the citizen of a 'new' nation for which the colonial experience is firmly in the past, a past somewhat theatrically symbolized in Gibreel Farishta's dream of Mirza Sayeed Akhtar's house *Peristan*, 'built seven generations ago', perhaps 'a mere contraction of *Perownestan*', after 'an English architect much favoured by the colonial authorities, whose only style was that of the neo-classical English country house' (SV 230).

Mirza Akhtar is a *zamindar* – member of a landowning class, collecting land-revenue for the British, created at the end of the eighteenth century. He and his wife thus mark modern Indian elite post-colonial public culture in rather an obvious way:

In the city [they] were known as one of the most 'modern' and 'go-go' couples on the scene; they collected contemporary art and threw wild parties and invited friends round for fumbles in the dark on sofas while watching soft-porno VCRs.

(SV 227)

Because the migrant as paradigm is a dominant theme in theorizations of post-coloniality, it is easy to overlook Rushdie's resolute effort to represent contemporary India. Whereas the topical caricature of the Bombay urban worlds of the popular film industry, of rhapsodic 'left' politics, of Muslim high society, of the general atmosphere of communalism, carries an idiomatic conviction, it is at least this reader's sense that so-called 'magical realism' becomes an alibi in the fabrication of Titlipur-Chatnapatna, the village and the country town. But then, these might be the constitutive asymmetries of the imagination – itself a fabricated word – that is given the name 'migrant'.

(And perhaps it is only in this sense that the drifting migrant imagination is paradigmatic, of the 'imagination' as such, not only of the historical case of post-coloniality. Here migrancy is the name of the institution that in-habits the indifferent anonymity of space and dockets climate and soil-type and the inscription of the earth's body. In this general sense, 'migrancy' is not derived.)

But since this general sense is never not imbricated with the narrow sense – our contemporary predicament – the trick or turn is not to assume either the metropolitan or the national as the standard and *judge* some bit of this plural landscape in terms of it. In learning to practise the turn, if only to sense it slip away, we can guess that the deliberate oppositional stance of the European avant-garde is itself part of an instituted metropolitan reversal, among the 'describers' – again.

Thus every canvas will have a spot that is less 'real' than others. Excusing it away as an entailment of migrancy in general is no less dubious a gesture than accusing it as a historical or sociological transgression. I do therefore note that, within the protocols of *The Satanic Verses*, it is contemporary rural India that clings to magical realism as an alibi and thus provides a clue to the politics of the writing subject, the scribe. This would lead us to a deconstructive gesture toward the claim of magical realism as a privileged taxonomic description, and a consideration of alternative styles and systems of the representation of rural India.[14]

Within the labyrinth of such gestures, we must acknowledge that, writing as a migrant, Rushdie still militates against privileging the migrant or the exilic voice narrowly conceived, even as he fails in that very effort. A *mise-en-abyme*, perhaps, the eternal site of the migrant's desire, but also a persistent critique of metropolitan migrancy, his own slot in the scheme of things. The message and the medium of his book are marked by this conflict.

In other words, I do not think the 'cosmopolitan *challenge* to national culture' is perceived by Rushdie as only a challenge.[15] Perhaps it is even an aporia for him, an impossible decision between two opposed decidables with two mutually cancelling sets of consequences, a decision which gets made, nonetheless, for one set, since life must operate as a passive or active *différance* of death, as we know from our most familiar experiences: 'I wanted to write about a thing I find difficult to admit even to myself, which is the fact that I left home'.[16]

The Indian world of the book is Muslim-based. India's Islamic culture, high and low, is too easily ignored by contemporary hegemonic constructions of national identity as well as international benevolence. Islamic India is another theme of migrancy, unconnected with the recent colonial past. For Islam as such has its head turned away from the subcontinent, across the Arabian Sea, perpetually emigrant toward Mecca. Within this turned-away-ness, Rushdie plants the migrant's other desire, the search for roots as far down as they'll go. The name of this radical rootedness is, most often, religion. Thus in the section called Mahound, Rushdie re-opens the institution of Revelation, the origin of the Koran. It is paradoxical that the protection against desacralization, writing in the name of the false prophet, Mahound rather than Mohammed, has been read, quite legitimately, by the Law where Religion is the 'real' (there can be no other Law), as blasphemy.

The question is not if the book is blasphemous. The question is not even the profound belief of heretics and blasphemers. The question is rather: how is blasphemy to be punished? Can it be punished? What is the distinction between punishment and nourishment? And further, in the name of what do we judge the punishers?

The story of Mahound in *The Satanic Verses* is a story of negotiation in the name of woman. As so often, woman becomes the touchstone of blasphemy.

One of the most interesting features about much of Rushdie's work is his anxiety to write woman into the narrative of history. Here again we have to record a failure.[17] (But I am more interested in failed texts. What is the use of a 'successful' text? What happens to the recorder of failed texts? As a post-colonial migrant, 'a tall, thin Bengali woman with cropped hair' (SV 536), like Swatilekha – the 'real' name of the woman playing the lead character in Ray's film version of Tagore's *The Home and the World* – an 'actress' acting out the script of female Anglicization – read emancipation – by male planning in the colonial dispensation, I am part of Rushdie's text, after all.) In *Shame*, the women seem powerful only as monsters, of one sort or another. *The Satanic Verses* must end with Salahuddin Chamchawalla's reconciliation with *father* and nationality, even if the last sentence records sexual difference in the idiom of casual here." "I'm coming," he answered her, and turned away from the view' (SV 547).

All through, the text is written on the register of male bonding and unbonding, the most important being, of course, the double subject of migrancy, Gibreel Farishta and Saladin Chamcha. The two are tortured by obsession with women, go through them, even destroy them, within a gender code that is never opened up, never questioned, in this book where so much is called into question, so much is re-inscribed.

Gibreel is named after the archangel Gabriel by his mother. But his patronymic, Ismail Najmuddin, is 'Ismail after the child involved in the sacrifice of Ibrahim, and Najmuddin, *star of the faith*; he'd given up quite a name when he took the angel's' (SV 17). And that name, Ismail, comes in handy in an echo of *Moby Dick*, to orchestrate the greatest act of male bonding in the book as an inversion of the angel of death, when Gibreel saves Saladin's life in the blazing Shaandaar Cafe: 'The adversary: there he blows! Silhouetted against the backdrop of the ignited Shaandaar Cafe, see that's the very fellow! Azraeel leaps unbidden into Farishta's hand' (SV 463). The allusion in the otherwise puzzling 'there he blows' is the white whale, of course.

Yet it must be acknowledged that in Mahound, we hear the satanic verses inspired by possible *female* gods. Gibreel's dream of Mahound's wrestling with himself, acting out an old script, restores the proper version, without the female angels, man to man. By the rules of fiction in the narrow sense, you cannot assign burden of responsibility here; although by the law of Religion, in the strict sense, the harm was already done. Rushdie invoked those rules against these Laws, and it was an unequal contest. We will not enter the lists, but quietly mark the *text*'s assignment of value. The 'reality' of the wrestling, the feel of the voice speaking through one, is high on the register of validity, if not verifiability. By contrast, in 'Return to Jahilia', prostitution is mere play. Ayesha, the female prophet ('historically' one of his wives), lacks the existential depth of 'the businessman' prophet. To her the archangel sings in popular Hindi film songs. Her traffic with him is reported speech.

If post-colonial plurality is one aggressive central theme of *The Satanic Verses*, the artist's identity is another. Rushdie's tactic is boldly old-fashioned here, and the tone reminds one of, say, George Meredith's 'Authorial voice' in *The Egoist*. Everything is taken care of by this overt comic self-undermining miming manipulation of 'dramatic irony' on so many levels. The multiple dreams, carried to absurdity, support as they take away the power of this planning genius. Here is the entire shift from Religions' God to Art's Imagination – a high European theme – played out in the staging of Author. Ostentatiously appearing as God or Devil (*upparwala* or *nichaywala* – the one above or the one below), he clearly produces error in Gibreel, who has a delusion of angelic grandeur and nearly gets run over by a motorcar as a result. Almost a hundred pages later, the authorial voice reveals that it had been the authorial voice posing as the Almighty, capable of 'mobiliz[ing] the traditional apparatus of divine rage ... [making] wind and thunder [shake] the room' (SV 319), and looking like photographs of Salman Rushdie 'medium height, fairly heavily built, with salt-and-pepper beard cropped close to the line of the jaw ... balding, ... suffer[ing] from dandruff and [wearing] glasses.' Does this make the author less reliable or more? Does this make the voice less real or more? Does this make the dream more true than truth? Is this a serious use of Romantic Irony in a contemporary comic format or a caricature of Romantic Irony? In an era of industriously de-centered subjects and radicalized citationality, these questions are disarmingly cozy. Are we obliged to repeat the argument that, as metropolitan writing is trying to get rid of a subject that has too long been the dominant, the post-colonial writer must still fore-ground his traffic with the subject-position?[18] Too easy, I think. Not because the migrant must still consider the question of identity, plurality, roots. But because fabricating de-centered subjects as the sign of the times is not necessarily these times de-centering the subject. There in the wake of the European avant-garde, is also a confusion of the narrow and general senses of the relationship between subject and center. The trick or turn is not to assume the representation of de-centering to *be* de-centering, and/or judge styles by conjunctures.

All precautions taken, there is no risk in admitting that Rushdie's book reads more like a self-ironic yet self-based modernism ('a myopic scrivener' setting two gentlemen a-dreaming) than an object-coded or subject-decentered avant-garde. Although he does broaden out to other Empires – notably Argentina through the Rosa Diamond sequence which also stages the Norman Conquest as immigration – once you have finished the phantasmagoric book, the global slowly settles into the peculiar locale of migrancy.

What are these dreams, these phantasmagoria, these shape-changes that convince not only the shape-changers themselves but the inhabitants of the world of the book as well? Like the taxonomy of migrancy, Rushdie legitimizing matrix. The story begins in a miracle, a series of super-natural events tamely accommodated into the reasonableness of the everyday. Vintage 'magical realism' – Asturias or Marquez – has taught us to expect a more intricate mosaic. Alleluia Cone's 'visions' can be validated by her personality and experience. Gibreel's fantasies have a firm diagnostic label: paranoid schizophrenia. But what about the peculiar authority of the many times repeated 'Gibreel dreamed' ... and then a noun of event or space? What is the relationship between this and the chain of 'and then ...' 'and then ...' that Deleuze and Guattari assure us is the mode of narrativization of the schizo?[19]

And what about the metamorphosis of the migrants in the hospital where Saladin is brought after the embarrassment of the discovery that he is a British citizen? What about his physical transformation into the Devil, setting a trend in the fashion world of 'Black Britain', only to be cancelled when he learns to hate Farishta? Saladin is never 'diagnosed', he is the side-kick that negotiates the book from beginning to end. And isn't that story about eating kippers at public school supposed to be a bit from Rushdie's own life-story? Is this a clue? Is Rushdie graphing his bio here as President Schreber, British-citizen-escaping-the-angel-of-god-by-demonic-metamorphosis-and-returning-home-for-a-wished-for-entry into the real?[20]

In *Capitalism and Schizophrenia*, Deleuze and Guattari have suggested that the schizo as a general psychic description entailed by capitalism stands as a critique of the Oedipal recuperation of the great branching-out of social – and desiring – production inscribing the unproduced. I should like to think that *The Satanic Verses* presents a portrait of the author as schizo under the desiring/social production of migrancy and post-coloniality, a displacement of the Oedipal project of Imperialism as bringing into Law of the 'favorite son'.

Farishta finds *The Marriage of Heaven and Hell* in Alleluia Cone's house. But the genius of this book is more the paranoid Schreber than the visionary Blake. This is no Prophet Against Empire, to quote the title of a well-known book on Blake.[21] The confident breaching of the boundaries between dream and waking in the *text* – not merely in the characters – and, indeed, in a text that sets store by the paradox of the so-called 'creative imagination' – can earn for *The Satanic Verses* a critic's subtitle: 'Imperialism and Schizophrenia'. Not because empire, like capital, is abstract, but because empire messes with identity.

Good and Evil, set up with such pomp and circumstance, have therefore no moral substance in the persons of the protagonists. They are no more than visual markers, inscribed on the body like special effects – a halo, a pair of horns. I am uncomfortable with this of course, but then ask myself if this is not the peculiar felicity of post-coloniality, good and evil as reactive simulation, overturning the assurance that 'a performative utterance will be *in a peculiar way* hollow or void if said by an actor on the stage, or if introduced in a poem'.[22]

I can anticipate critics suggesting that I give resistance no speaking part here. But the point is that a book such as this might at least be inviting us to consider the following question: who am I, or my critics, or indeed Salman Rushdie, to *give* resistance a speaking part? To 'state the problem' is not bad politics. In fact, it might be poor judgment to consider academy or novel as straight blueprint for action on the street. Chamcha gives himself the assurance that if a '"chimeran graft" ... were possible,' as shown on TV, 'then so was he; he, too, could cohere, send down roots, survive. Amid all the televisual images of hybrid tragedies ... he was given this one gift' (SV 406). In that very section, Rushdie's 'authorial voice' puts it in the first person singular in the classic tones of the psychotic as savant:

> But, it had to be conceded, and this was his [Chamcha's] original point, that the circumstances of the age required no diabolic explanation. I[authorial voice]'m saying nothing. Don't ask me to clear things up one way or the other; the time of revelations is long gone.
>
> (SV 408)

It is after this that we come to the only real act of intended, gratuitous, cunning cruelty and persecution represented in the book: the destruction of Farishta and Alleluia through the anonymous telephoned messages, in the pluralized ventriloquism of the radio-waves, of sexual innuendo couched in childish doggerel. No conceivable high allegorical connection with the great narrative of post-coloniality can be found in this important nexus of the book's narrative energy: this is rather the absurd discontinuity of the hyper-real. *Etre-pour-la-mort* is *être-au-téléphone*.

A word about the 'tall, thin Bengali woman with cropped hair', whom I cannot really leave behind. Rukmini Bhaya Nair gives her some importance:

> Narration in Rushdie's novels is shaped as gossip, an undervalued form of everyday talk that is now creatively empowered to reclaim the metaphors of an elite history. In S[atanic] V[erses], Rushdie, tongue very much in

cheek, presents the following case through one of his minor characters, an intellectual Bengali woman. [']Society was orchestrated by what she called *grand narratives*; history, economics, ethics. In India, the development of a corrupt and closed state apparatus had "excluded the masses of people from the ethical project." As a result, they sought ethical satisfaction in the oldest of the grand narratives, that is, religious faith.[']²³

Ms. Nair goes on to make a persuasive case for *The Satanic Verses* as 'satirical gossip'.²⁴

The case that I have made for religious faith as a counter-narrative with a generalized subject focussed on the moment when, *within the colonial rather than post-colonial context*, religious discursivity changed to militancy, gossip changed to rumor as vehicle of subaltern insurgency.²⁵ In the present essay, my opening point is that, in *post*-coloniality, the praxis and politics of life (the *Lebenswelt*) intercept aesthetic objects away from their destined ends. Thus, if the project of the *novel* is gossip, the post-colonial *Lebenswelt* wrenched it into rumor, criticism by hearsay, a text, taken as evidence, as talked about rather than read.²⁶ Upon the wings of that rumor, the metropolitan migrant subaltern (rather different from the colonial subaltern in the colony, though we tend to forget this) forged a collectivity which they could stage as a strike *for* the Imam *against* the West. The narrative of the State and the narrative of religion overdetermined the rumored book into a general mobilizing signifier for crisis.

II

I come now to the cultural politics of the specific (mis)reading of the book as disposable container of blasphemy, signifier of cultural difference, rather than the field of the migrant's desiring/social production. As Aziz Al-Azmeh comments:

> The enracinations, deracinations, alienations, comforts, discomforts and mutations which constitute the novel are kept entirely out of view by Rushdie's islamist critics, and his putative treatment of Muhammed and Abraham brought into view.²⁷

Literature is transactional. The point is not necessarily and exclusively the correct description of a book, but the construction of readerships. 'The birth of the reader must be at the cost of the death of the Author.'

A great deal has been written and said about the Rushdie affair in the last half-year. I will concentrate on a spectrum of historically constructed readerships here and assemble a highly selective dossier.[28] My main argument attempts to lay out the full implications of the statement made by Gita Sahgal, a member of the Southall Black Sisters, based in Britain: 'It is in this crisis where our own orthodoxies have collapsed that the doubters and transgressors must once more create a space for themselves.'[29]

India banned the book first: on October 5, 1988. Of the 21 deaths associated with *The Satanic Verses* at the time this article was written, 19 took place on the subcontinent. Of these, 12 were Muslim Anti-Rushdie demonstrators, shot in Rushdie's home-town, Bombay, on February 24, 1989. Ayatollah Khomeini called for Rushdie's death on February 14.

Why did India ban the book? In the name of the rights of a religious minority in a secular state, Syed Shahabuddin, an opposition Muslim MP, launched a campaign against the book. 'Doubters and transgressors must create a space for themselves' by taking a distance from mere rational abstraction, and here is the first one: 'rights of a religious minority in a secular democratic-socialist state.' Rational abstractions can be staunch allies, but *they can always also be used as alibis.* Gita Sahgal's '*this* crisis' is *always* implicit in the principle of reason. Her 'once more' is the activist's short-hand for what must be *persistent.*

In India it was not an islamist decision, but a decision related to the functioning of the rational abstractions claimed catachrestically by the post-colonial state. [30] Artists and intellectuals were immediately vociferous against the decision, but, from personal accounts that I have heard, the logic of the protests was extremely hard to manipulate, still in the realm of rational abstractions.

In addition, perhaps precisely because the rational abstractions of democracy are claimed catachrestically and therefore critically by the secularist in the post-colonial state, there was a voice raised in India against the West's right to claim freedom of expression. The best succinct statement of this may be found in a letter to *The Economic and Political Weekly* signed by, among others, Asghar Ali Engineer, one of the strongest analysts and critics of 'communalism' (religious sectarianism) in India: 'We do not for a moment belittle (the) Ayatollah's threat ... But we also see the danger of "freedom of expression" being fetishized and the embattled context in which a writer finds her/himself oversimplified.'[31]

Wole Soyinka, travelling to India in December wrote, as a native of Nigeria, of:

a nation which is, in the estimation of many, roughly equally divided amongst Muslims and Christians and animists, with the former two constituting a floating adherent population of the 'animist' in addition to being what they publicly proclaim ... I caught some flak from sections of the artistic and intellectual community for commenting that I quite understood the action of the Indian government in banning Salman Rushdie's book, ... I stated that, given India's harrowing situation of religious unrest, I probably would have done the same if I were the Prime Minister. I did not condone the ban; I merely tried to understand the horrible dilemma in which the government of India was placed.[32]

A dilemma, a crisis, an aporia, peculiar to democracy as checks and balances, rights and duties computed on the normative grid of rational abstractions inherited from the culture of imperialism. Bhikhu Parekh, a British-Indian political theorist has asked: 'Is there a release from this highly claustrophobic post-Enlightenment world view?'[33]

Rushdie's own reaction was straightforward:

> The right to freedom of expression is at the foundation of any democratic society ... My view is that of a secular man for whom Islamic culture has been of central importance all his life ... You know, as I know that [the Muslim parliamentarians] and their allies don't really care about my novel. The real issue is the Muslim vote.[34]

Still within 'the claustrophobic post-Enlightenment world-view', let us step back and ask, what exacerbated the situation of the Muslim vote so dramatically? It is of course idle to assign a single efficient cause to such trends but, for strategic reasons that I hope will be evident to at least a section of my readership, I choose the successful censoring of a woman, contained within national boundaries, a national *cause célèbre* for a time, but nothing about which it can be said 'Islam today has displayed its enormous mobilizing power.' I refer, of course, to the Shahbano case. I quote a few passages from 'Shahbano' by Rajeswari Sunder Rajan and Zakia Pathak:

> In April 1985, the Supreme Court of India ... passed a judgment in favor of Shahbano in the case of Mohammed Ahmed Khan, appellant, versus Shahbano and others, respondents. The judgment created a furor unequalled, according to one journal, since 'the great upheaval of 1857 [the so-called Indian Mutiny]' ... awarding Shahbano, a divorced Muslim woman, maintenance of Rs. 179.20 (approximately $14) per month from her husband ... and dismissed the husband's appeal against the award of

maintenance under section 125 of the 1973 Code of Criminal Procedure ...
When some by-elections fell due in December 1985, the sizeable Muslim
vote turned against the ruling party (the Congress-I) partly because it
supported the judgment . . . When Hindu fundamentalists offered to
'protect' her from Muslim men, her religious identity won ... In an open
letter, she denounced the Supreme Court judgment 'which is apparently
in my favour; but since this judgment is contrary to the Quran and the
hadith and is an open interference in Muslim personal law, I Shahbano,
being a Muslim, reject it and dissociate myself from every judgment which
is contrary to the Islamic Shariat.' . . . When the battle was carried to
Parliament and the government of India passed the bill that threw her on
the mercy of the male relatives of her natal family, her gender status was
again activated. She became a Muslim woman pursuing the case for the
return of her *mehr* (dower) under the provisions of the new act.[35]

Sunder Rajan and Pathak are quite right in saying that what is at issue
here is not 'whether this spacing, temporalizing self is a deferral of the
unified freely choosing *subject* or whether the latter is itself only a
metaphysic'.[36] What we are concerned with here is the question of *agency*,
even *national* agency within the effect of the nation in the real – just as
Rushdie's novel is concerned with the *migrant* agency represented in a
magical but none-the-less serious layout. 'Agent' and 'subject' are different codings of something we call 'being'. Shahbano, as citizen of the
same post-colonial nation invoked by Rushdie in his letter to Rajiv
Gandhi, has her *agency* censored by the script of religion and gendering.
In this context, to bring up the question of the staging of free will in the
subject has a hidden ethico-political agenda that may give support to the
very forces that recode her as gendered and therefore make her dependent upon the institution of heterosexual difference. This has something like a relationship with what militants in the Rushdie case have
pointed out: that arguments from cultural relativism are profoundly
complicit, when invoked at certain moments, with racist absolutism. It is
quite correct to point out the immense mobilization of national resistance
– the provisional fabrication of a collective agency on the occasion of
Shahbano. But woman *as* woman (unavailable to class agency in the
particular context) is still only an occasion here. The question of free will
should not be inscribed within arguments from subject-production; it is
rather to be seen in connection with the presupposition of individual
agency in collectivities. It is here that Shahbano stands censored. Within
this frame, there is no real polarization between self-censoring and other-

censoring (conversion and coercion); that is the opposition we must learn to undo. In the sphere of the production of political value, the mute as articulate in the service of 'orthodoxy' (to borrow Gita Sahgal's word) – a discontinuous naming of collective agency in the name of the 'sacred' rather than the 'profane' (in the other coding called 'secular', 'national') – is more spectacularly muted because so abundantly audible. And, in the context of the international collectivization brought about by way of Rushdie's book, of which she is among the first efficient causes, she has dropped out, become invisible. How can she *become* one of 'the doubters and transgressors' before she can participate in their 'clearing a space for themselves'? By counter-coercion through the orthodoxy of reason? *This* is the genuine dilemma, the aporia, the double bind of the question of agency. The condition of (im)possibility of rational collectivities must be seen, not as instrument, but as last instance.[37]

> By being categorized as a vagrant – the destitute woman – widow, divorcée, or abandoned wife – . . . fulfils her (anti-)social role. The psychological damage of potential vagrant status is partially minimized by the depersonalizing effects of legal action. Section 125 offers women 'negative' subjectivity: the new act responds by reinserting the divorcée within the family, this time as dependent on her natal family and sons.[38]

As impersonal instrument, rational abstractions can operate as *pharmakoi*, a poison that can be a healing drug.[39] It is thus that one must turn to the extraordinary and (ex)orbitant category of 'legal vagrant'. In the subordinate, gendered, de-colonized *national* space, the category of *female* 'vagrant' as 'access to public space' (section 125 of the Uniform Civil Code) must be recognized beside the category of 'migrant' within ex-colonial metropolitan space, where, as the migrant feminist group 'Women Against Fundamentalism' have pointed out 'women's voices have been largely silent' – and, I repeat, audible as muted ventriloquists – 'in the debate where battle lines have been drawn between liberalism and fundamentalism'.[40] Paradoxically, categorization as vagrant is 'psychologically damaging' only if the religious coding of gendered heterosexuality is implicitly accepted by way of a foundational concept of subject-formation. The freeing pain of a violent rejection from a system of self-representation (a mode of value-coding) is not confined to the franchised or disenfranchised.

This would take me into the arena where the reversal empire-nation is displaced, about which I have written elsewhere.[41] Here we are obliged to go forward to the most visible agent, the late Ayatollah Khomeini.[...]

III

I promised in the final section to provide an element of intellectual history. I will make no more than a few cryptic suggestions, remaining within the story of what Michel de Certeau has defined as a shift in the *Lebenswelt* – the formal praxis of life – 'from religious systems to the ethics of the Enlightenment'.[42] De Certeau must be read against the grain because, like most European intellectuals writing on the history of European consciousness, he does not take imperialism into account.

In section 4 of *The Writing of History,* de Certeau lays out a story that is not altogether unknown, although in the telling of it, a Derrida would emphasize Kant and Hegel, an Abrams the poets.[43] With his brilliant historian's eye, de Certeau tells us how 'the practical organization of Christianity is "socialized" in being stripped of its beliefs' (C 179), how in the seventeenth and eighteenth centuries Christianity is recoded, laundered and sublated into philosophy and ethics.

> *De-Christianizaton reveals in its formality the Christian practice*, but hereafter that practice is thrown out of the orbit of the *Logos* which had verified it … It 'betrays' Christianity in both senses of the term: it abandons it, and it unveils it. A social reinterpretation of Christianity is thus inaugurated, which will flow back over Christian milieus: in them it will develop missionary practices turned toward the 'other' … in them it will later provoke the reproduction of the ethics of progress in the form of a theology of history …
>
> (C 179)

Such a sublation/graduation of a monotheism into secularism as such at the end of the seventeenth and eighteenth centuries in a certain place has something like a relationship with the ideological requirements of the release of the abstractions of monopoly capitalist (rather than pre-capitalist) imperialism. To repeat that move with the other great monotheism, Islam, is not possible again precisely because the seventeenth and eighteenth centuries have taken place. The ethical has to entail the universal, although it must always also be accessible to a singular or a collective case. The attempt to fashion an ethical universal out of a religious base, which is subsequently not called Christian but simply secular, then goes out of joint with the conjuncture, especially with a (national) subject not of the monopoly-capitalist dominant. 'Conjuncture' is a word that would give its antonym in plain English as being 'out of joint'.

Thus it is futile (if not reactionary) to look for parallels between the seventeenth and eighteenth century Euro-Atlantic and contemporary West Asia/North Africa/South Asia. One glimpses asymmetrical reflections, as in a cracked mirror, only to put them aside:

> these movements are symptoms of *an order that is being undone* ... religious structures begin to 'turn' quite differently, as if they were taken up en masse into the political element ... Traditional 'heresy', a social form modeled on a theological truth, becomes less and less possible. The orthodoxy in terms of which this form was determined will now be more of a civil than religious nature ... The choice between Christianities is effected in terms of practices.
>
> (C 154, 158, 168, 162)

The residual appearances are not 'atheism, sorcery, mysticism'. Paradoxically, because the effort at globalizing Islam is wounded and incapacitated by the detritus of an imperialist formation already in place, we have to locate them on a much larger scale: the Khilafat movement, dismantled by Kamal Ataturk's modernization of Turkey; the Muslim contingency in the making of the Indian Constitution; and varieties of 'fundamentalism', a repetition and a rupture, and a reaction to the US–Israel combination.

'One of the tasks of history consists of measuring the distance or the relations between the formality of practices and their representations' (C 158). There is indeed a distance between the formality of historians' practices and their self-representation in the matter of imperialism. The invocation of 'missionary practices' cannot cover the distance altogether. And, where the descriptions are almost on target, the fact that colonialism/ imperialism remains conspicuous by its absence makes the distance intractable: 'State policy already turns the country into a mercantilist and capitalist enterprise', for example, or, worse, 'a dominant *political* ethics is born of the enormous effort that allowed the eighteenth century to create nations and pass from Christianity to modern Europe' (C 155, 176).

Given that the story of Christianity to secularism is the only story around, we tend to feel quite justified when we claim, in praise of reason, that reason is European. The peculiarity of historical narratives such as the one I have loosely put together in this section is that it is made up of contingencies which can also be read as Laws of Motion. I would like to suggest that it is the reading of one of those contingencies – the fit between monopoly capitalist imperialism and monotheist Christianity-into-secularism – as a Law of Motion that makes us presuppose that

Reason itself is European. It might be better to recode the gift of contingency rather than construct a fantasmatic present or future in the name of that presupposition. In aid of what? A competition about monotheisms? How about polytheisms or animisms? How far must discord be taken? Rather than lament reason, put it in a useful place, precisely to avoid these contingencies. Accept the limits of the contingency of history.

In place of mere secularism, the Southall Black Sisters might propose an instrumental universalism, always under the fire of doubt and transgression.[44]

IV

In this essay, I have first offered a literary-critical plot summary of the book because I think one must be a schoolteacher in the classroom when it becomes impossible. I have done it almost as an act of disciplinary piety towards what is, after all, a novel. Next I have presented a dossier trying to focus on what people who are diversely connected to this event are saying. I have paused for a moment upon the uses to which the spectacular rational abstractions of democracy can sometimes be put. I have gone on to sketch the possibility of questioning what we often take as given, that the idea of reason – since I see reason itself as a *pharmakon*, rather than an unquestioned good or an unquestioned evil – is *necessarily* Eurocentric.

Finally, then, an exhortation: whenever they bring out the Ayatollah, remember the face that does not come together on the screen, remember Shahbano. She is quite discontinuous with Salman Rushdie's fate as it is being organized on many levels. The Rani of Sirmur emerged in the East India Company records only when she was needed to make 'History' march.[45] Shahbano's emergence is structurally comparable. When the very well-known face is brought out, remember the face that you have not seen, the face that has disappeared from view, remember Shahbano.

Notes

1 Salman Rushdie, *The Satanic Verses*, Viking, New York, 1989. Page references have been included in the text, after the initial letter SV.
2 Peter Bürger, *Theory of the Avant-Garde*, tr. Michael Shaw, Univ. of Minnesota Press, Minneapolis, pp. 25–7.
3 James Atlas, 'What is Fukuyama Saying (Francis Fukuyama on the End of History)', *New York Times Magazine*, Oct. 22, 1989.

4   Roland Barthes, 'The Death of the Author?', tr. Stephen Heath, *Image-Music-Text*, Hill and Wang, New York, 1977, p. 148

5   'More on Power/Knowledge', 25–51 in Spivak (1993) *Outside in the Teaching Machine*, New York and London: Routledge.

6   Barthes, 'Death of the Author', p. 148.

7   Ibid., pp. 145–6.

8   Michel Foucault, 'What is An Author?', in *Language, Counter-Memory, Practice: Selected Essays and Interviews*, tr. Donald F. Bouchard and Sherry Simon, Cornell Univ. Press, Ithaca, 1977.

9   Barbara Johnson, *The Critical Difference: Essays in the Contemporary Rhetoric of Reading*, The Johns Hopkins University Press, Baltimore, 1981.

10 Jacques Derrida, 'Otobiographies: the Teaching of Nietzsche and the Politics of the Proper Name', in Peggy Kamuf, tr., *The Ear of the Other: Texts and Discussions With Jacques Derrida*, Schocken Books, New York, 1985.

11 Ibid., p. 10.

12 Salman Rushdie, '...' *Granta*, 28, Birthday Issue, Autumn 1989, p. 29. For reasons of security, I presume, this poem is irreproducible.

13 Derrida, 'Otobiographies', p. 11.

14 For the suggestion that 'magical realism' is a style that cannot narrativize de-colonization, see Spivak, 'Marginality in the Teaching Machine', 53–76, *Outside in the Teaching Machine* (1993). For a somewhat tendentious but intriguing genealogy of 'magical realism', see Jeffrey Herf, *Reactionary Modernism: Technology, Culture, and Politics in Weimar and the Third Reich*, Cambridge Univ. Press, Cambridge, 1984.

15 Timothy Brennan, *Salman Rushdie and the Third World: Myths of the Nation*, Macmillan, London, 1989. Perhaps because of his clear-cut position on the nation, Mr Brennan is weak in the presentation of the place of the novel in the Indian literary traditions (pp. 18, 79–80). Incidentally, Arjuna and Bhima are completely human characters in an epic, not 'figures in the Hindu pantheon' (p. 109). Rushdie's use of Hindu material gives us a sense of the non-sanctimonious 'secularism' which is a fact of the subcontinental everyday. It does matter in that context that we distinguish between Achilles and Zeus, and not call both gods. Mr Brennan's sense that *Midnight's Children* put 'the Indo English imagination on the map' (p. 80) is a step ahead of Alan Yentob's inspired polarization of India/Pakistan and the West as 'oral tradition' and the 'modern novel'! (Lisa Appignanesi and Sara Maitland, eds., *The Rushdie File*, Fourth Estate, London, 1989, p. 197). In Macaulay's day, Arabic and Sanskrit writing at least filled a school library shelf. With friends like these!

16 Rushdie, Interview with Sean French, in Appignanesi, *File*, p. 9.

17 I feel solidarity with men who let women in but cannot see this gesture as the performance of feminism. On this particular point, I must take exception even from my friend Srinivas Aravamudan's outstanding essay, a full-dress scholarly treatment of the novel. To create women as 'strong characters' is not necessarily to 'pursue ... [t]he issue of *feminism* and Islam' ('"Being God's Postman is no Fun, Yaar": Salman Rushdie's *The Satanic Verses*', *Diacritics* 19ii, summer 1989, p. 13: emphasis mine). And it is here that I must also split from Rukmini Bhaya Nair's impressive 'Text and pre-Text: History as Gossip in Rushdie's Novels': 'The Prophet's own intellectual, moral and practical dilemmas are brought closer to us through his wives, Khadijah and Ayesha, who implicitly believed in him, and the (un)common whores of Jahilia who imitated every move of the women proximate to the Prophet. Through the gossip

of women, we come to a truer understanding of the "sinuous complexities of history". Public facts alone are insufficient and unconvincing' (*Economic and Political Weekly* 24, xviii, May 6, 1989, p. 997). That private-public divide is old gender-coding. We must set these things on the move.

I repeat, I support men who make the effort. And it is in that spirit that I quote here my translation of a poem, just in from Bangladesh, by Farhad Mazhar, a secularist Muslim poet, where a desire is recorded and the possibility of an alternative history is glimpsed in a counter-factual complement. I have commented at greater length on such counter-factual moves in 'Marginality in the Teaching Machine'. I quote Mazhar's poem in full because I doubt that the readership of this book would otherwise have access to the work of this considerable poet-activist:

> I write these verses in Mistress Khadija's name:
> I'll not say bismillah, just take her name.
> Lord, permit me. No anger, please, just once.
> In her name I'll write my poem, Lord of Praise.
>
> Dear Prophet's name? No, his name neither, boss.
> Just'n Khadija's name – in exquisite Khadija's name
> For once I'll forget all other names on earth
> Forget you too, forget my Prophet.
>
> Only she, Lord, only in her wage work
> Was my dear Prophet ensconced, rapt with camel and trade.
> Don't show off – she was your beloved,
> But, for her, a salaried worker –
> All women know you are puny here
> But don't show it abroad for respect's sake.

18 This is the productive unease in Fredric Jameson, 'Third-World Literature in the Era of Multinational Capitalism', *Social Text* 15 (1986).

19 Gilles Deleuze and Felix Guattari, *Anti-Oedipus: Capitalism and Schizophrenia*, tr. Robert Hurley *et al.*, Univ. of Minnesota Press, Minneapolis, 1983, pp. 5, 36. See also p. 12.

20 For the notion of biography – the staging of the author is part of this – see Derrida, 'Otobiographies'. For Schreber, see Sigmund Freud, 'Psycho-Analytic Notes On An Autobiographical Account of A Case of Paranoia (*Dementia Paranoides*)', in James Strachey *et al.*, trs., *The Standard Edition of the Complete Psychological Works*, Hogarth Press, London, 1958, vol. 12.

21 David Erdman, *Blake, Prophet Against Empire: A Poet's Interpretation of the History of His Own Times*, Princeton Univ. Press, Princeton, 3rd ed., 1977.

22 J.L. Austin, *How to Do Things With Words*, Oxford Univ. Press, Oxford, 1965, pp. 21–2; quoted in Jacques Derrida, 'Signature Event Context', *Limited Inc.*, Gerald Graff (ed.), Northwestern University Press, Evanston, 1986, p. 16.

23 Nair, 'Text and Pre-Text', p. 995.

24 Ibid., p. 1000.

25 Spivak, 'Subaltern Studies: Deconstructing Historiography', in Ranajit Guha, ed., *Subaltern Studies: Writings on South Asian History and Society*, Oxford Univ. Press, Delhi, 1985, pp. 351–6.

26   The phrase 'criticism by hearsay', used in an academic context, comes from Paul de Man, 'The Resistance to Theory', in *The Resistance to Theory*, Univ. of Minnesota Press, Minneapolis, 1986, p. 15.

27   Aziz Al-Azmeh, 'More on "The Satanic Verses"', cited in *Frontier* 21. 25 (Feb. 4, 1989), p. 6.

28   Appignanesi, *File*, is, of course, now a much more extensive source.

29   Gita Sahgal, 'Transgression Comes of Age', *Interlink* 12 (May/June, 1989), p. 19. I am grateful to Peter Osborne and John Kraniauskas for help in assembling this dossier.

30   For post-coloniality and catachresis, see Spivak, 'Marginality in the teaching machine'.

31   'Dubious Defenders', *Economic and Political Weekly* 24.xvii (April 29, 1989), p. 894. Ali A. Mazrui strikes a similar chord in 'The Moral Dilemma of Salman Rushdie's *Satanic Verses*', in Appignanesi, *File*.

32   Wole Soyinka, 'Jihad for Freedom', *Index on Censorship* 18.5 (May/June, 1989), p. 20. All references to *Index* are to this issue.

33   'Identities on Parade: A Conversation', *Marxism Today* (June, 1989), p. 27.

34   'Open Letter to Rajiv Gandhi', *The New York Times* (Wednesday, Oct. 19, 1988).

35   Rajeswari Sunder Rajan and Zakia Pathak, '"Shahbano"', *Signs* 14.iii (Spring, 1989), pp. 558–9, 572.

36   Sunder Rajan and Pathak, p. 573. Emphasis mine.

37   For an explanation of the '(im)' of '(im)possibility', see Spivak, *In Other Worlds: Essays in Cultural Politics*, Methuen, New York, 1987, p. 263, 308 n. 81.

38   Sunder Rajan and Pathak, "Shahbano", pp. 576–7.

39   For *pharmakon*, see Derrida, 'Plato's Pharmacy', in Barbara Johnson tr., *Disseminations*, Univ. of Chicago Press, Chicago, 1981.

40   Sahgal, 'Transgression', p. 19.

41   See Spivak, 'Women in difference', 77–95 in *Outside in the Teaching Machine*.

42   Michel de Certeau, 'The Formality of Practices: From Religious Systems to the Ethics of the Enlightenment (the Seventeenth and Eighteenth Centuries)', in *The Writing of History*, Columbia Univ. Press, New York, 1988. All passages from de Certeau are from this chapter. Page references have been included in the text following the letter C.

43   See especially Jacques Derrida, *Glas* (Paris: Galilée, 1974), the left hand column; and M. H. Abrams, *Natural Supernaturalism*, Norton, New York, 1971.

44   For elaboration of a universalism of difference, see Spivak, 'Remembering the Limits: Difference, Identity and Practice: A Transcript', in Peter Osborne ed., *Socialism and the Limits of Liberalism*, Verso, London, 1993.

45   See Spivak, 'Reading the Archives: the Rani of Sirmur', in Francis Barker, ed., *Europe and Its Others*, Univ. of Essex Press, Colchester, 1985, vol. 1.

PART II
Essays on Postmodernism

Four: The Real and the True: Documentary Film

Introduction

During the early 1990s there were indications that the debate over postmodernity and postmodernism had begun to take a different direction, responding partly to the internal development of the arguments presented here, but reacting also to dramatic events in international politics. The collapse of the USSR as a state and world power, and the dissolution of the Eastern Bloc in Europe brought to an end the 45-year confrontation of the Cold War. This produced huge consequences, not only in Europe and North America, but wherever regional politics and cultures had been influenced by the contention between the East and the West. Writers and artists in the West who had drawn on libertarian socialist ideals for inspiration were presented with new dilemmas: did the post-Cold War world represent the triumph of the values of a global market economy as projected by postmodern theorists such as Baudrillard? Was there any future for the traditions of political theory and practice which derived from Marxism? The demise of the Cold War also contributed to the growing awareness of cultural diversity, both within Europe and America, and in the burgeoning economies of Asia, the Pacific and Latin America, and in the diversifying politics of Africa. These developments have brought increased urgency to questions which focus on the politics of representation and identity, at the level of nations, communities, and the individual (Giroux 1993).

Many of the debates over postmodernity and the postmodern are concerned with the nature of representation: how effectively and in what ways do different media and art forms portray the world? In part these debates are responding to the proliferation of means for reproducing images through contemporary audio-visual, communications and computer technology: it is easy to be intoxicated by the extraordinary achievements of technology such as the Voyager satellite which relayed computer-enhanced portraits of the frozen moons of Saturn from the edge of the solar system. But images are mute, and therefore have to be interpreted: the silence of pictures also makes them peculiarly vulnerable to manipulation and distortion (Owens 1992). Documentary, as a genre of film- and video-making which has always claimed to report on reality in the most direct ways, effectively illustrates a number of the central debates over postmodern representation. This final section therefore presents these issues through the writing and documentary films of Trinh T. Minh-ha whose work addresses key areas of these arguments. This introduction situates her article, 'The Totalizing Quest of Meaning', within the development of documentary film-making, because the ideal of the documentary film as a means of representing reality raises central questions which have been implicit throughout the arguments over postmodernism and postmodernity:

In what sense can documentary films represent the real and the true?

How is representation conditioned by the development of technology?

How can diverse cultures be portrayed without condescension or distortion?

Documentary: how is reality represented?

The ideal of the documentary as a truthful and compelling record of life had motivated film-makers from the moment of the medium's invention, and this kind of ambition was powerfully confirmed by the advent of synchronized sound in the late 1920s. Documentarists at this time felt that their new moving-and-speaking images of real people, if shaped into a narrative, should be able to convey an argument with great conviction. But this ideal of documentary film-truth demonstrates a central conundrum of the technology: the apparatus which appears most directly to allow authentic transcription of reality is itself an elaborate construction, utterly dependent on the operation of complex conventions (Owens 1992). And so immediately all of the assumptions about documentary's authenticity and conviction are unravelled before the audience's sceptical gaze: Why this selection of people? Surely that was rehearsed? What has been left out here? What are they trying to put over on us? (Gross, Katz, Ruby 1988).

By means of questions like these, the ideal of documentary's self-evident truth is revealed as a dangerously naive assumption. Showing and telling in themselves convey nothing, and documents also need artifice. The tension between documentary and feature film values

[246]

was expressed forcibly by the director Michael Powell, recalling the great achievements of his entertainment films such as *The Edge of the World* (1937) and *The Life and Death of Colonel Blimp* (1943), which were made during the period when the British documentary movement was producing its finest work: 'Our business was not realism, but surrealism. We were storytellers, fantasists. This is why we could never get on with the documentary film movement. Documentary films started with poetry and finished as prose. We storytellers started with naturalism and finished with fantasy' (Powell 1986: 532). The complex history of documentary film-making is that of a continuous struggle to present the pathos of actuality, of real people and events, within the most effective narrative and argumentative forms.

Documentary practice can be broadly defined by focusing on its three constitutive elements: these are (1) technological determinants, (2) didactic aims, and (3) formal organization (Collins 1986: viii–x). The camera and sound track offer the possibility of preserving a record of reality, and during the 1890s the first examples of documentary (as opposed to news and feature films) were called 'interest' or 'factual' films. Documentary transcribes aspects of the world for our attention, and we are interested in its images because we take them as evidence of the prior, real events or actions. Second, documentaries organize this evidence for a purpose which is either generally informative or more specifically didactic. Before the establishment of television as dominant medium, the vast majority of documentary films were made by government agencies or industry in order to convey information and propaganda. Documentary therefore has never disinterestedly presented images to its audience, but has always maintained particular agendas.

The work of John Grierson during the 1930s and 1940s was highly influential for both the content and form of documentary practice. *Drifters* (1929), the only film which Grierson personally directed, was a study of the Scots herring-fishing industry, and in it he drew on an unlikely combination of influences, ranging from Soviet avant-garde film technique to lessons taken from American 'public relations' theory. Grierson's organizational and polemical genius in the production of documentaries found expression because he could make use of government agencies for his particular vision. In 1930 he founded the Empire Marketing Board Film Unit, transferring to the General Post Office Film Unit in 1933. By the end of the 1930s Grierson had been responsible for the production of several hundred documentary films extolling British life and industry,

[247]

and he went on to direct the National Film Board of Canada throughout the Second World War. Basil Wright, one of the many prolific directors who worked for Grierson, emphasized the didactic content of documentary when he wrote 'it becomes quite plain that documentary is not this or that type of film, but simply a method of approach to public information' (Wright 1947: 38; and Hardy [1946] 1966).

Until the 1970s documentaries, unlike entertainment feature films, were rarely produced by purely commercial studios able to rely upon international distribution and rental networks. Because they did not generate box-office income, documentary films were necessarily funded by sponsorship, and this material fact largely determined the content, formal qualities and – crucially – the distribution, of most documentary work. Therefore, aesthetic qualities, the third aspect of this general definition of factual film, were heavily compromised by the constraints of the 'real' materials being shown, and the need to captivate an audience who by and large would rather be watching Charlie Chaplin or Deborah Kerr. It is a shock to learn, for example, that Robert Flaherty's *Nanook of the North* (1922) and *Man of Aran* (1934) which are classic founding examples of documentary art, were as closely scripted and acted as any feature film (Barnouw 1974: 33–51). The manipulations to which the factual material of documentary is subjected are therefore always open to question for a critical audience: documentary practice dramatizes the nature of audio-visual representation because we always have in mind the reality which it must in some way be mis-presenting.

There is a strong case for arguing that developments in the formal qualities of a medium are determined in the first instance by changes in the material circumstances of production and reception, and nowhere is this clearer than in mass communications where the medium is so intrinsic to the meanings which it carries. Some documentarists from the early years of the genre had already rehearsed the kinds of problem and questioning of convention which are raised by postmodern theory; the extraordinarily inventive work of 'Dziga Vertov' (pseudonym of Denis Arkadyevich Kaufman) and his collaborators in Russia during the 1920s is exactly the kind of modernist-experimental activity that anticipates late-twentieth-century practices and debates (Vertov 1984; Petric 1987). But it is the transformations brought about by technology and distribution during the last 30 years which have been decisive for new documentary styles. In 1960 the lightweight 16mm camera was perfected, replacing the less mobile 35mm technology for news gathering. An example of the immediate effect of this innovation was the dramatic coverage of Martin Luther King's freedom marches, and the attacks to which they were subjected, coverage which contributed powerfully to the debate over Civil Rights, first in the United States, and then throughout the world.

From this moment news coverage increasingly displaced any lingering hopes that documentary might have had to be the medium of mass information: 400 million viewers watched the funeral of John Kennedy, the first politician consistently to use television as an instrument of his presidency. It is television that now delivers a range of often impressive programmes in documentary format, from the kinds of personal film essay which John Grierson and Humphrey Jennings might have recognized, through to contentious investigations produced by news and current affairs departments. Therefore questions about the politics of representation in contemporary documentary are inevitably also questions of media-ownership and distribution, and these must be linked to careful assessment of the effects of television's dominant conventions of naturalism (Collins 1986).

Semiotic and feminist theorists have criticized documentary work that remains within the narrative and naturalist assumptions of broadcast convention, and have attempted to construct new rationales for critical film and documentary making. A celebrated documentary such as Barbara Kopple's *Harlan County, U.S.A.* (1976) was a significant commercial success because it narrated the events of a Kentucky miners' strike with such conviction. But even a politically engaged documentary like *Harlan County* can be criticized from the point of view of semiotic/feminist theory, precisely because of its implicit reliance on fictional conventions that gratify the audience without, so the argument goes, making them reflect sufficiently on the ways in which meanings are constructed within the film (Kaplan 1988: 81).

There are a number of problems inherent in the critique of successful dominant forms which also attempt to construct countervailing artistic practices, not the least of which is the consequent loss of the 'popular' audience. What kinds of critical pleasure could the theoretically informed documentary offer its audience in place of the purportedly false pleasures of satisfying narrative and realistic characterization? The work of Chris Marker and Trin T. Minh-ha in different ways provide examples of successful documentary films which do incorporate the process of critical reflection within their structures. The career of 'Chris Marker' (born

Christian François Bouche-Villeneuve, 1921) has produced a remarkable series of films that draw on the best critical traditions of early documentary making, and apply them to contemporary social and political developments. *Le Joli Mai* (1962) collaged a series of interviews conducted with a variety of Parisians during a dangerous period of the war in Algeria, from which France was then being forced to withdraw. A voice-over spoken by a woman provides commentary to the interviews, and the film attempts to diagnose the effects of the political crisis within the everyday lives of citizens.

Marker's *Sans Soleil* [*Sunless*] (1983) combines themes and techniques in ways which can be related very directly to debates over postmodern form. It also employs a voice-over spoken by a woman, who reads from letters addressed to her from three different locations, in Tokyo, Guinea-Bissau and Paris. The implied relationship conveyed by the voice-over is only ever implicit, and supplies a mysterious, emotional tone to the whole commentary. *Sans Soleil* is a rhapsody of visual editing over which Marker has also constructed a densely layered soundtrack, so that the film at one level provides a repertoire of virtuoso documentary practice. The film begins with what it offers as an image of pure happiness, of three children seen briefly outside a village in Iceland. The documentary then edits together imagery from the three disparate regions, weaving a complex essay on cultural difference, time, memory and anthropology. Throughout, the status of filmed footage as archival truth is put in question. At the level of its content, the film meditates (perhaps a shade too portentously) on the workings of memory and affection, while also displaying compressed political vignettes – the war of liberation in Portuguese Guinea-Bissau, a Japanese perspective on the Pacific offensive in the Second World War. Finally, *Sans Soleil* attempts to return to the image of happiness with which it began, but now the Icelandic village is buried under the lava of a volcanic eruption. As a conscious reflection on documentary truth, and the inter-relation of the personal and the political, *Sans Soleil* is an extraordinary achievement, whether or not we choose to classify it as postmodern.

A related example of the kind of allure which documentary truth offers to postmodern times can be found in the guerrilla film group '24fps', as portrayed in Thomas Pynchon's novel *Vineland* (1991). The group's enigmatic name means '24-frames-per-second', which is the film speed maintained by modern cameras in order to produce the illusion of lip-synchronous sound. This group dedicates itself to recording what they perceive as the slide towards totalitarianism within American society in recent decades:

> They went looking for trouble, they found it, they filmed it, and then quickly got the record of their witness someplace safe. They particularly believed in the ability of close-ups to reveal and devastate. When power corrupts, it keeps a log of its progress, written into that most sensitive memory device, the human face. Who could withstand the light? What viewer could believe in the war, the system, the countless lies about American freedom, looking into these mugshots of the bought and sold?
>
> (Pynchon 1991: 195)

Pynchon's novels, like those of Don DeLillo, are wonderfully alert to the ways in which images and TV broadcasts condition contemporary perception, and they are also alert to the kinds of deluded faith which can be placed in what are, after all, only pictures. The ambitions of the fictional 24fps group sound very like Chris Marker's actual achievement in documenting the political conflicts of the 1960s in his two-part, four-hour compilation film *Le Fond de l'Air est Rouge* (1977) (titled in English as *The Smile on the Face of the Cat*). This phase of documentary activity was developed with the lighter cameras of the 1960s and came to be known as 'cinéma vérité' or 'direct cinema', premised on the ideal of the film's direct contact with real event: it also encouraged a jagged style of feature film-making, as in the work of Jean-Luc Godard (Marie 1979: 35).

Trinh T. Minh-ha and the critique of documentary

Trinh T. Minh-ha emigrated from Vietnam to the United States in 1970. She is creative in many different media, having studied music and composition, ethno-musicology and French literature in America and Paris. She has taught music in the National Conservatory of Senegal, and is currently the Chancellor's Distinguished Professor in Women's Studies at the University of California, Berkeley, and Associate Professor of Cinema at San Francisco State University. Her films to date are *Reassemblage* (1982), *Naked Spaces – Living is Round* (1985), *Surname Viet Given Name Nam* (1989) and *Shoot for the Contents* (1991). Trinh Minh-ha's experience of divergent cultures and her use of a variety of forms of expression are important in the ways that they actively contribute to the specific articulations of her writing and film-making. Interviewed by Pratibha Parmar, Trinh Minh-ha defined her relationship to the experience of being a 'radical postcolonial intellectual' in this way: 'Since the self, like the work you produce, is not so much a core as a process, one finds oneself, in the context of cultural hybridity, always pushing one's questioning of oneself to the limit of what one is and what one is not... Fragmentation is therefore a way of living at the borders' (Trinh, Minh-ha 1990A: 72).

Making positive use of this experience of fragmentation and diversity consequently allows Minh-ha to maintain a critical view of dominant value systems and cultural hierarchies. Her Vietnamese-African-French-American perspectives give her a particular grasp of debates within feminism, and she combines reflection on issues within the women's movement with an active engagement with debates over postmodern practice. She regards both postmodernism and 'postfeminism' as attempts to learn from failure by returning to the possibilities created during the earlier phases of modernism and feminism: both terms are problematic, but both are potentially useful in the way they displace certainties in order to gain new ground (Trinh, Minh-ha 1990A: 66).

Minh-ha's writing and film-making are difficult to categorize because they continue this active process of crossing borderlines and intellectual demarcations. Her 'academic' text *Woman, Native, Other: Writing, Post-coloniality and Feminism* (1989), went the rounds of scholarly, militant, feminist and small presses before finding a publisher because each readership thought that the text's 'irrespectful mixing of theoretical, militant and poetical modes of writing' was 'impure' (Trinh, Minh-ha 1990A: 69). What is very exciting in Trinh Minh-ha's practice is her insistence that the writing of poetry is not inimical to theoretical work; she argues that this should be so, partly because on the evidence of the Asian, Hispanic, African and Native American literatures in the United States, 'poetry is no doubt the major voice of the poor and of people of colour' (Trinh, Minh-ha 1990A: 69). This mixing of different registers of writing and creative activity, through film, academic texts and lyric poetry, is also characteristic of many women active in feminist research and argument, for whom it is necessary to recast conventional assumptions about the separation of different kinds of cultural work, for example into the 'academic' and the 'creative'. Here, as in the discussion of visual arts from the women's movement (section Two above), feminism and postmodernism are in contention as the most appropriate descriptive category.

Poetry in Minh-ha's academic 'theoretical' writing allows the reader to make more effective use of the meaning of the text, to 'find tools for herself (or himself) to carry on the fight in her (or his) own terms' (Trinh, Minh-ha 1990A: 69). Similarly, the function of poetry within her films is to convey a very specific sense of the lives which the audience is watching, as in the African village filmed in *Naked Spaces – Living is Round*. This kind of lyrical practice is a recurrent feature of documentary film-making, and many earlier documentarists explored the possibilities of relating poetic, lyrical text to the actualities of the image track. Dziga Vertov's *One Sixth of the World* (1926) was actually titled a 'film-poem' and commented on its images through a series of linked inter-titles in the style of Walt Whitman; Humphrey Jennings supplied a mordant voice-over for *A Diary for Timothy* (1941), read by Michael Redgrave; Chris Marker provided characteristic poem-essays for *Sans Soleil* (1983).

Trinh Minh-ha's article, 'The Totalizing Quest of Meaning' is also written in a lyrical-reflective style, and it collages eloquent statements from documentarists together with argument and imagery from her own films. Minh-ha opposes the central assumptions of 'realist' documentary tradition and practices, and what she presents as the oppressive delusion of 'documentary truth'. Her analysis has four main arguments:

1 Most documentary practice is pernicious in the way that it claims to offer a version of the real as an unambiguous truth. The documentary maker presents a subjective narrative as if it constituted the objective facts of the case, and then dramatizes a moral agenda constructed on this selection. A voice, usually male, is granted, condescendingly, to the subjects of the documentary who are presumed to be somehow voiceless. Trinh Minh-ha argues for a style of film-making that avoids this kind of restricting moralism, and she constructs an aesthetic which can give new perspectives: 'In its demand to *mean* at any rate, the "documentary" often forgets how it comes about and how aesthetics and politics remain inseparable in its constitution. For, when not equated with mere techniques of beautifying, aesthetics allows one to experience life differently, or, as some would say, to give it "another sense", remaining in tune with its drifts and shifts' [p. 271–2]. Her argument here joins with a long debate which has its origins in romanticism over the ways in which avant-garde aesthetic experience may be a provocation which leads to new perception.

2 The style and techniques which are commonly assumed to be most appropriate for documentary reportage are themselves only

conventions, and they should be rejected because they are intrinsic to the mystique of documentary's supposed truth. For ethical-realist documentary, showing is equivalent to telling, and an 'ethics of technique' is developed which is intended to deliver the real in the most compelling, and (supposedly) least mediated style: this includes the use of carefully focused, synchronized sound; minimal editing; objectifying camera work and long takes; 'fly-on-wall' shooting, wide-angle lenses. 'Drama-documentaries' exhibit the paradoxes of documentary truth in a very clear form. The dramatic climax of Oliver Stone's documentary-style account of the Kennedy assassination, *JFK* (USA 1992) is built around 'Jim Garrison's' repeated showing in the courtroom of the Zapruder home-movie footage which fortuitously captured the moment of President Kennedy's death. The fixated and repetitious exploitation of this sequence in the feature film can be understood as documentary in the role of pornography, since it represents its audience with a spectacle of pure morbidity, again and again, inviting a thrilled pleasure in our awareness of the Real Presence of this death within the docu-feature melodrama of the film's narrative. *JFK* has become a notorious instance of the feature film which apes the manners of a documentary in order to gain credibility for its thesis. This confirms one strand of Trinh Minh-ha's argument: 'The documentary can thus easily become a "style": it no longer constitutes a mode of production or an attitude toward life, but proves to be only an element of aesthetics (or anti-aesthetics)' [p. 271].

3 Documentaries about the 'under-developed' world can be peculiarly pernicious because of the false values which they perpetuate through their technological inspection of pre-industrial societies. Compassionate reportage of 'third-world victims' which is addressed to 'concerned first-world' audiences fails to include in its frame of reference the complicity of the media with what it relays: 'how representation relates to or is ideology, how media hegemony continues its relentless course is simply not at issue' [p. 268]. Therefore unreflective documentary practice condescends to both its subject and its audience simultaneously through the simulacrum of 'the real' which it fatally offers as 'the true'. The claims of ethical-realist documentary to be able to record the world in a scientific manner are very clear in the genre of anthropological film-making. Documentary was in fact very largely developed during the first decades of the century through the record-

ing of exotic or 'primitive' peoples in the form of ethnographic travelogue films. Robert Flaherty's *Nanook of the North* or Dziga Vertov's *One Sixth of the World* were celebrated for their 'charming' portrayal of the strangeness of non-European cultures. But the procedural rigour of academic anthropological recording also fails in its effort to be objective: 'In its scientific "quest to make meaning", anthropology constantly reactivates the power relations embedded in the Master's confident discourses on Himself and His Other' [p. 275]. Trinh Minh-ha's own films *Reassemblage* and *Naked Spaces – Living is Round* challenge the conventions of anthropological film-making in precisely this way through their use of conspicuous editing techniques, voice-over and soundtrack.

4 Finally, her most abstract argument addresses the complicity of identity, meaning and representation in conventional documentaries. Her writing and film-making join with aspects of feminist and post-modern theory in the ways in which they question ascribed identity:

> there is no real me to return to, no whole self that synthesizes the woman, the woman of colour and the writer; there are instead, diverse recognitions of self through difference, and unfinished, contingent, arbitrary closures that make possible both politics and identity.
>
> (Trinh, Minh-ha 1990A: 72–3)

Further Reading and viewing

Chris Marker's *Sans Soleil* (1983) is available on video, as is *The Last Bolshevik* (1993), an extraordinary biography of the Russian director Alexander Medvedkin. Of Marker, Chris Petit writes, 'Few film-makers are as literate and literary' ('Insane Memory', *Sight and Sound* July 1994: 13). Trinh T. Minh-ha, *Framer Framed* (1992) presents the scripts and visuals from her film-essays in anthropology, *Reassemblage, Naked Space – Living is Round*, and *Surname Viet Given Name Nam*, together with inter-views.

Sean Cubitt *Videography. Video Media as Art and Culture* (1993) is a closely informed discussion about video as a specific medium for contemporary expression. Michael Renov edits a useful range of articles in *Theorizing Documentary* (1993). Ian Adam and Helen Tiffin (eds) *Past the Last Post: Theorizing Post-Colonialism and Post-Modernism* (1991), Linda Chisman and

Patrick Williams (eds) *Colonial Discourse and Post-Colonial Theory: A Reader* (1993), and Homi K. Bhabha *The Location of Culture* (1994) explore the relations between post-colonialism and postmodernity.

References

BARNOUW, Eric (1974) *Documentary: A History of the Non-Fiction Film,* New York: Oxford University Press.

COLLINS, Richard (1986) 'Seeing is believing: the ideology of naturalism' 125–38 in John Corner (ed.) *Documentary and the Mass Media,* London: Edward Arnold.

GIROUX, Henry A. (1993) 'Living dangerously: identity politics and the new cultural racism: towards a critical pedagogy of representation', in *Cultural Studies* 7/1, 'The Politics of Pedagogy/The Pedagogy of Culture(s)'.

GROSS, Larry, John Stuart KATZ, Jay RUBY (eds) (1988) *Image Ethics. The Moral Rights of Subjects in Photographs, Film, and Television,* New York and Oxford: Oxford University Press.

HARDY, Forsyth (ed.) ([1946] 1966) *Grierson on Documentary,* London: Faber.

KAPLAN, E. Ann (1988) 'Theories and strategies of the feminist documentary' 78–102 in Alan Rosenthal (ed.) *New Challenges for Documentary,* Berkeley, Los Angeles, London: California University Press.

MANVELL, Roger (1972) 'Documentary: the factual and specialized film', *The International Encyclopaedia of Film,* Roger Manvell (ed.), London: Michael Joseph.

MARIE, Michel (1979) 'Direct', 35–9 in *Anthropology–Reality–Cinema: The Films of Jean Rouch,* Mick Eaton (ed.), London: BFI.

OWENS, Craig (1992) 'Photography *en abyme*', 16–30 in *Beyond Recognition. Representation, Power, and Culture,* Scott Bryson, Barbara Kruger, Lynne Tillman, and Jane Weinstock (eds). Introduced by Simon Watney, Berkeley, Los Angeles, Oxford: University of California Press.

PETRIC, Vlada (1987) *Constructivism in Film. 'The Man with the Movie Camera' – A Cinematic Analysis,* Cambridge: Cambridge University Press.

POWELL, Michael (1986) *A Life in Movies. An Autobiography,* London: William Heinemann.

PYNCHON, Thomas (1991) *Vineland,* London: Octopus.

TRINH, T. Minh-ha (1987) 'Difference: "A Special Third World Women Issue"', *Feminist Review* 25: 5–22.

—— (1989) *Woman, Native, Other: Writing, Postcoloniality and Feminism*, Bloomington: Indiana University Press.

—— (1990A) 'Woman, native, other', Pratibha Parmar interviews Trinh T. Minh-ha, *Feminist Review* 36: 65–74.

—— (1990B) with Russell Ferguson, Martha Gever and Cornel West, *Out There: Marginalization in Contemporary Cultures*, New York and Cambridge, Mass.: The New Museum of Contemporary Art and MIT Press.

—— (1990C) with Laleen Jayamanne and Leslie Thornton, 'If upon leaving what we have to say we speak: a conversation piece', 44–66 in *Discourses: Conversations in Postmodern Art and Culture*, Russell Ferguson, William Olander, Marcia Tucker and Karen Fiss (eds), New York and Cambridge, Mass.: The New Museum of Contemporary Art and MIT Press.

—— (1991) *When the Moon Waxes Red. Representation, Gender and Cultural Politics*, New York and London: Routledge.

VERTOV, Dziga [Denis Arkadyevich Kaufman] (1984) *Kino-Eye. The Writings of Dziga Vertov*, edited and with an introduction by Annette Michelson, trans. Kevin O'Brien. London and Sydney: Pluto Press.

WRIGHT, Basil (1947) 'Documentary To-Day', *The Penguin Film Review* 2: 37–44. London and New York: Penguin Books.

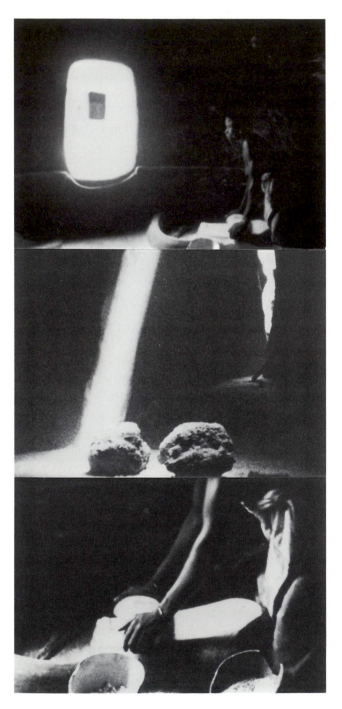

PLATE 15 Trinh T. Minh-ha, from *Naked Spaces – Living is Round*, 1985.

8
The Totalizing Quest of Meaning
TRINH T. MINH-HA

There is no such thing as documentary – whether the term designates a category of material, a genre, an approach, or a set of techniques. This assertion – as old and as fundamental as the antagonism between names and reality – needs incessantly to be restated despite the very visible existence of a documentary tradition. In film, such a tradition, far from undergoing a crisis today, is likely to fortify itself through its very recurrence of declines and rebirths. The narratives that attempt to unify/purify its practices by positing evolution and continuity from one period to the next are numerous indeed, relying heavily on traditional historicist concepts of periodization.

> *Nothing is poorer than a truth expressed as it was thought.*
>
> (Walter Benjamin)[1]

In a completely catalogued world, cinema is often reified into a corpus of traditions. Its knowledge can constitute its destruction unless the game keeps on changing its rules, never convinced of its closures, and always eager to outplay itself in its own principles. On the one hand, truth is produced, induced, and extended according to the regime in power. On the other, truth lies in between all regimes of truth. As the fable goes, What I Tell You Three Times Is True. To question the image of a historicist account of documentary as a continuous unfolding does not necessarily mean championing discontinuity; and to resist meaning does not necessarily lead to its mere denial. Truth, even when 'caught on the run', does not yield itself either in names or in (filmic) frames; and meaning should be prevented from coming to closure at what is said and what is shown. Truth and meaning: the two are likely to be equated with one another. Yet, what is put forth as truth is often nothing more than *a* meaning. And what persists between the meaning of something and its truth is the interval, a break without which meaning would be fixed and truth congealed. This is perhaps why it is so difficult to talk about it, the

[259]

interval. About the cinema. About. The words will not ring true. Not true, for, what is one to do with films which set out to determine truth from falsity while the visibility of this truth lies precisely in the fact that it is false? How is one to cope with a 'film theory' that can never theorize 'about' film, but only *with* concepts that film raises in relation to concepts of other practices?

> A man went to a Taoist temple and asked that his fortune be told. 'First,' said the priest, 'you must donate incense money, otherwise the divination might not be as accurate as possible. Without such a donation, in fact, none of it will come true!'
>
> ('The Words Will Not Ring True', *Wit and Humor from Old Cathay*)[2]

Concepts are no less practical than images or sound. But the link between the name and what is named is conventional, not phenomenal. Producing film theory (or rather, philosophizing with film), which is not making films, is also a practice – a related but different practice – for theory does have to be (de)constructed as it (de)construes its object of study. While concepts of cinema are not readymades and do not preexist in cinema, they are not theory *about* cinema either. The setting up of practice against theory, and vice-versa, is at best a tool for reciprocal challenge, but like all binary oppositions, it is caught in the net of positivist thinking whose impetus is to supply answers at all costs, thereby limiting both theory and practice to a process of totalization.

> I'm sorry, if we're going to use words we should be accurate in our use of them. It isn't a question of technique, it is a question of the material. If the material is actual, then it is documentary. If the material is invented, then it is not documentary ... If you get so muddled up in your use of the term, stop using it. Just talk about films. Anyway, very often when we use these terms, they only give us an opportunity to avoid really discussing the film.
>
> (Lindsay Anderson)[3]

In the general effort to analyze film and to produce 'theory about film', there is an unavoidable tendency to reduce film theory to an area of specialization and of expertise, one that serves to constitute a *discipline*. There is also advocacy of an Enlightenment and 'bourgeois' conception of language, which holds that the means of communication is the word, its object factual, its addressee a human subject (the linear, hierarchical order of things in a world of reification) – whereas, language as the 'medium' of communication in its most radical sense, 'only com-municates itself *in* itself'.[4] The referential function of language is thus not negated, but freed from its false identification with the phenomenal world and from its assumed authority as a means of cognition about that world. Theory can be the very place where this negative knowledge about the reliability of theory's own operative principles is made access-ible, and where theoretical categories like all classificatory schemes keep on being voided, rather than appropriated, reiterated, safeguarded.

How true is the film theorist's divination? As Sor Juana Ines de la Cruz (a name among many others) would probably defend in her devalued status as a woman in the Church, 'true' knowledge has to be separated from its instrumental use.[5] The link between money and fact surfaces in the very instances where it either goes unacknowledged or is adamantly denied. The question of quality in accuracy and truth seems to depend largely on the weight or on the quantity of donation money – incense money, as the priest specifies. Indeed, some of the questions invariably burned in film public debates with the filmmaker are: What's the shooting ratio? What's the budget? How long did it take you to complete the film? The higher the bet, the better the product; the larger the amount of money involved, the more valuable the film, the more believable the truth it holds out. The longer the time spent, the more prized the experience, the more reliable the information. Filmwork is made a *de facto* 'low-budget' or 'big-budget' product. This is what one constantly hears and has come to say it oneself. 'Low-tech', 'high-tech', 'High-class junk', 'low-grade footage'. Pressure, money, bigness does it all ... The wide-spread slogan in factual and 'alternative' realms may claim 'the larger the grain, the better the politics', but what exclusively circulates in mass media culture is undoubtedly the money image. Money as money and money as capital are often spoken of as one, not two. The problem of financial constraints is, however, not only a problem of money but also one of control and standardization of images and sounds. Which truth? Whose truth? How true? (Andy Warhol's renowned statement rings very true: 'Buying is much more American than thinking.') In the name of public service and of mass communication, the money-making or, rather, money-subjected eye remains glued to the permanent scenario of the effect- and/or production-valued image.

Documentary is said to have come about as a need to inform the people (Dziga Vertov's *Kino-Pravda* or *Camera-Truth*), and subsequently to have affirmed itself as a reaction against the monopoly that the movie as entertainment came to have on the uses of film. Cinema was redefined as an ideal medium for social indoctrination and comment, whose virtues lay in its capacity for 'observing and selecting from life itself', for 'opening up the screen on the real world', for photographing 'the living scene and the living story', for giving cinema 'power over a million and one images', as well as for achieving 'an intimacy of knowledge and effect impossible to the shimsham mechanics of the studio and the lily-fingered interpretation of the metropolitan actor' (John Grierson).[6] Asserting its independence from the studio and the star system, documentary has its *raison d'être* in a strategic distinction. It puts the social function of film *on the market*. It takes real people and real problems from the real world and *deals with* them. It *sets a value* on intimate observation and *assesses its worth* according to how well it succeeds in capturing reality on the run, ' without material interference, without intermediary'. Powerful living stories, infinite authentic situations. There are no retakes. The stage is thus no more no less than life itself.

> With the documentary approach the film gets back to its fundamentals ... By selection, elimination and coordination of natural elements, a film form evolves which is original and not bound by theatrical or literary tradition ... The documentary film is an original art form. It has come to grips with facts – on its own original level. It covers the rational side of our lives, from the scientific experiment to the poetic landscape-study, but never moves away from the factual.
>
> (Hans Richter)[7]

The real world: so real that the Real becomes the one basic referent – pure, concrete, fixed, visible, all-too-visible. The result is the elaboration of a whole aesthetic of objectivity and the development of comprehensive technologies of truth capable of promoting what is right and what is wrong in the world, and by extension, what is 'honest' and what is 'manipulative' in documentary. This involves an extensive and relentless pursuit of naturalism across all the elements of cinematic technology. Indispensable to this cinema of the authentic image and spoken word are, for example, the directional microphone (localizing and restricting in its process of selecting sound for purposes of decipherability) and the Nagra portable tape-recorder (unrivaled for its maximally faithful ability to document). Lip-synchronous sound is validated as the norm; it is a 'must'; not so much in replicating reality (this much has been acknowledged among the fact-makers) as in 'showing real people in real locations at real tasks'. (Even non-sync sounds that are recorded in-context are considered 'less authentic' because the technique of sound synchronization and its institutionalized use have become 'nature' within film culture.) Real time is thought to be more 'truthful' than filmic time, hence the long take (that is, a take lasting the length of the 400 ft. roll of commercially available film stock) and minimal or no editing (change at the cutting stage is 'trickery', as if montage did not happen at the stages of conception and shooting) are declared to be more appropriate if one is to avoid distortions in structuring the material. The camera is the switch onto life. Accordingly, the close-up is condemned for its partiality, while the wide angle is claimed to be more objective because it includes more in the frame, hence it can mirror more faithfully the event-in-context. (The more, the larger, the truer – as if wider framing is less a framing than tighter shots.) The light-weight, hand-held camera, with its independence of the tripod – the fixed observation post – is extolled for its ability 'to go unnoticed', since it must be at once mobile and invisible, integrated into the milieu so as to change as little as possible, but also able to put its intrusion to use and provoke people into uttering the 'truth' that they would not otherwise unveil in ordinary situations.

> Thousands of bunglers have made the word [documentary] come to mean a deadly, routine form of film-making, the kind an alienated consumer society might appear to deserve – the art of talking a great deal during a film, with a commentary imposed from the outside, in order to say nothing, and to show nothing.
>
> (Louis Marcorelles)[8]

because the film maker is not supposed to have a voice

The event itself. Only the event; unaffected, unregulated by the eye recording it and the eye watching it. The perfectly objective social observer may no longer stand as the cherished model among documentary-makers today, but with every broadcast the viewer, Everyman, continues to be taught that He is first and foremost a Spectator. Either one is not responsible for what one sees (because only the event presented to him counts) or the only way one can have some influence on things is to send in a monetary donation. Thus, though the filmmaker's perception may readily be admitted as being unavoidably personal, the objectiveness of the reality of what is seen and represented remains unchallenged.

[Cinéma-vérité]: it would be better to call it cinema-sincerity ... That is,

[263]

that you ask the audience to have confidence in the evidence, to say to the audience, This is what I saw. I didn't fake it, this is what happened ... I look at what happened with my subjective eye and this is what I believe took place ... It's a question of honesty.

(Jean Rouch)[9]

What is presented as evidence remains evidence, whether the observing eye qualifies itself as being subjective or objective. At the core of such a rationale dwells, untouched, the Cartesian division between subject and object which perpetuates a dualistic inside-versus-outside, mind-against-matter view of the world. The emphasis is again laid on the power of film to capture reality 'out there' for us 'in here'. The moment of appropriation and of consumption is either simply ignored or carefully rendered invisible according to the rules of good and bad documentary. The art of talking to say nothing goes hand in hand with the will to say and to say only to confine something in a meaning. Truth has to be made vivid, interesting; it has to be 'dramatized' if it is to convince the audience of the evidence, whose 'confidence' in it allows truth to take shape. 'Documentary – the presentation of actual facts in a way that makes them credible and telling to people at the time' (William Stott).[10]

The real? Or the repeated artificial resurrection of the real, an operation whose overpowering success in substituting the visual and verbal signs of the real for the real itself ultimately helps to challenge the real, thereby intensifying the uncertainties engendered by any clear-cut division between the two. In the scale of what is more and what is less real, subject matter is of primary importance ('It is very difficult if not impossible,' says a film festival administrator, 'to ask jurors of the documentary film category panel not to identify the quality of a film with the subject it treats'). The focus is undeniably on common experience, by which the 'social' is defined: an experience that features, as a famed documentary-maker (Pierre Perrault) put it (paternalistically), 'man, simple man, who has never expressed himself'.[11]

The socially oriented filmmaker is thus the almighty voice-giver (here, in a vocalizing context that is all-male), whose position of authority in the production of meaning continues to go unchallenged, skillfully masked as it is by its righteous mission. The relationship between mediator and medium, or the mediating activity, is either ignored – that is, assumed to be transparent, as value free and as insentient as an instrument of reproduction ought to be – or else, it is treated most conveniently, by humanizing the gathering of evidence so as to further the status quo. (Of course, like all human beings I am subjective, but nonetheless, you should have confidence in the evidence!) Good documentaries are those whose subject matter is 'correct' and whose point of view the viewer agrees with. What is involved may be a question of honesty (vis-à-vis the material), but it is often also a question of (ideological) adherence, hence of legitimization.

Films made about the common people are furthermore naturally promoted as films made for the same people, and only for them. In the desire to service the needs of the un-expressed, there is, commonly enough, the urge to define them and their needs. More often than not, for example, when filmmakers find themselves in debates in which a film is criticized for its simplistic and reductive treatment of a subject, resulting in a maintenance of the very status quo which it sets out to challenge, their tendency is to dismiss the criticism by claiming that the film is not made for 'sophisticated viewers like ourselves, but for a general audience', thereby situating themselves above and apart from the *real* audience, those 'out there', the undoubtedly simple-minded folks who need everything they see explained to them. Despite the shift of emphasis – from the world of the upwardly mobile and the very affluent that dominates the media to that of 'their poor' – what is maintained intact is the age-old opposition between the creative intelligent supplier and the mediocre unenlightened consumer. The pretext for perpetuating such a division is the belief that social relations are determinate, hence endowed with objectivity.

> By 'impossibility of the social' I understand . . . the assertion of the ultimate impossibility of all 'objectivity' . . . society presents itself, to a great degree, not as an objective, harmonic order, but as an ensemble of divergent forces which do not seem to obey any unified or unifying logic. How can this experience of the failure of objectivity be made compatible with the affirmation of an ultimate objectivity of the real?
>
> (Ernesto Laclau)[12]

The silent common people – those who 'have never expressed themselves' unless they are given the opportunity to voice their thoughts by the one who comes to redeem them – are constantly summoned to signify the real world. They are the fundamental referent of the social, hence it suffices to point the camera at them, to show their (industrialized) poverty, or to contextualize and package their unfamiliar lifestyles for the ever-buying and donating general audience 'back here', in order to enter the sanctified realm of the morally right, or the social. In other words, when the so-called 'social' reigns, how these people(/we) come to visibility in the media, how meaning is given to their (/our) lives, how their(/our) truth is construed or how truth is laid down for them (/us) and despite them(/us), how representation relates to or *is* ideology, how media hegemony continues its relentless course is simply not at issue.

> There isn't any cinéma-vérité. It's necessarily a lie, from the moment the director intervenes – or it isn't cinema at all.
>
> (Georges Franju)[13]

When the social is hypostatized and enshrined as an ideal of transparency, when it itself becomes commodified in a form of sheer administration (better service, better control), the interval between the real and the image/d or between the real and the rational shrinks to the point of unreality. Thus, to address the question of production relations as raised earlier is endlessly to reopen the question: how is the real (or the social ideal of good representation) produced? Rather than catering to it, striving to capture and discover its truth as a concealed or lost object, it is therefore important also to keep on asking: how is truth being ruled? 'The penalty of realism is that it is about reality and has to bother for ever not about being "beautiful" but about being right' (John Grierson).[14] The fathers of documentary have initially insisted that documentary is not News, but Art (a 'new and vital art form' as Grierson once proclaimed). That its essence is not information (as with 'the hundreds of tweedle-dum "industrials" or worker-education films'); not reportage; not newsreel; but something close to 'a creative treatment of actuality' (Grierson's renowned definition).

> If Joris Ivens has made the most beautiful documentaries that anyone has ever seen, that's because the films are composed, worked out, and they have an air of truth. Sure the documentary part is true, but all around the documentary sections there's an interpretation. And then you can't talk about cinéma-vérité.
>
> (Georges Franju)[15]

Documentary may be anti-aesthetic, as some still affirm in the line of the British forerunner, but it is claimed to be no less an art, albeit an art

[handwritten margin note:] Maybe IJ's found Drama is the only cinéma-vérité

PLATE 16 Trinh T. Minh-ha, from *Surname Viet Given Name Nam*, 1989.

within the limits of factuality. (Interpretation, for example, is not viewed as constituting the very process of documenting and making information accessible; it is thought, instead, to be the margin all around an untouched *given* centre, which according to Franju is the 'documentary part' or 'documentary section'.) When, in a world of reification, truth is widely equated with fact, any explicit use of the magic, poetic, or irrational qualities specific to the film medium itself would have to be excluded a priori as non-factual. The question is not so much one of sorting out – illusory as this may be – what is inherently factual and what is not, in a body of *pre-existing* filmic techniques, as it is one of abiding by the conventions of naturalism in film. In the reality of formula-films, only validated techniques are *right*, others are de facto wrong. The criteria are all based on their degree of invisibility in producing meaning. Thus, shooting at any speed other than the standard 24-frames-per-second (the speed necessitated for lip-sync sound) is, for example, often condemned as a form of manipulation, implying thereby that manipulativeness has to be discreet– that is, acceptable only when not easily perceptible to the 'real audience'. Although the whole of filmmaking *is* a question of manipulation – whether 'creative' or not –, again, those endorsing the law unhesitantly decree which technique is manipulative and which, supposedly is not; and this judgement is certainly made according to the degree of visibility of each.

[handwritten margin note: yet in reality 24 fps is only one speed among many that might have been chosen.]

> A documentary film is shot with three cameras: (1) the camera in the technical sense; (2) the filmmaker's mind; and (3) the generic patterns of the documentary film, which are founded on the expectations of the audience that patronizes it. For this reason one cannot simply say that the documentary film portrays facts. It photographs isolated facts and assembles from them a coherent set of facts according to three divergent schemata. All remaining possible facts and factual contexts are excluded. The naive treatment of documentation therefore provides a unique opportunity to concoct fables. In and of itself, the documentary is no more realistic than the feature film.
>
> (Alexander Kluge)[16]

Reality is more fabulous, more maddening, more strangely manipulative than fiction. To understand this is to recognize the naivety of a development of cinematic technology that promotes increasing unmediated 'access' to reality. It is to see through the poverty of what Benjamin deplored as 'a truth expressed as it was thought' and to understand why progressive fiction films are attracted and constantly pay tribute to documentary techniques. These films put the 'documentary effect' to advantage, playing on the viewer's expectation in order to 'concoct fables'. (Common examples of this effect include: the feelings of participating in a truth-like moment of reality captured despite the filmed subject; the sense of urgency, immediacy, and authenticity in the instability of the hand-held camera; the newsreel look of the grainy image; and the oral-testimony-like quality of the direct interview – to mention just a few.)

[268]

The documentary can thus easily become a 'style': it no longer constitutes a mode of production or an attitude toward life, but proves to be only an element of aesthetics (or anti-aesthetics) – which at best and without acknowledging it, it tends to be in any case when, within its own factual limits, it reduces itself to a mere category, or a set of persuasive techniques. Many of these techniques have become so 'natural' to the language of broadcast television today that they 'go unnoticed'. These are, for example: the 'personal testimony' technique (a star appears on screen to advertise his/her use of a certain product); the 'plain folks' technique (a politician arranges to eat hot dogs in public); the 'band wagon' technique (the use of which conveys the message that 'everybody is doing it, why not you?'); or the 'card stacking' technique (in which prearrangements for a 'survey' show that a certain brand of product is more popular than any other to the inhabitants of a given area).[17]

> You must re-create reality because reality runs away; reality denies reality. You must first interpret it, or re-create it … When I make a documentary, I try to give the realism an artificial aspect … I find that the aesthetic of a document comes from the artificial aspect of the document … it has to be more beautiful than realism, and therefore it has to be composed … to give it another sense.
>
> (Franju)[18]

A documentary aware of its own artifice is one that remains sensitive to the flow between fact and fiction. It does not work to conceal or exclude what is normalized as 'non-factual', for it understands the mutual dependence of realism and 'artificiality' in the process of filmmaking. It recognizes the necessity of composing (on) life in living it or making it. Documentary reduced to a mere vehicle of facts may be used to advocate a cause, but it does not constitute one in itself; hence the perpetuation of the bipartite system of division in the content-versus-form rationale.

To compose is not always synonymous with ordering-so-as-to-persuade, and to give the filmed document another sense, another meaning, is not necessarily to distort it. If life's paradoxes and complexities are not to be suppressed, the question of degrees and nuances is incessantly crucial. Meaning can therefore be political only when it does not let itself be easily stabilized, and, when it does not rely on any single source of authority, but rather, empties it, or decentralizes it. Thus, even when this source is referred to, it stands as one among many others, at once plural and utterly singular. In its demand to *mean* at any rate, the 'documentary' often forgets how it comes about and how aesthetics and politics remain inseparable in its constitution. For, when not equated with mere techniques of beautifying, aesthetics allows one to experience life differently or, as some would say, to give it 'another sense', remaining in tune with its drifts and shifts.

> It must be possible to represent reality as the historical fiction it is. Reality is a paper-tiger. The individual does encounter it, as fate. It is not fate, however, but a creation of the labor of generations of human beings, who all the time wanted and still want something entirely different. In more than one respect, reality is simultaneously real and unreal.
>
> (Alexander Kluge)[19]

From its descriptions to its arrangements and rearrangements, reality on the move may be heightened or impoverished but it is never neutral (that is, objectivist). ' Documentary at its purest and most poetic is a form in which the elements that you use are the actual elements' (Lindsay Anderson).[20] Why, for example, use the qualifying term 'artificial' at all? In the process of producing a 'document', is there such a thing as an artificial aspect that can be securely separated from the true aspect (expect for analytical purpose – that is, for another 'artifice' of language)? In other words, is a closer framing of reality more artificial than a wider one? The notion of 'making strange' and of reflexivity remains but a mere distancing device so long as the division between 'textual artifice' and 'social attitude' exerts its power.[21] The 'social' continues to go un-challenged, history keeps on being salvaged, while the sovereignty of the socio-historicizing subject is safely maintained. With the status quo of the making/consuming subject preserved, the aim is to correct 'errors' (the false) and to construct an alternative view (offered as a this-is-the-true or mine-is-truer version of reality). It is, in other words, to replace one source of unacknowledged authority by another, but not to challenge the very constitution of authority. The new socio-historical text thus rules despotically as another master-centred text, since it unwittingly helps to perpetuate the Master's ideological stance.

When the textual and the political neither separate themselves from one another nor simply collapse into a single qualifier, the practice of representation can, similarly, neither be taken for granted, nor merely dismissed as being ideologically reactionary. By putting representation under scrutiny, textual theory-practice has more likely helped to upset rooted ideologies by bringing the mechanics of their workings to the fore.

It makes possible the vital differentiation between authoritative criticism and uncompromising analyses and inquiries (including those of the analyzing/inquiring activity). Moreover, it contributes to the questioning of reformist 'alternative' approaches that never quite depart from the lineage of white- and male-centred humanism. Despite their explicit socio-political commitment, these approaches remain unthreatening – that is, 'framed', and thus neither social nor political enough.

Reality runs away, reality denies reality. Filmmaking is after all a question of 'framing' reality in its course. However, it can also be the very place where the referential function of the film image/sound is not simply negated, but reflected upon in its own operative principles and questioned in its authoritative identification with the phenomenal world. In attempts at suppressing the mediation of the cinematic apparatus and the fact that language 'communicates itself in itself', there always lurks what Benjamin qualified as a 'bourgeois' conception of language. 'Any revolutionary strategy must challenge the depiction of reality ... so that a break between ideology and text is effected' (Claire Johnston).[22]

To deny the *reality* of film in claiming (to capture) *reality* is to stay 'in ideology' – that is, to indulge in the (deliberate or not) confusion of filmic with phenomenal reality. By condemning self-reflexivity as pure formalism instead of challenging its diverse realizations, this ideology can 'go on unnoticed', keeping its operations invisible and serving the goal of universal expansionism. Such aversion for self-reflexivity goes hand in hand with its widespread appropriation as a progressive formalistic device in cinema, since both work to reduce its function to a harmlessly decorative one. (For example, it has become commonplace to hear such remarks as 'A film is a film' or, 'This is a film about a film.' Film-on-film statements are increasingly challenging to work with as they can easily fall prey to their own formulas and techniques.) Furthermore, reflexivity at times equated with personal view, is at other times endorsed as scientific rigor.

> Two men were discussing the joint production of wine. One said to the other: 'You shall supply the rice and I the water.' The second asked: 'If all the rice comes from me, how shall we apportion the finished product?' The first man replied: 'I shall be absolutely fair about the whole thing. When the wine is finished, each gets back exactly what he put in – I'll siphon off the liquid and you can keep the rest.'
>
> ('Joint Production', *Wit and Humor from Old Cathay*)[23]

[271]

One of the areas of documentary that remains most resistant to the reality of film as film is that known as anthropological filmmaking. Filmed ethnographic material, which was thought to 'replicate natural perception', has now renounced its authority to replicate only to purport to provide adequate 'data' for the 'sampling' of culture. The claim to objectivity may no longer stand in many anthropological circles, but its authority is likely to be replaced by the sacrosanct notion of the 'scientific'. Thus the recording and gathering of data and of people's testimonies are considered to be the limited aim of 'ethnographic film'. What makes a film anthropological and what makes it scientific is, tautologically enough, its 'scholarly endeavour [to] respectively document and interpret according to anthropological standards'.[24] Not merely ethnographic nor documentary, the definition positively specifies, but scholarly and anthropologically. The fundamental scientific obsession is present in every attempt to demarcate anthropology's territories. In order to be scientifically valid, a film needs the scientific intervention of the anthropologist, for it is only by adhering to the body of conventions set up by the community of anthropologists accredited by their 'discipline' that the film can hope to qualify for the classification and be passed as a 'scholarly endeavour'.

> The myth of science impresses us. But do not confuse science with its scholasticism. Science finds no truths, either mathematized or formalized; it discovers unknown facts that can be interpreted in a thousand ways.
>
> (Paul Veyne)[25]

One of the familiar arguments given by anthropologists to validate their prescriptively instrumental use of film and of people is to dismiss all works by filmmakers who are 'not professional anthropologists' or 'amateur ethnographers' under the pretext that they are not 'anthropologically informed', hence they have 'no theoretical significance from an anthropological point of view'. To advance such a blatantly self-promoting rationale to institute *a deadly routine form of filmmaking* (to quote a sentence of Marcorelles once more) is also – through anthropology's primary task of 'collecting data' for knowledge of mankind – to try to skirt what is known as the salvage paradigm and the issues implicated in the 'scientific' deployment of Western world ownership.[26] The stronger anthropology's insecurity about its own project, the greater its eagerness to hold up a normative model, and the more seemingly serene its disposition to dwell in its own blind spots.

In the sanctified terrain of anthropology, all of filmmaking is reduced to a question of methodology. It is demonstrated that the reason anthropological films go further than ethnographic films is because they do not, for example, just show activities being performed, but they also *explain* the 'anthropological significance' of these activities (significance that, despite the disciplinary qualifier 'anthropological', is de facto identified with the meaning the natives give them themselves). Now, obviously, in the process of fixing meaning, not every explanation is valid. This is where the role of the expert anthropologist comes in and where methodologies need to be devised, legitimated, and enforced. For, if a nonprofessional explanation is dismissed here, it is not so much because it lacks insight or theoretical grounding, as because it escapes anthropological control; it lacks the seal of approval from the anthropological order. In the name of science, a distinction is made between reliable and non-reliable information. Anthropological and non-anthropological explanations may share the same subject matter, but they differ in the way they produce meaning. The unreliable constructs are the ones that do not obey the rules of anthropological authority, which a concerned expert like Evans-Pritchard skillfully specifies as being nothing else but 'a scientific habit of mind'.[27] Science defined as the most appropriate approach to the object of investigation serves as a banner for every scientistic attempt to promote the West's paternalistic role as subject of knowledge and its historicity of the Same. 'The West agrees with us today that the way to Truth passes by numerous paths, other than Aristotelian Thomistic logic or Hegelian dialectic. But social and human sciences themselves must be decolonized' (E. Mveng).[28]

In its scientistic 'quest to make meaning', anthropology constantly reactivates the power relations embedded in the Master's confident discourses on Himself and His Other, thereby aiding both the *centri*petal and *centri*fugal movement of their global spread. With the diverse challenges issued today to the very process of producing 'scientific' interpretation of culture as well as to that of making anthropological knowledge possible, visually oriented members of its community have come up with an epistemological position in which the notion of reflexivity is typically reduced to a question of technique and method. Equated with a form of self-exposure common in field work, it is discussed at times as *self-reflectivity* and at other times condemned as individualistic idealism sorely in need of being controlled if the individual maker is not to loom larger than the scientific community or the people observed. Thus 'being reflexive is virtually synonymous with being scientific'.[29]

The reasons justifying such a statement are many, but one that can be read through it and despite it is: as long as the maker abides by a series of 'reflexive' techniques in filmmaking that are devised for the purpose of exposing the 'context' of production and as long as the required techniques are method(olog)ically carried out, the maker can be assured that 'reflexivity' is elevated to that status of scientific rigor. These reflexive techniques would include the insertion of a verbal or visual narrative about the anthropologist, the methodology adopted, and the condition of production – in other words, all the conventional means of validating an anthropological text through the disciplinary practice of head- and footnoting and the totalistic concept of pre-production presentation. Those who reject such a rationale do so out of a preoccupation with the 'community of scientists', whose collective judgment they feel should be the only true form of reflection. For an individual validation of a work can only be suspicious because it 'ignores the historical development of science'. In these constant attempts at enforcing anthropology as (a) discipline and at recentering the dominant representation of culture (despite all the changes in methodologies), what seems to be oddly suppressed in the notion of reflexivity in filmmaking is its practice as processes to prevent meaning from ending with what is said and what is shown – as inquiries into production relations – thereby to challenge representation itself while emphasizing the reality of the experience of film as well as the important role that reality plays in the lives of the spectators.

> Unless an image displaces itself from its natural state, it acquires no significance. Displacement causes resonance.
>
> (Shanta Gokhale)[30]

> After his voluntary surrender, Zheng Guang, a pirate operating off the coast of Fujian, was to be given an official post (in return for surrendering). When a superior instructed him to write a poem, Zheng replied with a doggerel: 'No matter whether they are civil or military officials they are all the same. The officials assumed their posts before becoming thieves, but I, Zheng Guang, was a thief before becoming an official.'
>
> ('The Significance of Officialdom', *Wit and Humor from Old Cathay*)[31]

As an aesthetic closure or an old relativizing gambit in the process nonetheless of absolutizing meaning, reflexivity proves critically in/ significant when it merely serves to refine and to further the accumulation of knowledge. No going beyond, no elsewhere-within-here seems possible if the reflection on oneself is not at one and the same time the analysis of established forms of the social that define one's limits. Thus to drive the self into an abyss is neither a moralistic stricture against oneself (for future improvement), nor a task of critique that humanizes the decoding self but never challenges the very notion of self and decoder. Left intact in its positionality and its fundamental urge to decree meaning, the self conceived both as key and as transparent mediator is more often than not likely to turn responsibility into licence. The licence to *name*, as though meaning presented itself to be deciphered without any ideological mediation. As though specifying a context can only result in the finalizing of what is shown and said. As though naming can stop the process of naming – that very abyss of the relation of self to self.

The bringing of the self into play necessarily exceeds the concern for human errors, for it cannot but involve as well the problem inherent in representation and communication. Radically plural in its scope, reflexivity is thus not a mere question of *rect*ifying and *just*ifying. (*Subject*ivizing.) What is set in motion in its praxis are the self-generating links between different forms of reflexivity. Thus, a subject who points to him/her/ itself as subject-in-process, a work that displays its own formal properties or its own constitution as work, is bound is upset one's sense of identity – the familiar distinction between the Same and the Other since the latter is no longer kept in a recognizable relation of dependence, derivation, or appropriation. The process of self-constitution is also that in which the self vacillates and loses its assurance. The paradox of such a process lies in its fundamental instability; an instability that brings forth the disorder inherent to every order. The 'core' of representation is the reflexive interval. It is the place in which the play within the textual frame is a play on this very frame, hence on the borderlines of the textual and extra-textual, where a positioning within constantly incurs the risk of de-positioning, and where the work, never freed from historical and socio-political contexts nor entirely subjected to them, can only be itself by constantly risking being no-thing.

A work that reflects back on itself offers itself infinitely as nothing else but work ... *and* void. Its gaze is at once an impulse that causes the work to fall apart (to return to the initial no-work-ness) and an ultimate gift to its constitution. A gift, by which the work is freed from the tyranny of meaning as well as from the omnipresence of a subject of meaning. To let go of the hold at the very moment when it is at its most effective is to allow the work to live, and to live on independently of the intended links, communicating itself in itself like Benjamin's 'the self is a text' – no more no less 'a project to be built'.[32] 'Orpheus' gaze ... is the impulse of desire which shatters the song's destiny and concern, and in that inspired and unconcerned decision reaches the origin, consecrates the song' (Maurice Blanchot).[33]

Meaning can neither be imposed nor denied. Although every film is in itself a form of ordering and closing, each closure can defy its own closure, opening onto other closures, thereby emphasizing the interval between apertures and creating a space in which meaning remains fascinated by what escapes and exceeds it. The necessity to let go of the notion of intentionality that dominates the question of the 'social' as well as that of creativity cannot therefore be confused with the ideal of non-intervention, an ideal in relation to which the filmmaker, trying to become as invisible as possible in the process of producing meaning, promotes empathic subjectivity at the expense of critical inquiry even when the intention is to show and to condemn oppression.

> It is idealist mystification to believe that 'truth' can be captured by the camera or that the conditions of a film's production (e.g. a film made collectively by women) can of *itself* reflect the conditions of its production. This is mere utopianism: new meaning has to *be manufactured* within the text of the film ... What the camera in fact grasps is the 'natural' world of the dominant ideology.
>
> (Claire Johnston)[34]

In the quest for totalized meaning and for knowledge-for-knowledge's sake, the worst meaning is meaninglessness. A Caucasian missionary nun based in a remote village of Africa qualifies her task in these simple, confident terms: 'We are here to help people give meaning to their lives.' Ownership is monotonously circular in its give-and-take demands. It is a monolithic view of the world whose irrationality expresses itself in the imperative of both giving and meaning, and whose irreality manifests itself in the need to require that visual and verbal constructs yield meaning down to their last detail. 'The West moistens everything with meaning, like an authoritarian religion which imposes baptism on entire peoples' (Roland Barthes).³⁵ Yet such illusion is real; it has its own reality, one in which the subject of Knowledge, the subject of Vision, or the subject of Meaning continues to deploy established power relations, assuming Himself to be the basic reserve of reference in the totalistic quest for the referent, the true referent that lies out there in nature, in the dark, waiting patiently to be unveiled and deciphered correctly. To be redeemed. Perhaps then, an imagination that goes toward the texture of reality is one capable of playing upon the illusion in question and the power it exerts. The production of one irreality upon the other and the play of non-sense (which is not mere meaninglessness) upon meaning may therefore help to relieve the basic referent of its occupation, for the present situation of critical inquiry seems much less one of attacking the illusion of reality as one of displacing and emptying out the establishment of totality.

Notes

1 *One-Way Street and Other Writings* (London: Verso, 1979), p. 95.
2 J. Kowallis, trans. (Beijing: Panda Books, 1986), p. 164.
3 Quoted in G. Roy Levin, *Documentary Explorations: Fifteen Interviews with Film-Makers* (Garden City, NY: Doubleday & Company, 1971), p. 66.
4 Benjamin, *One-Way Street*, pp. 109; 111.
5 See Jean Franco's re-reading of her work in *Plotting Women: Gender and Representation in Mexico* (New York: Columbia University Press, 1989), pp. 23–54.
6 In *Grierson On Documentary*, Forsyth Hardy, ed. (1966; rpt., New York: Praeger, 1971), pp. 146–7.
7 'Film as an Original Art Form', in *Film: A Montage of Theories*, R. Dyer Mac Cann, ed. (New York: E.P. Dutton, 1966), p. 183.
8 *Living Cinema: New Directions in Contemporary Film-making*, trans. I. Quigly (New York: Praeger, 1973), p. 37.
9 In Levin, *Documentary Explorations*, p. 135.
10 *Documentary Expression and Thirties America* (1973; rpt., New York: Oxford University Press, 1976), p. 73.
11 Quoted in *Living Cinema*, p. 26.
12 'Building a New Left: An Interview with Ernesto Laclau,' *Strategies*, No. 1 (Fall 1988): 15.
13 In Levin, *Documentary Explorations*, p. 119.
14 *Grierson on Documentary*, p. 249.
15 In Levin, *Documentary Explorations*, p. 119.
16 *Alexander Kluge: A Retrospective* (The Goethe Institutes of North America, 1988), p. 4.
17 John Mercer, *An Introduction to Cinematography* (Champaign, Il: Stipes Publishing Co., 1968), p. 159.
18 In Levin, *Documentary Explorations*, pp. 121; 128.
19 *Alexander Kluge: A Retrospective*, p. 6.

20 Ibid., p. 66.

21 This distinction motivates Dana Polan's argument in 'A Brechtian Cinema? Towards a Politics of Self-Reflexive Film?', in B. Nichols, ed., *Movies and Methods*, Vol. 2 (Los Angeles: University of California Press, 1985), pp. 661–72.

22 'Women's Cinema as Counter-Cinema', in B. Nichols, ed., *Movies and Methods*, Vol. 1 (Los Angeles: University of California Press, 1976), p. 215.

23 Kowallis, *Wit and Humor*, p. 98.

24 Henk Ketelaar, 'Methodology in Anthropological Filmmaking: A Filmmaking Anthropologist's Poltergeist?' in *Methodology in Anthropological Filmmaking*, N. Bogaart and H. Ketelaar, eds. (Gottingen: Herodot, 1983), p. 182.

25 *Did the Greeks Believe in Their Myths? An Essay on the Constitutive Imagination*, P. Wissing, trans. (Chicago: University of Chicago Press, 1988), p. 115.

26 See James Clifford, 'Of Other Peoples: Beyond the "Salvage Paradigm",' in *Discussions in Contemporary Culture*, Hal Foster, ed. (Seattle: Bay Press, 1987), pp. 121–30.

27 See *Theories of Primitive Religion* (Oxford: Clarendon Press, 1980).

28 'Récents développements de la théologie africaine', *Bulletin of African Theology*, 5: 9. Quoted in V. Y. Mudimbe, *The Invention of Africa: Gnosis, Philosophy and The Order of Knowledge* (Bloomington: Indiana University Press, 1988), p. 37.

29 Jay Ruby, 'Exposing Yourself: Reflexivity, Anthropology and Film', *Semiotica*, 30, 1–2 (1980): 165.

30 In *The New Generation. 1960–1980*, Uma da Cunha, ed. (New Delhi: The Directorate of Film Festivals, 1981), p. 114.

31 Kowallis, *Wit and Humor*, p. 39.

32 Benjamin, *One-Way Street*, p. 14.

33 *The Gaze of Orpheus and Other Literary Essays*, P. Adams Sitney, ed., L. Davis, trans. (Barrytown, NY: Station Hill Press, 1981), p. 104.

34 Johnston, 'Women's Cinema as Counter-Cinema', p. 214.

35 *Empire of Signs*, R. Howard, trans. (New York: Hill & Wang, 1982), p. 70.

Index

Aalto, Alvar 147
Abrams, M. H. 237
Abstract Expressionism 37
abstraction 150
academic journals 63
accumulation 119, 120, 165
Adorno, Theodor 29, 36, 95; *Aesthetic Theory* 145
advertising 54; and art 33–9, 53
aesthetic form 94–5
aesthetics 256, 271
affect, affectivity 54, 104, 158, 160–1
affective response 183
Africa 10, 16, 17, 60, 75
agency 55, 235–6
Aitken, Ian 4–5
Al-Azhar Institute, Cairo 197–8
aleatoric techniques 164
Algerian war 250
Alien 107, 141
allegory 44, 46, 163, 169–71, 174, 175, 177, 179–83; four kinds of 171
ambiguity 85
America *see* United States of America
American Revolution (War of Independence) 6
Americanization 8
Anderson, Laurie 77, 83, 87, 88, 89, 92, 93, 97n
Anderson, Lindsay 260, 270
Andrews, Bruce 216
androids (replicants) 101, 104–14
animism 234

anthropology 255, 272–4
anti-modernism 133–7
Apocalypse Now 33
aporia 226, 234, 236
appropriation 119–20, 157
Aravamudan, Srinivas 240n
Archigram 141
architecture 37, 39–42, 54, 117, 130–49
Are You Being Served? 49
Arista Records 96
arithmetic 131, 132, 136
Art & Language group 30
The Art Bears 93
'Art and Technique' (Shklovsky) 36
art-rock 90, 95–7
artificial intelligence 102
arts, visual 16–18, 24–5, 30, 118–49
Ashbery, John 189, 190–3; *And the Stars Were Shining* 190; *April Galleons* 190, 191; *Houseboat Days* 207; 'Litany' 44; *A Nest of Ninnies* (with James Schuyler) 190; *The New Spirit* 213; *Reported Sightings. Art Chronicles 1957–1987* 190; *Self-Portrait in a Convex Mirror* 59, 191, 215; *Three Plays* 190; *Three Poems* 45, 207–19
Asia 16, 75
assemblage 11, 17, 123, 154
Asturias, Miguel Angel 230
Ataturk, Kamal 238
Auden, W. H. 191, 211
Auerbach, Frank 163
Augustine, St, *The City of God* 218